Race, Rhetoric, and the Postcolonial

Race, Rhetoric, and the Postcolonial

Edited by
Gary A. Olson
Lynn Worsham

State University of New York Press

Published by
State University of New York Press, Albany

© 1999 State University of New York

All rights reserved. All material contained herein is published by
permission of *JAC: A Journal of Composition Theory*

Cover Art: "Just Desserts" by Denis Sargent, acrylic on canvas, 1996,
48" x 30", collection of the artist.

Printed in the United States of America
Designed and typeset by Gary A. Olson

For information, address State University of New York Press, State
University Plaza, Albany, N.Y., 12246

Production by Diane Ganeles. Marketing by Fran Keneston.

Library of Congress Cataloging-in-Publication Data

Race, Rhetoric, and the Postcolonial
  edited by Gary A. Olson and Lynn Worsham.

        p. cm.
Includes bibliographical references and index.
        ISBN 0-7914-4173-3 (hc: alk. paper)—
        ISBN 0-7914-4174-1 (pbk: alk. paper)
1. Rhetoric—Political aspects. 2. Race relations. 3. Feminist
theory. 4. Postcolonialism. 5. Intellectuals—Interviews.
I. Olson, Gary A., date.   II. Worsham, Lynn.

P301.5.P67R33   1999
808—dc21   98-34971
                                                        CIP

10   9   8   7   6   5   4   3   2   1

Para

Esperanza

Contents

Acknowledgments

We would like to acknowledge the support and friendship of Sara M. Deats and William T. Ross, both of whom have taken a personal interest in the success of scholarship in rhetoric and composition. Special recognition is due to Merry Perry for her hours of extensive research and technical assistance. Finally, we would like to thank both Priscilla Ross at SUNY Press for her editorial acumen and unflagging encouragement, and the anonymous manuscript reviewers of this book for their constructive suggestions.

Acknowledgments

Introduction

Race, Rhetoric, and the Postcolonial is a collection of six scholarly
interviews with internationally renowned intellectuals outside of
rhetoric and composition whose work has direct implications for
scholarship within the discipline. Included are interviews with
postcolonial theorist Homi Bhabha, postcolonial feminist and race
theorist Gloria Anzaldúa, African American race scholar Michael
Eric Dyson, British cultural studies scholar (and a founder of that
field) Stuart Hall, Argentinean political theorist Ernesto Laclau, and
French philosopher Chantal Mouffe. These interviews constitute a
cross-disciplinary dialogue among these influential scholars on
subjects related to rhetoric, writing, race, feminist theory, cultural
studies, and postcolonial theory.

Because rhetoric and composition is a uniquely interdisciplinary
field—drawing heavily on current scholarship in anthropology,
feminist theory, linguistics, literary criticism, philosophy, psychology, sociology, and other areas—a significant portion of its scholarship draws on the work of scholars and theorists prominent in
other disciplines. Consequently, the careful investigation of these
scholars' work is essential. Thus, the interviews in this book function
as a *primary source* in the discipline, in that they are direct, focused
opportunities for six of these scholars to address the key intellectual
questions in the discipline's scholarship.

The collection begins with a conversation with Homi Bhabha.
Bhabha suggests that the field of rhetoric and composition fulfills
important intellectual and social roles in that writing, the field's
principal preoccupation, is always already a "political" activity
linked to the acquisition of agency through critical literacy. Those
who are able to read their world and then have voice within it are
positioned to have a certain modicum of power within that world
and over their destinies. Teaching students to read and write the

world, then, is a way of helping them to achieve this power, to resist the dominating forces at play in their lives. This is why Bhabha believes that theory plays such a crucial role in literacy education, for it helps us to disrupt the continuity of "common sense," to challenge assumptions, preconceptions, fixed notions. It also helps us better understand cultural difference not as a question of fixed, monolithic groups of others defined by distinct borders, but as a constructed discourse about questions of power and hegemonic struggle over the ability to read and write the world—and, thus, to gain access to its resources. The work we do in rhetoric and composition, then, is crucial according to Bhabha.

In many ways, Bhabha's work is about the ability to speak—to have voice and thus to gain agency. This is also a main theme of Gloria Anzaldúa's work. Anzaldúa fiercely resists the "tradition of silence" in which she, as a woman of color, finds herself ensnared. Like Bhabha, she rejects the discursive dichotomies that bind us in such material ways—dichotomies of racial, ethnic, and sexual identity; dichotomies of reason and emotion, spirit and matter. She echoes Bhabha in insisting that identity knows no rigid borders, that we must struggle against the categorical violence of thinking cultural identity as prepackaged, fixed realities. For both writers, identity is fluid, washing over and through a person. Especially for those like Anzaldúa who inhabit a borderland space between multiple ethnic sites, achieving voice, subject position, is a matter of negotiating multiple identities, multiple voices. This is why Anzaldúa calls for new states of consciousness involving a multiplicity of writing strategies—what is referred to here as "mestiza rhetoric," or mestiza writing. For Anzaldúa, writing is a primary way of challenging rigid structures and transforming society's fixed categories; it is a "means of enabling the kinds of ongoing transformations necessary for inhabiting the borderlands." As a writer and a kind of writing theorist herself, Anzaldúa understands the double-edged nature of composition's project: as compositionists we are associated with the colonial, gatekeeping enterprise of enforcing "standard" ways of writing and "accepted" ways of thinking; but we can also associate ourselves with the emancipatory venture of enabling students to read and write their worlds.

While Anzaldúa speaks passionately about her struggles as a Chicana woman in a white, patriarchal society, Michael Eric Dyson is equally passionate about how constructions of race affect the

African-American experience. Straddling both the academic and outside worlds, Dyson hopes to disrupt traditional notions of race and to interrogate how race, class, and gender get constructed in ways that reinforce structures of domination. He believes that academics can indeed play an important role in the struggle for a more equitable society, that theory can help open up avenues of inquiry that can lead to material changes in the larger world. To Dyson, language and language instruction are at the forefront of these struggles. For example, he points out that narrativity is a central "component of self-understanding and the way in which African-American peoples constitute their own identities," and comprehending how narrativity works can lead to a better understanding of some racial and ethnic groups. Echoing both Bhabha and Anzaldúa, Dyson sees writing as a potentially revolutionary force in that it can contest narrow conceptions of self by situating writer and reader in a convergence of contested, conflicting identities. Thus, for all three theorists, writing is key to identity construction, to understanding and making use of the notion of self as protean.

Dyson is a champion of studying popular culture and of closing gaps between academic and popular cultures—the very same project that Stuart Hall has devoted his professional life to. Hall, however, does not share Dyson's exorbitant enthusiasm for importing cultural studies into the academy. While Hall agrees that culture deserves rigorous intellectual scrutiny and that cultural studies can serve important pedagogical ends, he worries that the institutionalization of cultural studies is dulling its political edge, diminishing its power as a discourse of disruption and resistance. Too much of what passes as cultural studies, according to Hall, is simply "a waste of everyone's time." Much more important are investigations of how culture constructs race, class, ethnicity, and gender. Like all of the theorists in this book, Hall is especially concerned about the liberal, pluralist notion of multiculturalism that tends either to erase and homogenize difference or to essentialize it. Like Bhabha and Anzaldúa, he calls for a "sliding and translation" among differences, among cultural identities. This more complex notion of difference will help scholars and other cultural workers to focus on the formation and material effects of race and ethnicity, how cultural identity contributes to social inequality and political powerlessness. This is why, for Hall, theory is a "deadly serious matter." He agrees with Dyson that theoretical work in the academy can have very real, material effects when new ideas are turned into everyday practice.

Ernesto Laclau, too, argues that intellectuals should not underestimate their potential to influence social policy. He points out that "high theory" and other intellectual developments have occasionally resulted in substantive change; however, he also believes that academics must begin to write specifically to nonacademic audiences if they wish to maximize their influence. Laclau's concern about intellectuals' maximizing their influence derives from the central concept of his work: hegemony. For Laclau, hegemony is not a one-way imposition of ideological structures on people by an elite; it is an ongoing struggle among various groups for the acceptance and ascendancy of their values and world view. Hence, hegemonic struggle is never-ending, and it therefore relies on constant persuasion—on rhetoric. Rhetoric, in its broadest sense, is central to hegemonic struggle, and this is why Laclau believes that literacy is necessary to revolutionary struggle. Literacy, for Laclau, is a "culture of questions," and it is the job of progressive academics to create such a culture in their classrooms—an important way in which our academic work can lead to real social change.

Laclau's frequent coauthor, Chantal Mouffe, further develops the notion of hegemony. She fears that the political left is abandoning hegemonic struggle, allowing the neoconservative right to triumph in such struggle by default. She calls on the left to establish a new hegemony, to transform the current relations of power, to offer an alternative to neoliberal discourse by redrawing political frontiers. Such an effort entails attempts to create consensus, but not some impossible or unreachable situation in which everyone agrees; rather, a fluid, flexible consensus in which parties join together in strategic solidarity to accomplish mutually beneficial goals. As in Laclau's political theory, rhetoric and argumentation are key to this process. In fact, Mouffe believes that rhetoric is crucial both to the construction of collective identities and to the functioning of an effective democratic political community, or *societas*. Like all of the theorists in this collection, Mouffe expresses optimism that proper action on the part of all of us can lead to a more equitable society.

Often in these interviews, the participants refer to the work or statements of the other interviewees, thereby creating a kind of cross-dialogue or polylogue. *Race, Rhetoric, and the Postcolonial* might thus be seen as a multi-level discussion in which these various theorists link their theoretical and political interventions to broader considerations of cultural struggle, whether such struggle focuses on race, national identity, writing, or teaching. These interviews are meant to clarify positions, provoke debate, and encourage response. We hope that they encourage compositionists to read these theorists' works and to incorporate them into their own scholarship; doing so, we believe, will enrich work being done in the field and lead to a deeper understanding of the functioning and interconnectedness of rhetoric, race, gender, and systems of power and domination.

Gary A. Olson
Lynn Worsham

Homi

Bhabha

Staging the Politics of Difference: Homi Bhabha's Critical Literacy

GARY A. OLSON AND LYNN WORSHAM

Postcolonial theorist Homi Bhabha sees writing, composition, as a "highly political" activity. Writing, defined in its broadest sense, is closely linked to the acquisition of agency. This is why it is important that we not treat writing as a simple medium of communication in which there is some transparent mediation between "already pregiven subjects, pregiven objects, and a preconstituted *mise en scène*." For Bhabha, writing constitutes, in a dialogic way, new relationships among these elements and is thus a "continually revisionary," perhaps even "revolutionary," activity. And, of course, the connection between writing and agency leads to issues of critical literacy. Bhabha believes that critical literacy is intimately connected to the question of democratic representation. For example, he says in the interview below that "literacy is absolutely crucial for a kind of ability to be responsible to yourself, to make your own reading within a situation of political and cultural choice." Yet, at the same time we must be cautious not to treat literacy as a panacea or to fetishize it. As Bhabha points out, racism often is the "leading ideology" of the most literate people. Thus, critical literacy in and of itself guarantees nothing, but it is an essential step toward agency, self-representation, and an effective democracy. Consequently, the kind of work we do in composition is extremely important socially, and more institutions need to understand that the work of composition is less about linguistic competence than it is about critical intervention in the world.

The acquisition of agency and critical literacy is linked to another subject central to Bhabha's project: the role of theory. Theory enables people, both in the academy and in the public domain, to "break the continuity and the consensus of common sense"—to break it and to break *into* it. As a kind of critical literacy itself, theory helps us "interrupt the dominant and dominating strategies of generalization within a cultural or communicative or interpretational community." That is, it helps us challenge assumptions, preconceptions, fixed notions; it helps us "deal with processes, subjects, or objects in transition," not as static entities. For example, postcolonial theory allows us to break into the mastering discourses of sententiousness and colonialism and reminds us that "what was some people's modernity was somebody else's colonialism." It also helps us see boundaries not simply as "the space between one nation and another," but as a "kind of internal liminal space." The awareness of sententiousness that critical theory provides underscores, again, the importance of the job of compositionists, for we both help students to "read" the sententiousness in their lives and to "write" from a position of agency. We are helping them, in Bhabha's words, to look "beyond" the sentence and to learn that "other logics" of signification exist and that "the sentence can sometimes sentence us" to a particular language form. Bhabha does caution, however, that just as we must not fetishize literacy, we must not permit the "arrogance of theory" to settle into its own mastering discourses.

Perhaps no other subject is as central to Bhabha's work as the question of cultural difference. First, it is important not to essentialize and therefore homogenize a culture or group simply because its members appear to share certain traits or traditions. Cultural difference, according to Bhabha, is a "particular constructed discourse." Also, we should not conceive of a cultural group independently of other types of cultural difference. Bhabha reiterates that "what we think of as the politics of difference, what we think of as the politics of multiculturalism, what we think of as the politics of new social movements do not allow us to think the subject of any one of those margins—race, gender, class, culture, geopolitical location, or generation—exclusively." That is, cultural location is always an articulation of various intersecting and often contesting positions, and essentializing difference or isolating it from other positionalities is counterproductive. Race, class, gender and other forms of difference are always being "constituted and negotiated in a cross-boundary process." But more importantly, the problem of cultural difference is not that various cultures exist in the world; it is that difference becomes a site of "contestation, abuse, insult, and discrimination" when "something is being challenged about power or authority." Cultural difference becomes problematic when it becomes linked with "the redistribution of goods between cultures, or the funding of cultures, or the emergence of minorities or immigrants in a situation of resources." Only at this point, says Bhabha, is cultural difference produced, and it is at this point that difference leads to a politics of discrimination. Of course, the typical response to difference is containment. Racial minorities, for example, are forced to represent themselves as subnations, and in that context they do not threaten the dominant hegemony; however, if they "seep in, disseminate in, and change and translate what is seen to be the dominant lines of the transmission of cultural tradition," they immediately become a threat. Much of Bhabha's work, including important parts of this interview, is concerned with these dynamics of cultural difference and with finding ways that the subaltern *can* have voice, *can* have representation.

Bhabha posits that one way to understand the politics of difference better is to learn more about the role of affect in the dynamics of power and social marginality. He claims that "the structures of feeling and the structures of affect are radically devalued in the language of political effectivity." The discourse of political action has, according to Bhabha, concentrated "too much on questions of interest and too little on questions of political passion." Because the politics of difference have such a "deep and strong affective charge," it is necessary to "understand the part that emotions, affects, play in the construction of community politics." Emotions such as anger and hatred are "substantial," not empty adjectives. Consequently, Bhabha intends to begin looking closely at the role of emotions in politics in his future work.

Bhabha professes a "great respect and desire for fine writing," and he speaks nostalgically of his attempts at creative writing during his college days at the University of Bombay. His fascination for word choice and carefully crafted prose has carried over into his theoretical writing. He sees himself as doing theory "*by* doing a certain kind of writing." He comments, "To me, the idea has to shape, enact the rhetoric. There is no concept, I feel, that can stand on its own with great clarity if the writing is workmanlike or clumsy." To Bhabha, writing is "the staging of an idea, and I use that term with its full theatrical and operatic and dramatic possibilities." In our view, the interview below provides another important stage for him to perform his theory in a way that will be useful and informative to us all.

Q. Much of your work deals with the centrality of discourse and the importance of writing, be it in the "inscription or writing of identity," the "writing of the hybrid colonial subject," or the writing of the narrative of nationness. You yourself have written a substantial body of works for both scholarly publications and more public forums such as *New Statesman and Society* and *Artforum*. Do you consider yourself to be "a writer"?

A. Yes, very much so. In fact, when I was an undergraduate at the University of Bombay, it always surprised me how completely absorbed I would be when I wrote my rather small and worthless poems. I was entirely enchanted by the form and the activity. Somehow the agony in "creative writing" (as they call it) seemed much sweeter than the agony in theoretical writing. It just surprised me how completely absorbing it was to decide to use one word rather than another. I wrote rather short poems; that was the form I worked in. The consequence of this for my present work is that I'm very fascinated by doing theory *by* doing a certain kind of writing. To me, the idea has to shape, enact the rhetoric. There is no concept, I feel, that can stand on its own with great clarity if the writing is workmanlike or clumsy. So to me the writing of the theory, the writing of the concept, is very very important. Quite often I sort of inspire myself by starting out— even my theoretical, conceptual pieces—by reading works that inspire me to a certain fineness of expression. One of the things I often do is to read some completely unconnected work before I start writing, most often poetry. For example, I often read W.H. Auden, who is a great favorite of mine, or I read Robert Lowell— just as a matter of practice, just as a sort of ritual to begin writing a piece, even though it has nothing to do with the piece.

So, I have a great respect and desire for fine writing. Often I will use a word that stretches a point just because I feel that it takes the thought somewhat further than it may need to go, but the suggestiveness of that word both enacts a kind of finer sense and sentiment, even though it would have been easier to close it down with a more workmanlike word that would have done the job and nailed it down. But I prefer to keep that open. I remember Toni Morrison saying to me once, "Writing is all." If you can't do it in the writing and through the writing, if you can't do this whole kind of revisionary history of slavery and sexuality that she's involved in in some of her work, if you can't do it in and through the actual writing, you can't do it by giving people ideas or thoughts. The two things really have to work together. That is what I try to do. In a way, writing to me is the staging of an idea, and I use that term with its full theatrical and operatic and dramatic possibilities, in the way in which the concept might be the armature or the architecture of the idea.

Q. In "The Postcolonial and the Postmodern," you discuss Barthes' attempt to think "outside the sentence." You write, "The hierarchy and the subordinations of the sentence are replaced by the definitive discontinuity of the text, and what emerges is a form of writing that Barthes describes as 'writing aloud.'" You continue, "If you seek simply the sententious or the exegetical, you will not grasp the hybrid moment outside the sentence—not quite experience, not yet concept; part dream, part analysis; neither signifier nor signified. This intermediate space between theory and practice disrupts the disciplinary semiological demand to enumerate all the languages within earshot." This is an elegant theoretical intervention, and it is useful on a number of levels; however, those of us in rhetoric and composition are charged with helping students to "be in the sentence," to compose clear, sententious prose. Do you believe that teachers of writing should problematize the dynamics of discourse by introducing discussions of sententiousness?

A. Yes, I think so. Sententiousness is a particular ideology of rhetoric, and it has a particular history. Eighteenth-century sententiousness, for instance, was a very dominant form. It was related to various discourses like the law or political edicts. It is part of a rhetoric of governance and authority. So, I think some awareness of what sententiousness is—as a production, as a process of communication, its conditions—is very important. I also think that it is very important to teach students, people, to write in a way that is clear, to communicate what it is that they want to say effectively so that they can feel represented. There is no totality of representation, but I think people should feel—in the sentence, if you will, in the language—that they can represent themselves. I know that this links to the question of literacy, which is a very important subject that we'll discuss later. However, like all pedagogical forms, I think sententiousness must also keep open for itself the possibility that the place where the sentence falls, where it will be taken up again, where the pause occurs in the sententiousness, where there is a hesitation within it, is not just a disturbance. It's not just an abnormality of the sententiousness, but it could be the place for resistance to its authority, for the reelaboration of its object of attention.

What's important to me is the possibility of seeing the borders of sententiousness as porous, not in some simple dyadic form in which sententiousness is the authoritative and nonsententiousness is the marginal or the subaltern or the resistance, not at all like this—but to continually see sententiousness as transforming. As Henry James once said, these are forms of relationship that really don't end anywhere; sententiousness is itself an emergence. Understanding that it is itself not an origin but an emergence is very important because then one is open to other residual and emergent and marginal forms of meaning-making or communication or subject identification. So I think my suggestion that we should look in a way beyond the sentence is not to say, as is often said now in a kind of flippant way, that we should move beyond rationalism or something of that kind, or rationality. Rather, it is to say that there are other logics of signification to which we should be open, and the sentence can sometimes sentence us, in the imprisoning sense, to the kind of prison house of a particular language form.

Q. "The Commitment to Theory" represents a carefully elaborated view of the interaction of politics, rhetoric, and theory. You write, "Political positions are not simply identifiable as progressive or reactionary, bourgeois or radical, prior to the act of *critique engagée*, or outside the terms and conditions of their discursive address. It is in this sense that the historical moment of political action must be thought of as part of the history of the form of its writing. This is not to state the obvious, that there is no knowledge—political or otherwise—outside representation." It is to suggest that "the 'political' as a form of calculation and strategic action dedicated to social transformation" must acknowledge "the force of writing, its metaphoricity and its rhetorical discourse, as a productive matrix which defines the 'social' and makes it available as an objective of and for action." Some compositionists may understand this view as a confirmation that writing is *the* central political act and therefore that writing instruction is an important form of political activism. Do you place any limits on the political effectivity of writing (or, for that matter, on the field of composition itself), and, if so, what are they?

A. Before I answer, let me just interject that as somebody who, as you quite rightly detected, is very keen on writing, I would like to compliment you on the form of the writing of these questions. I had the experience when reading them that each question antici- pates a thought that will develop in the next one. They really move very well, and the interconnections are not only serial; they go in many directions. They are very finely cast.

   To return to your question, I certainly do believe that writing is a political form. By *writings*—if I might use that word—and *inscription*, I'm not only talking about printed writing or writing as we usually understand it. I'm talking about the possibility of making a determining mark on a surface. It may be a social surface; it may be a visual screen. I'm talking about writing in the widest sense: a kind of ordering of things or ordering of commu- nication in one way in the context of a wider contingent structure. That's what I'm talking about. Certain forms of ritual could be inscribed in that way; certain modes of political organization could be inscribed in that way too. Having said that, let me say that I do feel that even in the more narrow sense writing is—and composition is—a highly political activity. It's a political activity. There is a politics of instruction, a politics of composition. Too often writing—in the broadest sense—is treated as a communica- tional medium where the subjects of that communication are constituted prior to the writing, where the objects of that com- munication are also constituted prior to that writing, and where the task of writing is seen as transparently mediating between already pregiven subjects, pregiven objects, and a preconstituted *mise en scène*. My interest is in suggesting that the agency of writing actually constitutes in a dialogic way new relationships between elements that may or may not be pregiven such that the pregivenness is questioned, the preconstitutedness is questioned. Of course, there are certain conditions, certain determinants that precede a particular act of communication, or writing, or mediation; but what happens in and through the writing is the reconjugation of those given conditions, and that is what I believe to be the effectivity of writing as a kind of agency, as a performance, as a practice, and as a process which is too little understood.

I chose here to talk here about metaphoricity because metaphoricity is one of those even more widely recognized moments when you have to stop and think where the writing act is going, what it is trying to constitute beyond what it is in some transparent way saying—the doubleness of the inscriptive act. So, I do think the activity of writing is, in that sense, a continually revisionary, and in some ways revolutionary, activity. I don't mean "revolutionary" with a capital *R*, not in some sort of political-adventurist sense, as I could be understood to mean. I'm just saying that it's a continual movement. In the "Minority Maneuvers and Unsettled Negotiations" essay in *Critical Inquiry*, it was my purpose to talk about political movement as movement, and indeed writing itself as a kind of movement.

I just want to add that we've talked about this active and even proactive—indeed, even revisionary—sense of writing. And I've tried to think, in the widest sense, of what politics might be conceived in that way. I just want to add that writing, therefore, is itself a mediation. It's not a medium; it's a mediation. Critics, philosophers, and political thinkers are so easily able to conceive of the mediatory nature of individuals, for instance, or of a particular kind of institutional form. But in a way, writing, which scribbles over all these things, subtends them—writing in the widest sense as the inscription of a mark, the making of an order—is somehow relegated to a transparency, as if it is following on from positions, objects, subjects already constituted. So it's this that I'm trying to get at in that passage you highlighted.

Q. You comment that you have tried to "erase" the popular binarism between theory and politics, the intellectual and activist, and you say that, it is a sign of "political maturity" to accept that "there are many forms of political writing whose different effects are obscured when they are divided between the 'theoretical' and the 'activist.' It is not as if the leaflet involved in the organization of a strike is short on theory, while a speculative article on the theory of ideology ought to have more practical examples or applications. They are both forms of discourse and to that extent they produce rather than reflect their objects of reference. The difference between them lies in their operational qualities." Of course, such a position enters into the larger debate over the efficacy of theoretical work in the public domain, whether critical theory can ever be truly "activist" or achieve ends in the world beyond the academy. What do you see as the role of theory in the world outside the academy, and what are the "operational qualities" that distinguish the work of theory from that of other kinds of writing?

A. I see that the section you have chosen is from "The Commitment to Theory," and I think it took me some time to write that. Let me just say, if I can cut to the bone, that I think that the operational quality of theory in the public domain is to break the continuity and the consensus of common sense. It is to break it and to break into it. Too often, the breaking into common sense has been represented as some deconstructive work of ideological critique or symptomatic reading which then takes that commonsensical false-consciousness or ideological perspective and puts a kind of carapace of conceptual order around it. I can see both historically and philosophically why that should happen and when it has happened. In the last two decades, for instance, the very useful and brilliant work of Louis Althusser, not so much in itself but in his followers, produced precisely that kind of response. People looked "theoretically" for the fissures in common sense, and then instead of actually occupying those fissures and seeing where else it will get you (which is what I think the work of theory is: if your ontology or your genealogy is a fissured one, then where else will it get you, and how would you work through it?), what they did was to pour the cement of their own theoretical position into the fissure and cover it up. I have always felt uncomfortable with that, even when I didn't have the theoretical language to deal with it. I'm now talking of seminars in the mid to late '70s in Oxford when there wasn't any theoretical work except through the brilliance and the generosity of Terry Eagleton—one seminar a week where we would go to discuss such matters. But even at that time, it felt for me conceptually that this filling up of the fissure, detecting it and then filling it up, was not the appropriate thing. For me it's always been a matter of asking, "If you actually now reposition yourself in the fissure as a form of knowledge, as a mode of signification, as a place of enunciation, where would you get to? What would you do? What possibilities would be opened up for you?" Not to come with your own already constituted resolution to the fissure. Of course, you come with a whole lot of reconstituted baggage, but the whole point is how can your baggage be thrown around? How can it be challenged by the fissure?

That's why I say again that the use of theory must be both to intervene in the continuity and consensus of common sense and also to interrupt the dominant and dominating strategies of generalization within a cultural or communicative or interpretational community precisely where that community wants to say in a very settled and stentorian way: this is the general and this is the case; this is the principle and this is its empirical application as a form of proof and justification. I think that the importance of theory is to unsettle the complacency of those relations. If I might speak both theoretically and figuratively at once, the role of theory is precisely that kind of alienation and distanciation that, say, Brecht talks about. It's also, in another kind of philosophical register (and I'm being translative here), the snatching of the moment that flashes out in a situation of danger or emergency that Benjamin talks about. I want to give you a third example in which theory does its work: it is often seen to be an applicative or bridging work. In some ways it is, but it's bridging in the sense that Heidegger talks about. Until you throw the bridge across the river, you don't quite know what the banks are. You don't know what you're calculating. And I think theory works in that way.

There is a second emphasis in your question, which has to do with the operational nature of the theoretical, the operational qualities that we need to distinguish. For me, the purpose of the theoretical—which I said a moment ago is part of this intervention into the consensus and continuum of common sense—is to make us aware of what it would be to deal with processes, subjects, or objects in transition. Transitionality has been for me a guiding problem. That's exactly what it is, a problem: how to deal with the transitional. And various things that I've emphasized in the construction of social reality, the construction of subject formation, and the construction of meaning—things like ambivalence—are to me important and become subjects for theoretical speculation because they have within them this agonistic, unresolved moment of transition. They also demand a certain kind of ethical responsibility to negotiate that. Theory has been important for me operationally in these ways.

Q. You write in *The Location of Culture*, "I have chosen to demonstrate the importance of the space of writing, and the problematic
of address, at the very heart of the liberal tradition because it is
here that the myth of the 'transparency' of the human agent and
the reasonableness of political action is most forcefully asserted.
Despite the more radical political alternatives of the right and the
left, the popular, common-sense view of the place of the individual in relation to the social is still substantially thought and lived
in ethical terms moulded by liberal beliefs. What the attention to
rhetoric and writing reveals is the discursive ambivalence that
makes 'the political' possible." This view suggests that the crucial
function of the textual and the rhetorical is to make political
struggle possible by drawing attention to discursive ambivalence.

A. Yes, I think that's a fair reading, but let's flesh it out. What
address does is to draw your attention—if I may be figurative—
not only to the place where the sign emerges in a particular
discourse or a particular speech act, but how it flies and then falls
at a point of relocation. That's what address is—how it moves
from one space to another. Now, ambivalence is very important
in order to contest forms of rationalism (not rationality but
rationalism) that want to ascribe certain kinds of intentionality and
achieved intentionality, as somehow flying through this transparent and immaterial medium. My emphasis on address is always to
suggest that where the sign emerges and where it ends up may
have incommensurable and contradictory terrains of inscription
at either end. So to that extent, where address addresses the
problem of the construction of social meaning or the ascription
of a person or peoples, and so on, the important thing about
writing and indeed the ambivalent structure of the sign in its
emergence and its destination is to be aware that politically we are
continually constructing the constituencies that we address, just as
we are constructing the objects of value that we are transmitting.
This, therefore, does not enable you to give a universal and
transhistorical value to things like virtue or tolerance or secular-
ism—or indeed the sacred. I think this makes you each time
reinterrogate, because you are constructing the constituency and,
indeed, the consistency of language and thought which you are
then pointing to digitally.

Q. In "The Commitment to Theory," you effectively challenge
critical theorists (particularly materialists) to avoid the kind of

political idealism in which theory merely develops and augments an a priori political principle or commitment—or, what you call "identikit political idealism." The language of critique is effective, you argue, not because it keeps separate the terms of opposition, "but to the extent to which it overcomes the given grounds of opposition and opens up a space of translation: a place of hybridity, figuratively speaking, where the construction of a political object that is new, *neither one nor the other*, properly alienates our political expectations, and changes, as it must, the very forms of our recognition of the moment of politics." The opening up of this space of translation is a sign that "history is *happening*—within the pages of theory." Here you offer a view of theory that is more rhetorical than that of identikit political idealism. You claim it is "deeper" and more "dangerous." What makes the passage of history in theory more dangerous?

A. When I used the term "passage of history in theory," I wanted to suggest three ways of reading the notion of passage. First, "passage" more spatially, as in opening up a space. Second, "passage" as a kind of movement, as in a rite of passage. A rite of passage is a way not only of thinking transformation but of thinking the transition that is involved in making the transformation, and I want to make a distinction there. And then I also want to think about "passage" as a piece of inscription, as we might say a passage in a book, which also has many of those meanings: it opens up something; it takes you from somewhere to somewhere; and also, in itself, it holds you in that moment of transition. So there are three ways of thinking of passage in that phrase in *The Location of Culture*. My interest there relates to something we talked about earlier, which is to unsettle the kind of conceptual mastery of what is understood to be theory, as some kind of x-raying mechanism that will take you to the bare bones of a situation, on the one hand; but also, to contest the authority that is given very often to historical event, as if it is somehow there and it is there preceding our theoretical attention, that when we attend to it we attend to it already given an established reality. What I stress is really the need to open a passage between those two in order to make either of those positions untenable, and my language is somewhat Benjaminian, particularly from the essay "On Language as Such and on the Language of Man," where he says that the important thing about translation is to focus on the continuum of transformation, all those small micromovements which if you only look at the large arch, and if you only look at the dominant passage of history, you will miss. It's those micromovements that happen *in the midst of* moments of change, of transformation, that I think need to be attended to, because if you don't attend to them, the temptation is always to fall into large claims about identity and difference, not to see the negotiatory strategies by which positions, or persons, or cultures get constituted. It's for that reason that I think such a passage, in the various meanings that I've given to the term, must be kept open as a way between, or in order not to allow the arrogance of theory—or, indeed, the arrogance of history—to settle into their own mastering discourses.

Q. One of the most important theoretical innovations you offer is the distinction you draw between cultural diversity and cultural difference. You say that "Cultural diversity is the recognition of pre-given cultural contents and customs; held in a time-frame of relativism it gives rise to liberal notions of multiculturalism, cultural exchange or the culture of humanity. Cultural diversity is also the representation of a radical rhetoric of the separation of totalized cultures that live unsullied by the intertextuality of their historical locations, safe in the utopianism of a mythic memory of a unique of collective identity." To trouble, if not displace, this notion of cultural diversity and the liberal and left-progressive projects of multiculturalism it underwrites, you suggest a rather complex notion of "cultural difference" as a kind of "adding to" that "doesn't add up." Would you explain more specifically what you mean by cultural difference?

A. Let me start with a rather abstract formulation which I'll then try to flesh out. You take the "adding to without adding up" from "DissemiNation," and in that same essay I also say that we should never simply conjoin or elide the difference between the repetition of the symbol and the iteration of the sign. (This relates back to what you were talking about in terms of address.) Quite often, the difference of cultures is in fact read on the similarity of certain signs that work their ways through cultures, as, indeed, particular cultures are unified by finding—through the concept of tradition, for instance—similarities over time, as the phrase has it. My concern is that cultural difference is constituted in a kind of agonistic and unresolved tension between those two things, the moment of recognition where a community or a culture recognizes itself in some generalizing practice. But then, there has to be the other work, which is, however, that the particular practice—it could be a practice of inheritance; it could be a practice to do with a certain ritual—affects different members of that culture very differently and, indeed, in the translation from the general more pedagogical level to the performative level, there can be oppositionality within that culture.

So to me cultural difference is the awareness that first of all you have the problem of difference not because there are many cultures, preconstituted cultures. The notion that cultural diversity is a problem because there are already many different cultures is not the reason why you have cultural difference. Cultural difference is a particular constructed discourse at a time when something is being challenged about power or authority. At that point, a particular cultural trait or tradition—the smell of somebody's food, the color of their skin, the accent that they speak with, their particular history, be it Irish or Indian or Jewish—becomes the site of contestation, abuse, insult, and discrimination. Cultural difference is not a natural emanation of the fact that there are different cultures in the world. It's a much more problematic and sophisticated reproduction of a ritual, a habit, a trait, a characteristic. That reproduction has to bear a whole set of significations, tensions, anxieties. And it becomes the sign of those tensions and anxieties. Cultural difference is not difficult, if you like, because there are many diverse cultures; it is because there is some particular issue about the redistribution of goods between cultures, or the funding of cultures, or the emergence of minorities or immigrants in a situation of resources—where resource allocation has to go—or the construction of schools and the decision about whether the school should be bilingual or trilingual or whatever. It is at that point that the problem of cultural difference is produced. So, it's really an argument against the naturalization of the notion of culture.

Q. In your discussion of what the prefix "post" in "postcolonialism" means, you write: "Postcoloniality . . . is a salutary reminder of the persistent 'neo-colonial' relations within the 'new' world order and the multinational division of labour. . . . Beyond this, however, postcolonial critique bears witness to those countries and communities constituted . . . 'otherwise than modernity.'

Such cultures of a *postcolonial contra-modernity* may be contingent to modernity, discontinuous or in contention with it, resistant to its oppressive, assimilationist technologies; but they also deploy the cultural hybridity of their borderline conditions to 'translate,' and therefore reinscribe, the social imaginary of . . . modernity." Postcoloniality, in your view, is clearly neither another school of criticism, nor a mere extension of postmodernism as the celebration of the fragmentation of the grand narratives of post-enlightenment rationalism, which you call a "profoundly parochial enterprise." What is striking here, and what we would like you to explain further, is your view of postcolonialism as a spatial and temporal project that opens up an intervening space and revisionary time in modernity.

A. This is a very large question, so I'll have to restrict my answer somewhat. I want to follow very closely your suggestion that I should locate the notion of the postcolonial in and as a spatial and temporal project, and, in addition to that, as a revisionary temporal and spatial project. Let me say, then, that I think it is the responsibility—theoretical, ethical, aesthetic, political—of what we may call postcolonial discourse (which is a term that has its own problems) to remind us that what was some people's modernity was somebody else's colonialism. Therefore, I would say to those who suggest that the word *postcolonial* bucks the responsibility of a word like *neocolonial* that these terms are not exclusive; the one does not obliterate the other. The usefulness of that ambiguous and ambivalent "post" before "colonial" is that it draws attention to this anteriority, this early emergence when modernity is emerging in and through a very complex negotiation with its own colonial double life. That's the point, that at the point at which the notion of universality as an ethical and political value is emerging, at that very moment a discourse in the name of universality—a discourse of discrimination, of marginalization, of the negation of autonomy—is being produced by those very cultures themselves in the colonial site. So, I think "the postcolonial" not only refers us to indigenous agencies in the colonial world, it also gives us a sense of how western modernity has its own colonial anteriority and not the kind of claims to origin that it claims for itself. Very often modernity in its desire for democracy might make a claim to some Greek ideal, but I think it should also, at that point, make a claim to the colonial reality in relation to which it has elaborated its own modernity, whether that modernity be the notion of nationhood or civility or civil society or civic society or civic virtue.

So to me the most important thing about the postcolonial project is to make one aware of the global and transnational history of those very early moments of modernity and the various obdurant, incommensurable, and aporetic tensions that modernity has to become ethically and politically aware of (and that postmodernity also has to become ethically and politically aware of) in claiming some discursive or political or spatial authority for itself. That's absolutely crucial, and that's why the idea that people who talk about the postcolonial somehow neglect the very important neocolonial social and political arrangements of the contemporary world—the international division of labor, the inequities of the international monetary fund, and so on—are somewhat missing the point, because first of all, they're not exclusive. And secondly, it would enhance such a reading of neocolonialism or neocoloniality if it were able to date the emergence of the history of modernity to that place that postcolonialism is trying to indicate. So I think that this is really the key to that question.

Q. Hybridity is a central concept in your critical project. You write, "Hybridity . . . is no jejune post-Modern lark, nor is it simply my invention. It comes from [James] Baldwin's profound meditation on the unique power and pathos of the American color line." "Hybridity is not . . . about new 'alloys' conceived in an amoral state of historical amnesia; it is not about cultural appropriation or assimilation subsumed in a celebration of citizenship. Hybridity, as Baldwin testifies, is a form of social and psychic recognition; it is an awareness of the graftings, transitions, and translations through which we define our present and articulate an ethics equal to the way we live now." Would you explain how hybridity, as a form of social and psychic recognition, is not assimilable to a liberal politics of recognition but instead must disrupt it and its nondifferential concept of cultural time?

A. Let me just take us back to a question you asked me earlier that really prepares us for this particular problem. I want to remind ourselves of what I said about writing and communication and discourse. The important issue is that there's a similarity here, in this respect: that just as the notion of inscription does not allow there to be a preconstituted subject (that doesn't mean that people are not there prior to the speech act; it just means that in and through the performance of the speech act, those positionalities have acquired different significances), in the same way, when we talk about hybridity, as opposed to the politics of recognition, we are making a similar distinction. The politics of recognition assumes—whether it's in the Hegelian master-slave model or in any other model of a kind of mutual culturally relativistic recognition—that there are these kinds of in-place subjects in and through whom the process of recognition happens. The question of hybridization is precisely to draw attention to the way in which the process of negotiation is continually placing and replacing the members of that act of cultural or social or political interaction. First of all, the "subject" of hybridization is a different subject than the subject of the politics of recognition. The subject of hybridization is an enunciatory subject.

In the enunciatory subject—which is a subject in performance and process, the notion of what is to be authorized, what is to be deauthorized, what difference will be signified, what similarity or similitude will be articulated—these things are continually happening in the very process of discourse-making or meaning-making. They are not subjects which are already given to that process of enunciation. The most important thing about the process of enunciation as a kind of borderline concept is that it is aware that it is through the process of enunciation that the borders between objects or subjects or practices are being constituted. Therefore, it really does contest most of the liberal theories of individualization as being the process of subject formation, and it attacks precisely the punctuality of the notion of a liberal individual subject. That means that there is no naivete in the construction of the liberal individualist subject. It's not as if (as often it is represented as being) it's some kind of completely ahistorical conceit in an ahistorical and universal way; it's not even *that* that bugs me particularly or that I find difficult. What I do find difficult is that somehow that subject is always on time. Its priority always depends upon it being absolutely timely, so timely in fact that its universality is each time affirmed. Its position prior to the process of enunciation is each time valorized. It's that punctuality of the subject that the concept of enunciation, which is central to the process of hybridization, contests.

If you think for just a moment about some influential theoretical images of the subject, you'll find that each of them contests punctuality. For instance, if you think about the Althusserian concept of interpellation as one very popular notion of the way of thinking about the subject in contemporary theory (in cultural studies certainly, although Althusser is no longer in vogue, but much of Jameson, much of Eagleton, much of a whole materialist Marxist cultural studies group still works around that subject willy-nilly), you have in the structure of interpellation, in the interpellated subject, the contest to what I've called individualist punctuality by saying that the subject by its very nature is overdetermined or displaced. Althusser has to, therefore, make his move toward Lacan to construct that subject, Freud and Lacan. Now of course, the limitation of that is dictated much more by a desire to enshrine a kind of structuralist Marxism where the subject can't also be terribly errant and in movement. The subject has to be fixed. So what he gives with one hand he takes away with the other. He gives this notion of overdetermination and displacement by his move toward Lacan and toward the unconscious, but then he pulls back at that point and says, however, "As you know, the subject is not an individualist subject; it's a produced subject of displacement, an overdetermined subject, but it is the subject of the Lacanian imaginary." By making that move, he takes the subject out of the flux and gives it a kind of punctuality, the imaginary relation being the most stable of all the relations of identification in Lacan. So, what I'm saying is not that we've got to move from the one kind of subject to another kind of subject, that we've got to move from timeliness to eternal belatedness. If we choose between those things, then there is no real choice; all we're doing is moving from one to another.

I think, therefore, that the reason why ambivalence is important as a theoretical idea is that we've got to continually calculate the tensions between these positions. That's why I've always been opposed to the way of doing cultural theory or doing theory in general that is always looking for more and more accurate notions of contradictions, subject, or whatever: "We no longer want the Lacanian one, so now we've got to do the Lacanian/Kantian version of it. If only we could get the subject right, if only we could get the object right, and so on." I've always been opposed to that. It's this opening up of the question of the subject, by opening up the question of its nonpunctual evocation, that's important. That's why I've been so insistent upon raising questions of disjunctive temporality at the point of enunciation. That's why to me the question of cultural difference is not the problem of there being diverse cultures and that diversity produces the difference. It is that each time you want to make a judgment about a culture or about a certain element within a certain culture, in the context of some kind of social and political condition that puts pressure on that judgment, you are standing at that point in this disjunctive difference-making site. And you cannot avoid that this is where, in that disjunctive and slippery and problematic terrain, your foot cannot fixedly grow.

Q. In "The Postcolonial and the Postmodern" you write, "The postcolonial perspective forces us to rethink the profound limitations of a consensual and collusive 'liberal' sense of cultural community. It insists that cultural and political identity are constructed through a process of alterity. Questions of race and cultural difference overlay issues of sexuality and gender and overdetermine the social alliances of class and democratic socialism. The time for 'assimilating' minorities to holistic and organic notions of cultural value has dramatically passed. The very language of cultural community needs to be rethought from a postcolonial perspective." Is the liberal concept of community inherently flawed, and, if so, what do you think of critical projects, such as Ernesto Laclau and Chantal Mouffe's, that propose a hegemonic strategy for the left that does not renounce liberal-democratic ideology but attempts to deepen and expand it?

A. The answer to that question must rest on what we understand by "deepening and expanding." That's the issue here. Much of what Chantal is developing is a kind of agonistic democracy, and this is something for which I have a good deal of time. So in terms of that difference, I don't so much want to define it against what they're doing because there are many ideas that we share, a whole history of thinking that we share. But I think that what I'm concerned about is the basis on which consent and consensuality as a guiding principle of liberal community puts into place a particular notion of what a subject is, which is where I think I would differ. Another area is what culture is as signification, which I've talked about in terms of enunciation; it is very difficult to accommodate that notion of the disjunctive ground of the enunciative. Liberal communities can deal with contradiction and, indeed, need contradiction to test the mettle of tolerance. That they absolutely need. But can they deal with the disjunctive? Can they deal with the aporetic? Can they deal with ambivalence in the way in which I've suggested it? Isn't there a tendency each time to deal with difference or tolerance by preconstituting communities and giving each community its authenticity and integrity and saying that difference is actually integrally and expressively contained within each one we're choosing between, and between them we choose with various criteria? But *my* thinking of an enunciative community starts out very differently. The whole basis on which constitution takes place is different, so I think that this is another way in which the notion of the liberal community in my view would be different. Finally, I think that really within liberal theories of community—and I realize that I'm biting off a large chunk and trying to be succinct about it—there isn't often adequate attention given to the fact that the group as an agent cannot be conceived of as a group of individuals, that we need another way of thinking about what a group interest or a group demand is that does not simply conceive of groupishness as a position negotiated among individuals.

I think that what I'm saying would need us to complicate the whole notion of group identification in and through a more psychoanalytic way of thinking. So, theoretically I can see what needs to be done, but I'm not, at this point, in a position to say that if we started thinking like that, how it would cash out in terms of very important policy-driven, practical, political consider-ations. It would be like asking, if you raised the question of the phantasmatic, fantasy, social fantasy, in the construction of a particular political position, how would a court recognize that? Or how would a policy institution recognize that? That's the question I'm not entirely clear on at the moment. But I think it's for those reasons that I would say that what I'm suggesting would require not so much a deepening of the liberal ideology as it would a necessary erasure of it, in the Derridean sense. And by that I do mean—and I think you have highlighted to me some-thing that I knew but had not seen demonstrated—that among the various theories and positions and forms of discourse that I have been in conversation with, right from the very beginning I seem to have been more or less naively in conversation with the history of liberalism, something that you really have made me aware of in studying your questions and thinking of a response to them.

Q. In "The Commitment to Theory" you offer an important view on the concept of hegemony, saying that the work of hegemony is "itself the process of iteration and differentiation. It depends on the production of alternative or antagonistic images that are always produced side by side and in competition with each other. It is this side-by-side nature, this partial presence, or metonymy of antagonism, and its effective significations, that give meaning (quite literally) to a politics of struggle *as the struggle of identifications* and the war of positions. It is therefore problematic to think of it as sublated into an image of the collective will." Doesn't the work of hegemony and political struggle also involve an attempt to fix and pre-fix images, meanings, and values and thereby subsume and sublate social antagonism?

A. Yes it does, but within a general landscape of the iterative, within a general landscape of the contingent. It's a different thing to think about fixation within an economy of iteration and contingency than to think of fixation within a more universalistic or a more communicational or expressive model of the subject or of meaning. It's that the question of hegemonic fixation as I'm suggesting depends upon the profound liminality and instability of the question of representation. That's what we've been talking about in trying to move away from the notion of the subject of recognition toward the subject of enunciation. That's where we've been moving, and I think rather neatly; and, therefore, I feel that fixation has a very different value when you see it in the trammels of representation as opposed to if you see it as the destiny and the teleology of representation.

Your very interesting question also made me think of something else. There is a kind of narrative or image of power—which has also been one of the specters, the ghosts we've been dealing with in our discussion—that somehow assumes that power works because somewhere prior to a particular exercise of authority it has been fixed. It works because it has already been institutionalized; it's been prefixed in a way. And I think that to some extent, of course, this is true. You enter into a negotiation only because there is a disequilibrium or an inequality. But I think how you negotiate depends very much on how you read the weight and sedimentation of that prior fixing or prefixing of power or authority or domination. It's to try and rethink the context of that prefixing, to suggest that this prefixing may also be disarticulated or unfixed, that I've always suggested lets us think about the moment of prefixing as a kind of anteriority that does itself in the present—in the moment w en you're negotiating—produce its kind of anteriority. That's how I also want to try and rethink the *pre*; the *pre* is not a givenness, but an anteriority.

Q. Much of your work insists on the importance of interrogating the mode of representation of otherness. In "The Other Question," for example, you write, "An important feature of colonial discourse is its dependence on the concept of 'fixity' in the ideological construction of otherness." But fixity, as you remind us, is a paradoxical mode of representation: "it connotes rigidity and an unchanging order as well as disorder, degeneracy and daemonic repetition." As you point out, one of the principal strategies of fixity is the stereotype, which "is not a simplification because it is a false representation of a given reality. It is a simplification because it is an arrested, fixated form of representation" that denies the play of difference. The consequence is that the stereotype "impedes the circulation and articulation of [for example] the signifier 'race' as anything other than its fixity as racism." What strategies might we take to rethink race beyond the limitations of fixity?

A. One of the ways in which history or historical situations or political struggles have made us rethink race beyond the limitations of its fixity has been the way in which race theory, so popular in the nineteenth century, and the integrity of race theory as a discourse, has itself been generally questioned. Its object is no longer unitary or fixed. But I also think that the history of political movements has shown us that what we think of as the politics of difference, what we think of as the politics of multiculturalism, what we think of as the politics of new social movements do not allow us to think the subject of any one of those margins—race, gender, class, culture, geopolitical location, or generation—exclusively. We do not or we cannot think those things exclusively in themselves because, I believe, of the concept of difference that I've been trying to explore that underlies them. As I say in that piece on minority maneuvers, we are always in the middle of difference. If there is anything about the theoretical work that

I've been doing, it has been to shift—whether it's at the level of
enunciation, whether it's at the level of subject formation—away
from this idea that the politics of difference consists in the putting
together of one originary marking with another originary marking
and a third one—one being race, one being sex, one being class.
These are always in a way being constituted and negotiated in a
cross-boundary process. That does not mean that at any particular time you may not want to emphasize one particular strategy of
difference or one particular form of identification rather than
another. That is perfectly possible. But as we know it, what is
impossible is to, in a sense, take the textuality of difference and
separate its threads because somehow the effectivity of thinking
through difference is to keep thinking through these nodal textiles
and not to give any one of them temporally a prior or an a priori
authority. So I think that's very important to understand within
the framework of the theory of difference.

Now, let me say something else: it's very important to understand that what the theory of identification allows us to understand—identification as a process of the iterative and the
enunciatory—is not just that we identify one on one or one on the
another, if I might play with these terms. It's not just who you
identify with, but what you identify with in that object. That's a
way of thinking the politics of difference. So in the articulation
between, say for instance, a certain feminist position and a certain
position on race, both of these positions will be substantially
transformed because of the object around which they decide to
negotiate an articulation between themselves. It could be housing
or education, for example. If it's education in an African-
American community in the U.S., then the coming together of
feminism and the question of race will not be defined by the prior
given signs—race and gender. They will be reconstituted in and
through a negotiation with this third space or third thing which in
a way disjuncts any sense of the two of them doing just some kind
of simple dealing with each other. Negotiation is always a double
dealing—a doubling dealing, not a mere double dealing. So it
seems to me that context is of course very important. If you're
thinking then about class issues and education issues and race
issues for Muslim minorities in Paris, there's a very different sign
of what class is because that sign of class will be class through a
certain kind of postcolonial migration and resettlement; the sign

of gender will be constituted partly through certain French republican ideas but also through certain other ideas that the migrant community brings with it. So, to return to what I said in response to your question about adding to without adding up, the sign each time, in each of its iterations, constitutes a different set of priorities and choices and significations in each iterative moment. So my sense is that we think beyond the limitations of fixity because the form of difference and enunciation that I've been suggesting pushes us never to be contained by any sign for longer than its rearticulation or translation demands.

Q. Given what you've just said, in the national discourse on race here in the U.S., the media now regularly call on people of color to represent divergent political positions on various issues. Does this development suggest that fixed notions of race may be loosening up somewhat?

A. This is a very interesting issue to bring up in this context because it calls on people of color to represent divergent political positions on various issues so long as their diversity is contained by a kind of ideological and political matrix that always makes them into little nations. They have to be subnations. They have to see their context as subnational. One of the most influential works recently in this area is Will Kymlicka's *Multicultural Citizenship*. You cannot read anything without reference to Kymlicka's work. He says very clearly that the only way in which minorities, in the long run, will be able to conceive of themselves as being participants in wider cultures is to accept the national or subnational form. But that's the issue: represent yourself as a little national minority and of course we will support you; but seep in, disseminate in, and change and translate what is seen to be the dominant lines of the transmission of cultural tradition, of national ritual, then we're not so sure. Become a virus and we don't want you; remain virtuous in the national mold and you can come and join "the mixed salad," or "the melting pot," or the consommé, or the casserole, or whatever else you'd like. Sit at our table.

Q. In several of your works you theorize a cultural construction of nationness as a form of social and textual affiliation. For example, you say that the project of *Nation and Narration* is to "explore the Janus-faced ambivalence of language itself in the construction of the Janus-faced discourse of the nation." You write, "To study the nation through its narrative address does not merely draw attention to its language and rhetoric; it also attempts to alter the conceptual object itself. If the problematic 'closure' of textuality questions the 'totalization' of national culture, then its positive value lies in displaying the wide dissemination through which we construct the field of meanings and symbols associated with national life." You seem to believe, then, that critical theory has the potential to help rewrite the nation, to alter the material realities as well as the symbolic content of nationness. What specific strategies do you see critical theory developing to effect such changes?

A. First, in its obstruction to the processes of totalization, critical theory allows us to reconceive of a very potent myth in the construction of a homogeneous society: the myth of the national past. I think it's obvious from what I've been saying about enunciation and the iterative temporality of national culture why that would unsettle the notion of a continuous past. But for reasons that take us right back to the question of sententiousness, in allowing us to break down, or break through, or write across, or run across the sententiousness of the discourse of the national life, critical theory allows us to see the residual and emergent forces often linked with communities of interest—with the way in which, say, national self-belonging can for AIDS and gay communities be mediated through the notion of mourning, melancholia, illness, citizenship, and effective citizenship. Just to give you one example of what I think the sententiousness of citizenship once broken down can open up into, we could think about similar ways in which women's movement can emerge out of this trumping, or negotiating, or displacing the sententious.

So, rethinking what authority and tradition is through the treachery of trumping the sententious not only allows for sites of emergence; that emergence—and I've talked about the emergence of, say, the gay community—allows you to rethink the notion of the people. What is the people? What is the national people? If the past is the myth of the nation in a displaced time, "the past," the people is the recurrent myth of every national discourse about its presentness. The presentness of the nation, let me propose, is often symbolized in a notion of a people. Its contemporaneity is always the people. And I think that to study nationhood through its narrative address must make you question what it means to construct a people, or how a people is inscribed, or how a discourse creates its own authority by referencing "a people." It makes you rethink that. In fact, in *Nation and Narration*, where I deal with the concept of the pedagogical and the performative as a kind of agonistic and ambivalent construction of the nation, the fulcrum of that argument is how we may rethink the notion of the people. So the past, I think, can be rethought. I think the present, the notion of the people, can be rethought.

Another way in which critical theory can do its work is to help us to see boundaries not as simply the space between one nation and another, one self and another, but to see the boundary as always also facing inward, as some kind of internal liminal space; this allows us to think more generally of a way of connecting nations or countries, not by using the national form as a currency of exchange, but by using those kinds of minorities within nations who are always seen as both partly belonging to and not belonging enough; that partial condition becomes a way of making a transnational articulation. For instance, ecological movements very often—and a number of minority groups who by the nature of the demand they make, or by who they are, or by the voice they articulate are seen to be neither inside nor outside—find their theater of action by moving across boundaries to those other groups who occupy similar ambivalent and liminal positions outside. So I think there is a different way of elaborating the transnational than using the nation as the counter of exchange.

Q. In "DissemiNation," you make what is for us a provocative but underdeveloped statement that identifies literacy as one of the instruments for narrating the nation. In this context, you say that historians and political theorists (and we might add, compositionists) ignore literacy in an effort to evade "the essential question of the representation of the nation as a temporal process." Would you elaborate on what you see as the role that literacy and literacy instruction play in the constitution and interrogation of the nation?

A. This is a very important question, and coming as I do from India, it has a very specific significance for me. I feel that literacy is connected intimately and institutionally with the question of democratic representation. It's more complex than saying that you can't really have a one-person one-vote system unless you have literacy because people are open then to all kinds of pressures, particularly in poorer countries where votes can be bought and sold. (Of course, votes can be bought and sold in Chicago or in any other place.) It's not limited to the South. But I do think that literacy is absolutely crucial for a kind of ability to be responsible to yourself, to make your own reading within a situation of political and cultural choice. In the Indian context, fascinatingly, the state of Kerala in the south has the highest literacy, that literacy fostered very much by Jesuit and other Catholic missionaries. And Kerala has been (or was until recently; I'm not sure of the situation at the moment) the state which had communist rule in an unbroken period of fifteen or twenty years. So there was a particular collaboration between Catholicism, communism, literacy, and democratic development.

Literacy is very important for the representation of "self," by which I don't mean individuals, just self-representation within a democratic foundation. But I think that there's no doubt that literacy is also in some ways an equalizing force. There is a danger of course in fetishizing literacy, the kind of fetishism when people say (and I'm talking about literacy in the more general sense), "We have this terrible racism, and it's because people don't know enough about another's culture. They don't know how to appreciate another's language or cuisine." That's a load of crap. Racism is often the leading ideology of the most educated and literate people. So, that's not important. But I think the kind of composition, the kind of writing, the kind of literacy that *we* have been talking about—which is not merely about competence but is about intervention, the possibility of interpretation as intervention, as interrogation, as relocation, as revision—is often not taught even at the best institutions and should be talked about and taught much more.

Q. How do we counter the growing popularity of the claim that the unity of the nation as a symbolic force has been superceeded by "those new realities of internationalism, multinationalism, or even 'late capitalism'"? In other words, how do we demonstrate that there is little that is new in the rhetoric of these global terms, for they are most often underwritten, as you say, "in that grim prose of power that each nation can wield within its own sphere of influence"?

A. First, let me take up the issue of there being little that is new in the rhetoric of these global terms. Of course, there are many new things. Digital technology has speeded up this transnational process, and I accept that this speeding up is not just a quantitative issue; it's a qualitative issue. It can be fetishized as a kind of technophilia, and I think that this is a very important issue, the belief that because you can conjure up anybody you want at any time through e-mail, we have therefore somehow transcended time and space and geographies and inequalities and disjunctions. Only so long as both of you have connectivity and access.... Well, you know that argument; it's too familiar, so I won't rehearse it here. I do want to remind myself that really the first globalization was mercantilism and colonialism. Of course, there is a big difference in time there. I once calculated (and this is not an accurate calculation) that it took something like five or six months in that era—the early and mid-nineteenth century—to make colonial connectivity. In London, they produced an edict that was to be enacted in India, then they sent it by ship, then they distributed it through India, then the viceroy wrote a report as to whether it worked or not, and then they sent it back. So before they could actually reconsider what they'd done, it took about five or six months. Now, of course, it takes about two minutes for some global organization to effect a change in policy.

What I'm getting at is that there is an obduracy of certain power blocks and power forces that can translate, particularly at the economic level, the power of the transnational for very parochial even nationalist concerns at the level of institutions, at the level of ideologies, and at the level of economies. So there is no guarantee that translationality and transnationality (which I see as being linked) will not be used for the most nationalistic ends. For instance, if you speak to the Hindu nationalists in India who are now very seriously contesting the cosmopolitanism of the Indian subcontinent, which is remarkable, with their anti-Muslim acts (political acts, not just propaganda), they will say, "Our notion of nationalism, our notion of Hinduism is very much a western concept of the nation. Hinduism is a very tolerant religion; we believe in peace. All we are saying is that we want to have that kind of hegemonic function that, for instance, Protestantism as a state religion has in Britain. And then we will happily tolerate Muslims or Parsees or Christians. So we are not archaic; we are absolutely out there in the transnational discourse. We see our desire for what we call *Hindutva*, the Hindu state, as being absolutely in a translational relationship with western nation forms. We're in fact modernists in a western sense, and we're demanding this because we have a modern faith in Hinduism which will be this umbrella; it'll be a normative form, but it'll be an umbrella very tolerant to all kinds of religions." So I do feel that there is grim prose of nationalist and national authority.

My sense is not to say that in many ways this blurring of the boundary of nation has not taken place; it has. And it has often taken place through refugees, the eighteen million people displaced for one reason or another (you have eighteen to twenty million according to some United Nations figures). And I think they are producing what must be recognized as a kind of vernacular or vernacularizing or vernacular cosmopolitanism, internationally. But at the same time as we recognize the liminal form of the nation form, we have to recognize possibilities of actually using the transnational in a very national sense. I mean, you can sign whatever transnational agreement you want, but very often what you find is that the ruling national elite channels and filters its benefits in its own direction. So I think that we should be more cautious in celebrating the transnational, and we should be aware that we are, certainly historically at the moment, at the level of or in the place of liminal nationality or nationhood.

Q. In your discussions of nationness, you write that "the concept of the 'people' emerges within a range of discourses as a double movement. The people are not simply historical events or parts of a patriotic body politic. They are also a complex rhetorical strategy of social reference." That is, "The nation's people must be thought in double-time; the people are the historical 'objects' of a nationalist pedagogy, giving the discourse an authority that is based on the pre-given or constituted historical origin *in the past*; the people are also the 'subjects' of a process of signification that must erase any prior or originary presence of the nation-people to demonstrate the prodigious, living principles of the people as contemporaneity: as that sign of the *present* through which national life is redeemed and iterated as a reproductive process." Thus, "the people are the articulation of a doubling of the national address, an ambivalent *movement* between the discourses of pedagogy and the performative." What are the implications of thinking "the people" in this double-time? Does such a conceptualization have the potential of generating social agency?

A. This is a very thoughtful question. There are two immediate effects implied by thinking of the people in a double-time. One I've already referred to: to see the nation as an internally liminal formation. The second follows from that: to see the way in which minorities or minoritization are very much part of the other side of the national people, that the problem of minoritization should be seen as the problem of nation construction. It's usually seen as the abnormal, the thing that didn't work, or the adjacent thing, or the accidental. I'm saying that the construction of minorities is as much a process of nation formation as the construction of a national people. In fact, the two may be as closely linked as I believe the emergence of modernity is to the emergence of coloniality. The effects of this would be to change the way in which we think of the citizenship of communities, interests, minorities, migrants. I believe we would have to rethink those questions of citizenship if we did think in terms of what I call the double-time. So it's really to try to make us reconsider the question of cultural membership and national membership.

Q. You have said that your concern is "with other articulations of human togetherness as they are related to cultural difference and discrimination"—other than the liberal vision of togetherness. "For instance, human togetherness may come to represent the forces of hegemonic authority; or a solidarity founded in victimization and suffering may, implacably, sometimes violently, become bound against oppression; or a subaltern or minority agency may attempt to interrogate and rearticulate the 'inter-est' of society that marginalizes its interests." Do you envision contingent, temporary, strategic alliances as a way to bind individuals in social agency, as a way to rearticulate human togetherness?

A. I made that statement because there was a sense that human togetherness had a kind of inherent value. Solidarity was what happened to the left, and a sort of rather evil hegemony was what happened on the right. *They* formed power blocks; *we* formed solidarities. There's some truth in that, but I've always wanted to suggest that the real power of the political is the power of understanding how the political object, aim, or constituency was actually a result of the ethical and practical labor of construction and negotiation. I made that statement to get away from this idea of the power block versus solidarity, but also to get away from the idea that if you had a kind of more social constructionist way of thinking, you would automatically come out on the right side. I've always wanted to suggest that you can come out completely on the wrong side. That's what politics is about: to be vigilant about that very moment in which groups are being constituted, or objects are being created.

But yes, I think that much of my work—I'm thinking especially of the piece on Indian mutiny in *The Location of Culture*—has been an attempt to see social agency where it has mostly been denied or where it hasn't ended up in great acts of revolutionary transformation. But then it has also been my purpose to say that revolution or radical social transformation cannot be seen altogether, at the same time, from one place. You've got to look at it in different moments and times, and things add to rather than necessarily add up. I've always been interested, therefore, in stressing that in a way this togetherness is also (if I may produce a rather bad sort of pun) to be aware of the "to-gatheringness," the gathering as an important assumption of togetherness. It's been my desire to suggest that this expressive togetherness—that we assume that the category of woman or the category of class already is an expressive subject—is problematic. And I've tried to problematize that. My use of the concept of enunciation and psychoanalytic identification has also led me to want to understand not only, as I said a moment ago, agency in times and places where it is least acknowledged, but also to try and understand forms of agency that do not emanate from individual intention. I've wanted to see the way in which in the construction of the collectivity, something else, some other body gets constituted as the site of a community or a togetherness. And I only use that awkward phrase "to gather" because it actually stresses the important disseminatory potential that there must be in order to be able to think about collective agency.

Q. In "The Postcolonial and the Postmodern," you write that "a range of contemporary critical theories suggest that it is from those who have suffered the sentence of history—subjugation, domination, diaspora, displacement—that we learn our most enduring lessons for living and thinking. There is even a growing conviction that the affective experience of social marginality—as it emerges in non-canonical cultural forms—transforms our critical strategies. It forces us to confront the concept of culture outside *objets d'art* or beyond the canonization of the 'idea' of aesthetics, to engage with culture as an uneven, incomplete production of meaning and value, often composed of incommensurable demands and practices, produced in the act of social survival." In the idea that the affective experience of social marginality has the potential to transform living and thinking, there is suggested the important role of political emotions, those emotions (for example, anger and outrage) that are produced in the act of survival. Do you think that political emotions provide an occasion for social solidarity, if not community? Are the affective experiences of social marginality incommensurable, just as are cultural meanings and values?

A. The answer to both questions is yes. Yes, I do think that the structures of feeling and the structures of affect are radically devalued in the language of political effectivity, cultural identity, and so on. I'm going to have to elaborate on that, but I also think that the possibility that affect is both effective and incommensurable in a social and cultural sense must be entertained fully, and we must learn to work with that and to understand it. My longer response is that the discourse of political action and political choice has concentrated too much on questions of interest and too little on questions of political passion. Of course, this was not always the case. In fact, that great book, *The Passions and the Interests* by Albert Hirschman, was written in a way to track the history of the shift. But I do think that in our contemporary moment, the politics of difference, the politics of community, the politics of communities of interest have such a deep and strong affective charge that we now have to start to understand the part that emotions, affects, play in the construction of community politics. For instance, almost all the very effective journalism on Bosnia has never failed to describe the almost perverse and pathological passion involved in the most horrific acts. If we see that, then we're seeing something that is motivating that construction of the group, or that construction of the group in action, that construction of a performative subject. The something that is constructing that is not just ethnic hatred or racial hatred; there is another charge that is working there that is actually creating solidarity, creating a camp. And I think it is our responsibility to begin to understand it. Anger, violence, hatred—these are seemingly just adjectives always attached to what is seen as something more substantial, but I don't think that this is the right way to see it.

So a history of affect as well as an affective history are very important tasks, certainly for me, for the future. I've worked on the question of ambivalence in quite a sustained way, and now some of my new work is focusing around anxiety as an affect of social transition and translation. Let me also say that I believe that one of the great contributions of Franz Fanon was to raise this question of the psychoaffective moment in the wider moment of political autonomy. His theory of violence, I believe, is not (as it is often read as) some kind of surrealist excess; it is part of this process of taking seriously the question of the body, the question of the emotions, the question of affect at the level of political identification.

Q. In "Black and White and Read all Over" you write, "When a figure arises from behind the black mask to address a range of publics—black, white, academic, vernacular, church congregations, *Newsweek* readers—there is a palpable anxiety about his or her 'representative' status. It is commonly held, after all, that the authenticity of the intellectual, whether conservative or radical, is founded on the possibility of free and unfettered choice among competing ideas and interests. . . . By this logic, minority intellectuals lack the ethical autonomy to be properly representative because they lack the conditions of freedom: they are, so to speak, parti pris." The position you appear to be taking here seems to support the work of various feminist standpoint theorists such as Donna Haraway, Sandra Harding, and Nancy Hartsock, who argue that positionality is actually a strength in the production of knowledge rather than a liability. Do you see any theoretical affinities between your work and feminist standpoint theory?

A. Yes, to the extent to which I think what we're both talking about is the importance of recognizing what the conditions of one's situatedness are. What is one's situation? I think my notion of enunciation affirms the need to each time understand what is happening at the place of utterance, what each iteration and reiteration of a particular sign is, how it produces its own strategy, its own authority. This is an emphasis on situatedness that I think the feminist standpoint theorists also have. As I understand it, the other shared idea would be an attempt to think about political action not merely as liberation, but also as an active process of survival—survival as a very positive thing, not just as what you do when you're not running around winning arguments and battles. I think those would be the two shared ideas.

Q. In "Are You a Man or a Mouse?" you suggest that in the study of masculinity the aim should not be "to deny or disavow masculinity, but to disturb its manifest destiny—to draw attention to it as [an enunciative site and] a prosthetic reality—a 'pre-fixing' of the rules of gender and sexuality" and a kind of "blocked reflexivity" that is masked by "an appeal to universalism and rationality." Do you see the new men's studies movements (particularly those inspired by and responsive to feminism and gay studies) bringing greater self-reflexivity to the history of the construction of masculinities? To polemicize the point slightly: are there significant limits to the self-reflexivity that a white straight man can bring to the study of white straight masculinities?

A. I don't know what to say about this question because I've not really followed the men's movement. On the one hand, if it's in response to certain feminist or queer interrogations, well one would say it's not a bad thing. On the other hand, there must be a way in which that kind of work, even in the process of interrogation, makes you fetishize something about your own group. I suppose what I would say *there* is that I'm interested in responding to the interrogations of masculinity. I'm interested in what a white, straight, male group would want to identify itself as, and in what would be its conditions of solidarity under those specific signifiers. Why would it want to foreground those signifiers to identify itself? The most progressive parts of the women's movement don't just come together only because its members happen to be women; they come together because women as signs signify certain things about inequality. Queer movement, gay movement, race movement come together because, again, those signs signify certain terrains of political action. I'm interested in finding out if you are a white straight male how you engage in discourse. Do you say, "We're straight white men and we're exploiters?" How do you enter that discourse? Do you say, "Now we want to understand the conditions under which we are exploiters?" I would be as untrusting of a group that's actually pronouncing itself guilty as I would be of a group that's saying that everybody's trying to make them feel guilty and they don't feel guilty. I would want to know what claims these people are making for themselves.

Q. In *The Location of Culture*, "translation" becomes almost the paradigmatic instance of "the performative nature of cultural communication. It is language *in actu* (enunciation, positionality) rather than language *in situ (énoncé,* or propositionality). And the sign of translation continually tells, or 'tolls' the different times and spaces between cultural authority and its performative practices. The 'time' of translation consists in that *movement* of meaning, the principle and practice of a communication that, in the words of [Paul] de Man 'puts the original in motion to decanonise it, giving it the movement of fragmentation, a wandering of errance, a kind of permanent exile.'" Your self-conscious use of the word *tolls* is provocative. Would you more fully explain your view of the task and responsibility of translation?

A. Let me respond to the use of the word *tolls* straightaway. I used it to emphasize that in the very telling—that is, in the discursive act of the translational process—there has to be a sense that every translation is at once the death of something and its revival, that there's a sort of spectral logic, as Derrida would say, in the construction of translation. In fact, somewhere (I think when talking of translation) Derrida, stimulated by Benjamin, has said that translation is about survival, *sur vivre*, to live on—living on a borderline, as well as *living on*, just the act of living on. I used the word *tolls* to indicate that complex sense of both the death of meaning and its relocation in the act of translation or in the act of cultural translation. That's why I used that particular word.

The task and responsibility of translation—which is after all the task not only of transferring or relocating meaning but the responsibility of setting up a site of revisionary meaning, which means that what you receive is also being revised—produces an enormous responsibility to the present, to the future, and to what has gone before, if you put it in temporal terms. It produces this responsibility because through this whole process of the rearticulation of these temporalities, you are also addressing your "self"; you are addressing your "self" to an act of judgment about where you stand in the process of transition, where you will go to through translation. But I think, as I have said before, that translation as a form of enunciation is an ethical act because one is from a position of midstness, of being in the middle of difference, taking the responsibility to deauthorize something that has put itself about as being the place of the powerful or the original; and one is revaluing a genealogy in order to revise, to empower, to resituate a set of concerns, or a set of identifications. Both the acts of empowering and deauthorizing must be undertaken with the greatest reflection, circumspection, and modesty.

Q. In your writings you have taken numerous controversial, and some say "radical" positions. And given the complexity of the ideas you are struggling with, it would not be unusual that some readers might misconstrue some of your positions. Are there any misunderstandings or critiques of your work that you'd care to address at this time?

A. Well, this for me has been such a rich exploration of what I've done that, entirely due to your skill, I feel myself completely understood in a moment of luminous clarity, which I'm sure is completely wrong. It's entirely due to you and not to me or what I've written. Yes, people point to a whole range of aspects of my work, often in a complimentary way, sometimes in a critical way. But there are some things that are misunderstood. I'll just list them. Very often what I've talked about as ambivalence is misunderstood as ambiguity, and they're radically different things. Ambivalence is a struggle for identification; ambiguity is a much more hermeneutic process. There may be some ambiguity in ambivalence, but these terms are not the same thing. Where I have tried to, in a way, contest certain traditions of intentionality in order to be able to open up the question of agency and to see agency in acts that are often not seen as agential, people have sometimes misunderstood that (I think rather ludicrously) as a complete loss of any agency.

Where I have tried in the same vein, in pursuit of the same kind of value, to address myself to archival moments, literally moments in the historical or discursive or theoretical archive that have been overlooked (moments where I actually go into the archive to reconstruct the missionary discourse, as in "Signs Taken for Wonders" or in "By Bread Alone"), people have seen these moments as purely anecdotal and they ask, "Where is the history there?" The fact that in these moments I talk about the printing industry, the ideological and the discursive practices of missionaries, the fact that I locate this within the kind of quasi-state governance of the East India Company, somehow is not history enough for some people. They want a different kind of narrative history. Because I will not give them an easily continuous, conjoined history loaded with large generalizations about state formations or "exploitation" or "resistance" or whatever, they feel that this is not history. That's not my problem in a way. I want to do a different kind of work. I feel that the task demands historicity, which I believe I to some extent satisfy, but I think there is a demand by critics for a kind of "historicism," a particular kind of narrative history. It's not that I've never produced such work, but it's not my dominant mode.

Finally, I think there is a misunderstanding about my notion of hybridization. For me, hybridization is really about how you negotiate between texts or cultures or practices in a situation of power imbalances in order to be able to see the way in which strategies of appropriation, revision, and iteration can produce possibilities for those who are less advantaged to be able to grasp in a moment of emergency, in the very process of the exchange or the negotiation, the advantage. Hybridization is much more a social and cultural and enunciative process in my work. It's not about people who eat Chinese food, wear Italian clothes, and so on; but sometimes, in a very complimentary way to me personally, it's been taken to mean some kind of diversity or multiple identities. For me, hybridization is a discursive, enunciatory, cultural, subjective process having to do with the struggle around authority, authorization, deauthorization, and the revision of authority. It's a social process. It's not about persons of diverse cultural tastes and fashions.

Gloria

Anzaldúa

Toward a Mestiza Rhetoric: Gloria Anzaldúa on Composition and Postcoloniality

ANDREA A. LUNSFORD

> I will have my voice: Indian, Spanish, white. I will have my
> serpent's tongue—my woman's voice, my sexual voice, my poet's
> voice. I will overcome the tradition of silence.
>
> Gloria Anzaldúa

Gloria Anzaldúa has not had an easy time of having what she calls her "own voice." Born (1942) and raised in the border country of south Texas (in Jesus Maria of the Valley), Anzaldúa learned early that she was different, an "alien from another planet" who didn't quite fit with the norms and expectations of her family and community, didn't "act like a nice little Chicanita is supposed to act" ("La Prieta," 199, 201). Describing some of her early experiences in "La Prieta" (from the landmark 1981 collection *This Bridge Called My Back: Writings by Radical Women of Color*), Anzaldúa rejects ongoing efforts to label her differences in various ways—as lesbian, as feminist, as Marxist, as mystic, as "other": "Ambivalent? Not so. Only your labels split me," she says (205).

In this early essay, Anzaldúa announces the multiplicity of her "self" and her "voice": she is a "wind-swayed bridge, a crossroads inhabited by whirlwinds"; she is "Shiva, a many-armed and legged body with one foot on brown soil, one on white, one in straight society, one in the gay world, the man's world, the woman's, one limb in the literary world, another in the working class, the socialist, and the occult worlds. A sort of spider woman hanging by one thin strand of web" (204). And indeed, much of Anzaldúa's work has been devoted to making a space where such multiplicity could be enacted. *This Bridge Called My Back* (1981; 2nd ed. 1983), edited with Cherie Moraga, grew out of an experience at a 1979 women's retreat during which Anzaldúa was made (once again) to feel she was being labeled—tokenized as a "third-world woman" and as an outsider, an exoticized other to the white feminists there. Characteristically, Anzaldúa turned that experience into a means of affirming her commitment to women of color by providing a forum in which their multiple voices—and her own—could be heard. In 1987 came her groundbreaking *Borderlands/La Frontera*, the book in which she has most thoroughly rendered and theorized the borderland space that is home to her multiple identities and voices. And then in 1990—after years of waiting for someone "to compile a book that would continue where *This Bridge Called My Back* left off"—Anzaldúa edited the luxuriant and sprawling collection *Making Face, Making Soul/Haciendo Caras*. (She has also given voice to two bilingual children's picture/story books—*Prietita Has a Friend/Prietita tiene un amigo* [1991] and *Friends from the Other Side/Amigos del otro lado* [1993]).

Taken together, Anzaldúa's work (including a number of essays I haven't cited here) stands testimony to her personal triumph over the "tradition of silence" and to her ability to imagine, enact, and inhabit spaces that go beyond dichotomies of all kinds: beyond male/female; beyond reason/emotion; beyond gay/straight; beyond other/white; beyond mythic/real; beyond mind/body; beyond spirit/matter; beyond orality/literacy; beyond I/you. In every case, Anzaldúa rejects either/or in favor of both/and then some, of an identity that is always in process. As she says in "To(o) Queer the Writer," identity can never be reduced to a "bunch of little cubbyholes. . . . Identity flows between, over, aspects of a person. Identity is a river, a process" (252-53). This process—which Anzaldúa represents both as occurring on the borderland, on the in-between, and in the act of making faces/souls—can enable transformations that, while often brutally painful, can allow for non-binary identity, for new states of mestiza consciousness, and for multiple writing strategies (what AnnLouise Keating calls "mestizaje ecriture" and what I am calling a "mestiza rhetoric").

In these moments, it is possible to take in the labels of society and to transform them, to find all others in one's self; one's self in all others. Learning to live such transformations calls for a "new mestiza" who has "a tolerance for contradictions, a tolerance for ambiguity," who "learns to be an Indian in Mexican culture, to be Mexican from an Anglo point of view. She learns to juggle cultures. Not only does she sustain contradictions, she turns the ambivalence into something else" (*Borderlands* 79). In turn, living in and rendering such contradictions and transformations calls for a new kind of writing style. In Anzaldúa's case, this means a rich mixture of genres—she shifts from poetry to reportorial prose to autobiographical stream of consciousness to incantatory mythic chants to sketches and graphs—and back again, weaving images and words from her multiple selves and from many others into a kind of tapestry or patchwork quilt of language. It also means an insistence that visual images and words belong together in texts of all kinds as well as a rich mix of languages—some English, some Spanish, some Tex/Mex, some Nahuatl—and registers. In "How to Tame a Wild Tongue," she denounces "linguistic terrorism," saying "I am my language. Until I can take pride in my language, I cannot take pride in myself. Until I can accept as legitimate Chicano Texas Spanish, Tex-Mex and all the other languages I speak, I cannot accept the legitimacy of myself. Until I am free to write bilingually and to switch codes without having to translate, . . . my tongue will be illegitimate" (*Borderlands* 59). In the interview that follows, Anzaldúa comments on all of these issues. In addition, she also has much to say about her prior experiences with and current relationship to writing and to a form of collaboration, aspects of her work that will be of special interest, I think, to compositionists.

As we might expect, Anzaldúa's relationship to language and to writing is extremely complex. If books, as she says in the preface to *Borderland/La Frontera* "saved [her] sanity" and taught her "first how to survive and then how to soar," she often figures the act of writing as daring and dangerous (*Bridge* 171) or as painful, as a terrifying ride in the "nightsky" (*Borderland/La Frontera*, 140-41), as like "carving bone," as giving birth, an endless cycle of "making it worse, making it better, but always making meaning out of the experience," as a "blood sacrifice" (73, 75). Writing is for Anzaldúa inextricably related to the process of making (or writing) faces/ souls as well as a primary means of enabling the kinds of ongoing transformations necessary for inhabiting the borderlands. "*There is no separation between life and writing*," she says in "Speaking in Tongues: A Letter to Third World Women Writers," so "*Why aren't you riding, writing, writing?*" Most important, she cautions, "It's not on paper that you create but in your innards, in your gut and out of living tissue—*organic writing*, I call it" (*Bridge* 172).

Given her commitment to multiplicity and inclusivity, Anzaldúa is naturally drawn to forms of collaboration: with artists in her children's books, with co-editors and with collectives in other works, even—as she says in the following interview—with the architect and designers who have helped to expand her home. Anzaldúa represents herself as in constant conversation, a dialogue among her many selves, her multiple audiences/readers, and the texts that emerge in the process (with their own intertexts and interfaces) that hum along on her computer screen. "That's what writers do, we carry on a constant dialogue between language and hands and images, one or another of our identities trying desperately to get in a word, an image, a sound" she says in a passage in *Making Face* that is highly reminiscent of Bakhtinian dialogism (xxiv). In fact, Anzaldúa's discussions of the crucial role audiences/others play in her own writing provides a fine example of what Bakhtin means by "answerability," which Anzaldúa refers to as "responsibility," literally the ability to respond, to answer, to join in a conversation that is always ongoing. As she says in this interview, "I do the composing, but it's taken from little mosaics of other's people's lives, other people's perceptions." These mosaics are her own collaborative response-abilities (for a further explanation of this aspect of Anzaldúa's work, see Bickford) and reveal the degree to which she is aware of the politics of address, of her need to answer or respond in ways that will create a readership at the same time that it teaches how to "read" her respondings (*Making Face* xviii).

During this interview, Anzaldúa remarks that she has been shocked to "find composition people picking me up," (she was interviewed at a CCCC meeting in 1992 by Donna Perry). Given that composition has long been equated with the hegemony of "standard" English and with gatekeeping, Anzaldúa's surprise is—well, not surprising. As this interview reveals, however, she has experienced in her own schooling both the limiting—and the liberatory—impulses in composition, the latter in the company of long-time writing teacher, theorist, and critic Jim Sledd. Close attention to this doubled experience with composition and a close reading of this interview suggests to me that, among her many selves, Anzaldúa includes a theorist of writing as well as an accomplished rhetor and a prolific writer. She is also a teacher. When I asked her whether she thought mestiza consciousness could be taught, she said yes, though with great difficulty and pain. In *Making Face*, she speaks directly of her own teaching goals: "I wanted a book which would teach ourselves and whites to read in nonwhite narrative traditions" (xviii). Moreover, she wants to teach others to acquire voices without becoming *periquitas* (parrots) and to use theory to "change people and the way they perceive the world" (xxv). "We need *teorias*," she says, "that will enable us to interpret what happens in the world, that will explain how and why we relate to certain people in specific ways, that will reflect what goes on between inner, outer, and peripheral 'I's within a person and between the personal 'I's and the collective 'we' of our ethnic communities. *Necesitamos teorias* that . . . cross borders, that blur boundaries—new kinds of theories with new theorizing methods" (xxv). Here and elsewhere Gloria Anzaldúa calls for a new rhetoric, a mestiza rhetoric, that she is clearly in the process of helping to make.

Q. What are some of your very early memories of writing? I'm using "writing" very broadly here to include drawing, marking, any kind of language use that seems like writing.

A. *Sí*, the whole activity of writing and the conditions that surround it as distinct from writing on a piece of paper started very early on orally with me: it started as a defense against my sister. When we were growing up, we had to work after school. We had chores, we had field work, we had housework. And then it was time for bed, and I didn't get to do my reading. So I would read under the covers with a flashlight in bed with my sister. And my brothers were in the same room, but my sister and I shared the same bed. And she was ready to tell my mom. To keep her entertained, and to keep her from going to my mom, I would tell her a story. I would make up a story—just something that had happened during the day—and I would make it all kind of like an adventure or a quest of the happenings of these little girls, my sister and myself, and, you know, I kind of embroidered it. And so she would settle down and go back to sleep and wouldn't tell my mom the next day. And then the following night she would want the same thing. Every night I learned to tell a little story. So I was writing stories very early.

Q. Your own version of *A Thousand and One Nights?*

A. And then this is what happened: she wanted two. So I got into doing serials. I would tell a part of the story and then break it off and say, "You know, if you don't tell, you'll get the rest of it tomorrow." It was like I turned the tables on her. So for me, writing has always been about narrative, about story; and it still is that way. Theory is a kind of narrative. Science—you know, physics—that's a narrative, that's a hit on reality. Anthropology has its narrative. And some are master narratives, and some are outsider narratives. There's that whole struggle in my writing between the dominant culture's traditional, conventional narratives about reality and about literature and about science and about life and about politics; and my other counter narratives as a *mestiza* growing up in this country, as an internal exile, as an inner exile, as a postcolonial person, because the Mexican race in the United States is a colonized people. My ancestors were living life on the border. The band was part of the state of Tamaulipas, Mexico, and then the U.S. bought it, bought half of Mexico, and so the Anzaldúas were split in half. The Anzaldúas with an accent, which is my family, were north of the border. The Anzalduas without an accent stayed on the other side of the border, and as the decades went by we lost connection with each other. And so the Anzaldúas and the Anzalduas, originally from the same land, the state of Tamaulipas in the nation of Mexico, all of a sudden became strangers in our own land, foreigners in our own land. We were a colonized people who were not allowed to speak our language, whose ways of life were not valued in this country. Public education tried to erase all of that. So here I am now, a kind of international citizen whose life and privileges are not equal to the rights and privileges of ordinary, Anglo, white, Euro-American people. My narratives always take into account these other ethnicities, these other races, these other cultures, these other histories. There's always that kind of struggle.

Q. I know that art and drawing are central to much of your work, and I think of drawing as a kind of writing too. As a child, did you draw a lot?

A. Yes. I wanted to be an artist. I wasn't sure whether I wanted to be a visual artist or a writer, or something else, but I started out as an artist. In fact, the teaching that I did in high school as a student teacher was in literature and in art. But I never could get a job teaching art in the public schools. I got one teaching composition, teaching English, teaching literature, but not art. But I have a degree in art. I had two areas of focus in my MA, "majors" I guess was the word, and one was art education and the other was literature.

Q. If you define writing broadly enough to include drawing, then you certainly began writing very, very early in your life.

A. Yes. I started drawing very early on. Besides telling my sister these narratives, these stories, I started keeping a journal because my sister, my whole family is. . . . I don't know how to explain it. We would talk a lot and fight a lot and quarrel a lot.

Q. You were a very verbal family?

A. Very verbal. In some ways like your average family in the U.S.: abusive verbally, or not aware of the vulnerabilities a child might have. So I was always gotten after for being too curious, for reading. I was being selfish for studying and reading, rather than doing housework. I was selfish because I wasn't helping the family by reading and writing. So anyway I had all of these emotions. I wanted to fight back and yell, and sometimes I did. But I would watch my sister have temper tantrums, and she would have temper tantrums so severe that she would pee in her pants.

Q. She is younger than you, right?

A. A year and three months. And she would eat dirt. She would get so upset, and I didn't want to be with her. I started shutting down emotions, but I had to find a release for all these feelings. I was feeling alienated from my family and I was fighting against society—you know, your typical pre-adolescent and adolescent *angst.* So I started keeping a journal. I attribute my writing to my grandmothers who used to tell stories. I copied them until I started telling my own, but I think it was my sister who forced me to find an outlet to communicate these feelings of hurt and confusion. So I started keeping journals.

Q. Did you keep them throughout school?

A. Yes. I have all of them lined up on top of my closet, but I think the earlier ones are still back home, so I'm going to try to hunt those up. I always keep journals and I do both my little sketches and some texts. The pamphlet I gave you [which includes several drawings] came from a workshop in Pantla that I did at the Villa Montalbo, a writer's residency right here in Saratoga. These people saw an essay that I had done about *Nepantla,* the in-between state that is so important in connecting a lot of issues—the border, the borderland, *Nepantla*. It was an essay I had done for a catalog, on border art as being the place that a lot of Chicanas do our work from—you know, the site of cultural production. These people wrote up a grant and got some money, and so five of us (I got to pick some of the other artists) worked for five weeks on a project together and had an exhibit at the San Jose Latino Arts Center. My presentation was both textual and visual. I had the visual image and I had the text, and they exhibited them together on the wall.

So yes, if you define writing as any kind of scribble, any kind of trying to mark on the world, then you have the oral, the dance, the choreography, the performance art, the architects—I had a feminist architect help me design this addition to my study. It's all marking. And some of us want to take those marks that are already getting inscribed in the world and redo them, either by erasing them, or by pulling them apart, which involves deconstructive criticism. Pulling them apart is looking at how they are composed and what the relationship is between the frame and the rest of the world. In this country it's white. The dominant culture has the frame of reference. This is its territory, so any mark we make on it has to be made in relationship to the fact that they occupy the space. You can take any field of disciplinary study, like anthropology: that frame is also Euro-American, it's Western. Composition theory, that's very Euro-American. Thus, any of us that are trying to create change have to struggle with this vast territory that's very, very powerful when you try to impinge on it to try to make changes. It's kind of like a fish in the Pacific Ocean, with the analogy that the Pacific Ocean is the dominant field and the fish is this postcolonial, this feminist, or this queer, or whoever is trying to make changes. I think that before you can make any changes in composition studies, philosophy, or whatever it is, you have to have a certain awareness of the territory. You have to be familiar with it and you have to be able to maneuver in it before you can say, "Here's an alternative model for this particular field, for its norms, for its rules and regulations, for its laws." And especially in composition these rules are very strict: creating a thesis sentence, having some kind of argument, having kind of a logical step-by-step progression, using certain methods, like contrast, like deductive versus inductive thinking. I mean all the way back to Aristotle and Cicero with the seven parts of a composition.

So for anyone like me to make any changes or additions to the model takes a tremendous amount of energy, because you're going against the Pacific Ocean and you're this little fish and you have to weigh the odds of succeeding with the goal that you have in mind. Say my goal is a liberatory goal: it's to create possibilities for people, to look at things in a different way so that they can act in their daily lives in a different way. It's like a freeing up, an emancipating. It's a feminist goal. But then I have to weigh things: okay, if I write in this style and I code-switch too much and I go into Spanglish too much and I do an associative kind of logical progression in a composition, am I going to lose those people that I want to affect, to change? Am I going to lose the respect of my peers—who are other writers and other artists and other academicians—when I change too much? When I change not only the style, but also the rhetoric, the way that this is done? Then I have to look at the students, the young students in high school and in elementary school who are going to be my future readers, if my writing survives that long. And I look at the young college students, especially those reading *Borderlands*. How much of it is a turn-off for them because it's too hard to access? I have to juggle and balance, make it a little hard for them so that they can stop and think, "You know, this is a text, this is not the same as life, this is a representation of life." Too often when people read something they take that to be the reality instead of the representation. I don't want to turn those students off. So how much do you push and how much do you accommodate and be in complicity with the dominant norm of whatever field it happens to be?

Q. So if you are a fish in this vast ocean, which is the Anglo-European framework, you can't just reject the water outright but rather try to change it?

A. Yes. Let me show you a little drawing, so you can see what I am saying. I want to speak of the *nosotras* concept. It used to be that there was a "them" and an "us." We were over here, we were the "other" with other lives, and the "*nos*" was the subject, the white man. And there was a very clear distinction. But as the decades have gone by, we—the colonized, the Chicano, the blacks, the Natives in this country—have been reared in this frame of

Nos ▌otras

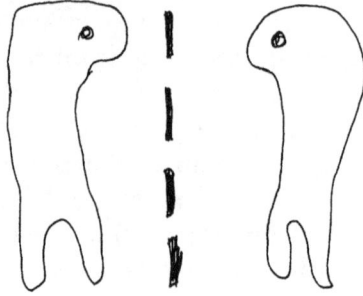

subject	Other
dominance	subordination
us	they
we	them

disrupts binary oppositions

reference, in this field. So all of our education, all of our ideas come from this frame of reference. We are complicitous for being in such close proximity and in such intimacy with the other. Now I think that "us" and "them" are interchangeable. Now there is no such thing as an "other." The other is in you, the other is in me. This white culture has been internalized in my head. I have a white man in here; I have a white woman in here. And they have me in their heads, even if it is just a guilty little nudge sometimes. So, when I try to articulate ideas, I try to do it from that place of occupying both territories: the territory of my past and my ethnic community, my home community, the Chicano Spanish, the Spanglish; and the territory of the formal education, the philosophical educational ideas and the political ideas that I have internalized just by being alive. Both of these traditions are inherent in me. I cannot disown the white tradition, the Euro-American tradition, any more than I can disown the Mexican, the Latino or the Native, because they are all in me. And I think that people from different fields are still making these dichotomies.

Q. Would you describe yourself as being in one or more "fields"?

A. Composition, feminism, postcolonialism—I didn't even know I belonged to this postcolonial thing until Patricia Cloud said in a bookflap that I am a feminist, postcolonial critic. And then there is me the artist, me the teacher, and all the multicultural stuff. It's hard to keep up with the reading, so I don't even try anymore. For preparation for this interview, one of your questions was "Who has influenced you as a postcolonial critic?" and I couldn't think of anyone. All of the reading that I've done has been in terms of particular articles for a class. When Homi Bhabha was here, I did some reading and I went to his lecture, which I couldn't understand. When Spivak was here it was the same thing. I took a class with Donna Haraway in feminist theory, and when I had to read "Can the Subaltern Speak?" it took me weeks to decipher one sentence. Well, not weeks, but you know what I'm saying. And then I read a couple of JanMohammed's essays too; of course, way back I read a little bit of Frantz Fanon's *The Wretched of the Earth*, and Paulo Freire's *The Pedagogy of the Oppressed*, but just little snippets. And then for your interview I got a copy of a postcolonial studies reader. But you know, I didn't have time to study a lot, so I made little notes about the things that I wanted to think about and maybe respond to in writing.

Q. One of the reasons that Lahoucine and I wanted particularly to talk to you about postcolonial studies is that we are interested in why there hasn't been more confluence between postcolonial studies and composition studies. One reason is no doubt the historical association of the English language with colonialism. We think that another of the reasons may well be that postcolonial studies has very quickly theorized itself into very high abstract language that is inaccessible. I think Homi Bhabha is a very good example of the kind of scholar who is speaking on a level of abstraction that just seems completely foreign to a student in a first-year writing class, who may come from southern Texas and be a speaker of Spanish as a first language. Yet it seems a shame that these fields don't talk more to one another. In our perspective, you're a person who does talk to both fields, and in ways that are accessible. My first-year students read parts of *Borderlands*, for example, and they are more threatened than they are puzzled. They are threatened because they think they can't imagine you. Many of my students are from small farming communities in

Ohio. Most of them are Anglo, and they say things like, "She sounds so mad. Is she mad? And who is she mad at?" So that's one of the reasons we wanted to talk with you, and to see if in doing so we could find some means of getting both composition and postcolonial studies to think about their own discourses, and the ways in which some of those discourses are very exclusionary—they shut people out.

A. I think that you came at the right time, because the first half of one of the book projects that's currently on my back-burner is about composition and postcolonial issues of identity. Most of the questions that you've asked are there, plus others. I have about four different chapters of notes and rough drafts for this book in my computer that have to do with the writing process, that have to do with rhetoric, that have to do with composition. Not just that, but taking it over into how one composes one's life, how one creates an addition to one's house, how one makes sense of all the kinds of coincidental and random things that happen in one's life, how one gives it meaning. So it's my composition theme, *compustura*. In fact, that's the title of one of the chapters: "*Compustura*." *Compustura* used to mean for me being a seamstress; I would sew for other people. *Compustura* means seaming together fragments to make a garment which you wear, which represents you—your identity and reality in the world. So that's why when you and Lahoucine called me, I thought, yes, there's finally somebody out there who's making the connection.

Q. You have already talked about the risks you take and about the stylistic borders you cross. Are there any things about writing that are particularly hard for you? Or easy?

A. Yes, there are. I think one problem is for me to get into a piece of writing, whether it is theory, or a story, or a poem, or a children's book, or a journal entry. I am always rethinking and responding to something that I value, or rethinking somebody else's values. If the value is competition, then I start thinking about how when you compete, there is a certain amount of violence, a certain amount of struggle. Okay, behind that violence and that struggle I experience some kind of emotion: fear, hesitancy, sadness, depression because of the state of the world, whatever. In order to backtrack to the theoretical concepts, I have to start with the feeling. So I dig into the feeling and usually the feeling will have a visual side while I'm pulling it apart. One of the visuals that

I use is Coyochauqui, the Aztec moon-goddess who was the first sacrificial victim. Her brother threw her down the temple stairs and when she landed at the bottom she was dismembered. The act of writing for me is this kind of dismembering of everything that I am feeling, taking it apart to examine it and then reconstituting it or recomposing it again but in a new way. So that means I really have to get into the feeling—the anger, the anguish, the sadness, the frustration. I have to get into this heightened state, which I access sometimes by being very, very quiet and doing some deep breathing, or by some little tiny meditation, or by burning some incense, or whatever gets me in there. Sometimes I walk along the beach. So I access this state, I get all psyched up, and then I do the writing. I work four, five, six hours; and then I have to come off that. It is like a withdrawal. I have to leave that anger, leave that sadness, leave that compassion, whatever it is that I am feeling; I have to come off of that heightened, aware state. If I want to do some honest writing, I have to get into that state. If you want to do a mediocre job, you do a kind of disembodied writing which has nothing to do with your feelings or with your self or with what you care about. You care, maybe, only intellectually about putting out this essay so that your peers can respect you. So that is one problem of writing for me: engaging in an emotional way, and then disengaging. To disengage you have to take another walk, wash the dishes, go to the garden, talk on the telephone, just because it is too much. Your body cannot take it. So that is one problem.

There are other things that come up for me, and I wrote them down because I knew you were going to ask me this. One other problem is that you want to avoid that stage. You do avoidance; you procrastinate. It takes you awhile to go to the computer. You circle around the stuff over and over. You do not want to get to the dissertation, to the master's thesis, to that paper that is due for this quarter, because you are going to be struggling with these things. That is the problem of avoidance, of not doing the work. Every day I have to recommit myself to the writing. It is like making a date with myself, having an appointment to do this writing. Some days I don't feel like meeting that appointment. It's too hard on my body, especially since I have diabetes; it takes out too much.

Q. Do you try to write at a regular time? Every day?

A. Not in terms of clock time, but in terms of my routine, because my internal clock changes. I get up later and go to bed earlier and sometimes I write at night and sometimes I write during the day; but yes, I have a certain routine. I get up and I inject myself with insulin and I have my food. Generally, after that I have some activity like this interview. Or maybe two hours of filing and returning people's calls and letters—the stuff that I don't like to do. And then a walk, and then I dive into four, five, or six hours of this appointment with myself. Sometimes I can only do two or three hours, and other times I can do it around the clock. After writing, I take a break for lunch or the second meal, whenever that is, and then I do some reading: serious theoretical stuff for maybe an hour or two, and then some escapist reading. I love mysteries and horror.

Q. Do you compose at the wordprocessor?

A. Yes, I do, at my desk, and sometimes I take my little laptop to the coffee house or to the beach, or just outside.

Q. Do the words seem to come out as well from the ends of your fingers typing as they did when you were scripting?

A. Yes, except that when I was at an artist's retreat for four weeks just last month, my computer broke down and I had to resort to handwriting. What started happening was that I started writing poems. I had gone there to revise *Twenty-Four Stories*, which is this book I'm working on. I had taken nineteen of the stories in hard copy, so I was able to revise on paper, but the rest of the time I was doing poems and I was doing composition theory. I ended up doing a lot of stuff on composition theory. I also did work on a large book that I have in progress—the creative writing manual that I told you about. I did writing exercises for that book: some meditation, some hints and elements of writing, some fictive techniques. I didn't plan on doing any of that. I just wanted to do the stories, but not having a computer switched me over.

So anyway, those are two problems: the problem of engaging and disengaging, and the problem of avoidance. Then there is the problem of voice. How am I going to write the foreward for the encyclopedia I agreed to do? What voice, tone, am I going to take? How much can I get away with the Spanish? How much can I get away with the Spanglish? This is a pretty formal reference book. Another example is the bilingual series of children's books. How much can I get through the censors in the state of Texas in any particular children's book? The state of Texas has more stringent censorship rules than the other states, and most publishers can only do one book for all of the states. So the publishers tend to be conservative, because they want to get these books into the schools. How much can I get away with pushing at the norms, at the conventions? That's another problem, and sometimes it's my biggest problem: if I can't find a voice, a style, a point of view, then nothing can get written. All you have are those notes, but you don't have a voice to speak the style. The style is the relationship between me, Gloria, the author; you, the person reading it, my audience, the world; and the text. So there are three of us. Or are there more than three of us?

Q. More, probably. At least four, maybe, when you bring the text in?

A. Well, in the author there is the outside author, there is the author who is the writer, and there is the narrative-voice author; and then in the reader there are all these different readers. And then the text changes according to the reader, because I think that the reader creates the text.

So I'm grappling with this voice and how much I can push in order to make people think a little bit differently, or to give them an emotional or intellectual experience when they can go and say, "Oh, so that's the Pacific Ocean?" Not quite that blatantly. Another example is Toni Morrison's *The Bluest Eye*. You never quite look at another black child without what you took from that text. It has changed your way of looking at black children. The problem of voice is the third problem.

I think another more external problem is one of censorship. With the very conservative path that this country has taken in terms of the arts, these times are hard. I know artists who can't exhibit nude photographs of their children because that's like an obscenity. When you apply for the NEA or any of these grants, you're limited. That's external censorship from the Right, of morality and family values. Then there is the external censorship from my family. "Gloria don't write about that, that's a secret." You're not supposed to devalue the Chicano culture. I was being disloyal to my mother and my culture because I was writing about poverty and abuse and gender oppression. So there's a kind of weightiness on you *not* to write, not to do your art in as honest a way as possible. You're supposed to make nice, like you were talking about being Southern girls.

I write a lot about sexuality in my stories. I don't know if you read "Immaculate, Inviolate" in *Borderlands*, but when I sent my brother the book and he read it, he had a fit. He was going to show it to my uncle, and my uncle was going to sue me, because that was his mother I was talking about, my grandmother. I talked about how my grandfather lifted her skirt to do his thing, and how he had three other *mujeres con familia*. He would spend three days and three nights with my grandmother, and two days and two nights with the next mistress, and two days with the next one. The children from all the families played together, and my grandmother was ashamed of that and felt humiliated. I'm not supposed to write about that. I'm constantly asked by my family to choose my loyalty: when I choose who I'm going to be loyal to, myself or them, I'm supposed to choose them. I don't and I never have, and that's why I'm accused of betraying my culture, and that's why I'm a bad girl: selfish, disobedient, ungrateful.

Q. And also why you are a writer.

A. To take the problem of censorship one step further, there is also internal censorship. I've internalized my mom's voice, the neoconservative right voice, the morality voice. I'm always fighting those voices.

Q. I was just going to ask you about that again. The visual that you showed me earlier had "us" and "them," and you said very beautifully that both of these—the "them" and the "us"—are now in you. You're very aware of that mixture of voices inside yourself. I think that many teachers of composition would like to be able to find ways to help students recognize their own multiple voices, especially the Anglo students who don't see themselves as having any race, any ethnicity; and often they don't even think they have any range of sexuality. They're just "man" or "woman," that's it. How do we help those students hear those other voices? How do we help them get Gloria's voice in them? They have the *nos* so much in their head that they don't have any other voices. One of the reasons work like yours is so important to the future of composition studies is that it gives concrete evidence of many voices in a text, many voices speaking out of who you are, many voices that you allow to speak. Many, on the other hand, are not only monolingual in the strict sense of English being the only language, but deeply, internally monolingual as well. Composition studies hasn't done much of anything to help them out of that.

A. I think that the only recourse is a kind of vicarious move of immersing themselves in the texts of people who are different, because the fastest way for them to recognize that they have diversity, that they have these values, that they have these experiences and beliefs, is to jerk them out into another country where they don't speak the language, where they don't know the food. It's like taking a fish out of water. The fish doesn't know that it lives in the element of water until it jerks onto the beach and can't breath. You can't do that to every student. But sometimes a traumatic experience can do that, it can open up a window. What education and the schools can give is this vicarious experience via the text, via reading *The Bluest Eye*, or *Borderlands*.

In terms of composition , I think teachers need to look at alternate models. What I want to do with the chapters of the textbook that I've been talking to you about is to offer other ways of considering how to write a story, a poem, or a paper. And again, that alternate way is colored by the Western frame of everything. What I'm trying to present to you is another way of ordering, another way of composing, another rhetoric; but it is only partly new. Most of it is cast in the Western tradition, because that's all that I was immersed in. The symbol is to see the university as this walled city, and somebody brings the Trojan Horse, the Trojan *Burra*, into the city gates. At night the belly of the *burra* opens, and out comes the "other" trying to make changes from inside. And I have a visual for that. . . . There's your Trojan *Burra*. It's kind of hard, because the university wall or city is very seductive, you know? There's something very seductive about fitting in, and being part of this one culture, and forgetting differences, and going with the way of the norm. Western theory is very seductive, and pretty soon instead of subverting and challenging and making marks on the wall, you get taken in.

Q. Certainly some in composition studies have thought that that's what the university was for, that that's what the composition teacher was for: to help the students become assimilated into the university rather than to help them challenge the reality of the university.

A. Yes. This is also what traditional therapy tries to do. It tries to assimilate you to life, to reality, to living.

Q. So here, in the night, out of the *burra*, come the challengers?

A. Yes, these different ways of writing: the inappropriate ways, the bad girls not making nice. It's really hard because you are one of only a few.

Q. One of the things I like best about teaching composition is that sometimes I can make a place, as a teacher, for students to do dangerous and experimental kinds of writing. But then they have to go and pass the tests and pass the history essays and do the inside-the-lines kind of writing.

A. This is what I was talking about earlier: that in order to make it in this society you have to be able to know the discipline, if it's teaching, if it's composition, if it's carpentry. Whatever field it is, you have to know your way around. You have to know how to wire the house before you can start being an innovative electrician. The question is, how can you change the norm if the tide is so tremendous against change? But you can do something. You are in the field of composition, right? And somehow you respect my ideas and my writing. Otherwise, you wouldn't be here. So for me to be effective in making whatever little changes I can, I have to get this respect, this acceptance, this endorsement from my peers. All of these academics who teach my writings are endorsing me, and they make it possible for me to reach a wider audience. Whatever little changes I can make in people's thoughts, it is because they first allowed me through the gate. If you absolutely hated my stuff and everybody else hated my stuff, no matter how innovative it was, nobody would ever see it because it wouldn't get through the peer gate. I couldn't do any of this without you.

Q. Well, you could do it, and you have done it; but reaching the very, very largest audience in the United States certainly does take that.

A. Which is my next step. One of my goals is to have a larger audience, which is what I'm trying to accomplish with this book of fiction. Fiction is a genre that more than just people from the academy can accept. I mean, community people do read my books—the children's book especially goes into the community, and *Borderlands*— but it's still beyond the scale of most people. My family doesn't do any serious reading. They will look at my stuff—my sister will read a little bit of it, and my brother—but they don't do serious reading. They don't sit down on a daily basis like you and I do and read stuff on composition and theory.

Q. But they might read a book of stories.

A. Yes, and what I'm trying to convey to you about composition and postcoloniality, I am trying to do through story. You can theorize

through fiction and poetry; it's just harder. It's an unconscious
kind of process. The reader will read this and wonder about it.
Instead of coming in through the head with the intellectual
concept, you come in through the back door with the feeling, the
emotion, the experience. But if you start reflecting on that
experience, you can come back to the theory.

Q. I wonder if that's partly why the boundaries between fiction and
nonfiction seem to be so permeable right now. It's hard sometimes to say what is a short story and what is an essay.

A. The way that one composes a piece of creative nonfiction and the
way one composes fiction are very similar. In composing nonfiction, you're very selective and you take little fragments here and
there and piece them together in a new way. So right off the bat
you're not being true to the nonfiction. It's fiction already, just in
manipulating it.

Q. And then the representation itself—you said earlier that the
representation is not the same as the experience; it's the representation.

A. The borders are permeable, and I like the fact that at this turn of
the century these borders are transparent and crossable. And
when we get past the millennium, the *fin de siècle*, some of these
things will settle down into another kind of reality. At every turn
of the century everything is up for grabs: the categories are
disrupted, the borders are crossable. Then you get to another
plateau where things become more fixed in cement, but not really.
Then you wait for the next period of insurgency, when everything
is up for grabs again. I think it goes like that in cycles. So this is
why I'm so hopeful and so glad that I'm alive right now, because
I can partake of this confusion. But still, back to your students,
what's going to help them?

Q. Well, the book you're working on may help them, but I often find
students so anxious to be able to work within the framework and
to be part of the system, and so fearful of what will happen if
they're not part of the system (and often with very good reason),
that they resist taking risks and they resist trying to get in touch
with things that might hurt.

A. Yes, we come back to the same thing: fear of being different. They
don't want to stick out, to be different—especially at their age.
You and I have already passed mid-life. We can have a sense of
identity and of self that is not so much based on other people's

reactions anymore. But theirs is very much a relational type of identity, so that if this group of people disapproves of them and finds their difference to be problematic, they won't be able to function. They won't be able to get their degree, they won't get the grant, they won't get the job. So how do you teach them to take risks? How do you teach them to stand up and say, "I'm different and this is who I am, and your way is maybe a good way, but it's not the only way." How do you get them to do that? I think that writing and postcolonial studies are trying to do that in terms of getting people to think about how they are in the world.

Writing is very liberating and emancipatory; it frees you up. In the process of writing, you're reflecting on all of the things that make you different, that make you the same, that make you a freak. You're constantly grappling with identity issues. Postcoloniality looks at this power system discipline—whether it's a government, whether it's anthropology, or composition— and it asks, "Who has the voice? Who says these are the rules? Who makes the law?" And if you're not part of making the laws and the rules and the theories, what part do you play? How is that other system placed in your mind? You get into the neo-colonization of people's minds. You get into the erasure of certain histories, the erasure of ideas, the erasure of voices, the erasure of languages, the erasure of books. A lot of the Mayan and Aztec codices were burned, and a whole system of knowledge was wiped out. Postcoloniality comes and asks these questions. What reality does this disciplinary field, or this government, or this system try to crush? What reality is it trying to erase? What reality is it trying to suppress? Writing is about freeing yourself up, about giving yourself the means to be active, to take agency, to make changes. So I see both writing and postcoloniality as emancipatory projects, about how to get from here to there.

Q. May I ask a question about English? One of the first things that brought me to your work was your mixture of languages. As a teacher of writing who believes that writing and literacy can be liberatory, it was very frightening and disorienting and hurtful when I began to realize the degree to which writing and language could be just the opposite: the ways in which they could enslave, keep down, exclude, hurt, silence. To have to face my own doubleness within the discipline of writing was hard for me, because I wanted to embrace the goals of liberation, and I didn't want to face the fact that teaching any kind of a system involves constraints and hurts, or the degree to which English is hegemonic and silencing, the way in which English tends to drown out. I also think about the way in which English, throughout its whole history as a language, has been like a sponge, sucking up words from Norse, or German, or French, or I think now of Spanish, from which English is absorbing enormous amounts. I don't know how I feel about that. I don't know whether I think that it's good that the language is alive and growing, or whether I think that English is exerting its power once more and trying to surround Spanish, let's say, and take it in. Those are very confusing issues to me. I'm also very much aware that students quite often fear other languages in the same way that they fear other people that they perceive as different. So how are you feeling about the state of English today? How do you feel about the English-only legislation which passed in the Congress last summer?

A. Well, I think that English is the dominant symbology system. Language is a representational system, a symbology system. But what happens with the language, this particular symbolic system, is that it displaces the reality, the experience, so that you take the language to be the reality. So say you had Hindi, or Spanish, or Hopi, or whatever the language happens to be. That language attempts to create reality: not just shape it but create it; not just mold it but create it and displace it. I think all languages do that. Then you take a country like the United States, where via the industrial age and the electronic age and the age of the Internet, the dispersal of English is faster and more widespread than any other language thus far. It's going to become the planetary language if we're not careful. Other countries are going to become—I don't want to say "Americanized" because I don't want to use the word "America" to represent the United States—but it's going to have this kind of United Statesian-culture-swallowing-up-the-rest-of-the-world kind of mouth. As for me, I like English and I majored in English at a time that I wasn't allowed Spanish. I never took any Spanish courses other than a Spanish class in high school. I took some French and some Italian—which didn't do any good because I can't remember any of it now. The way that I grew up with my family was code-switching. When I am my most emotive self, my home self, stuff will come out in Spanish. When I'm in my head, stuff comes out in English. When I'm dealing with theory, it's all in English, because I didn't take any classes in which theory was taught in Spanish. So the body and the feeling parts of me come out in Spanish, and the intellectual, reasoning parts of me come out in English.

Q.Do you dream in Spanish?

A.I dream in both Spanish and English. What's happening more and more is that I get the ideas in Spanish and I get them in visuals. Like one of the ideas that I'm working with is *conocimiento*, the Spanish word for knowledge, for ways of knowing. Those ideas come to me in Spanish and in visuals. So when I think *"conocimiento,"* I see a little serpent for counter-knowledge. This is how it comes to me that this knowledge, this "counter-knowledge," is not acceptable, that it's the knowledge of the serpent of the garden of Eden. It's not acceptable to eat the fruit of knowledge; it makes you too aware, too self-reflective. So how do you take this *conocimiento* and have the student speculate on it, when all the student knows and is immersed in is the kind of knowledge that crosses this one out? For a student to do this, there has to be some kind of opening, some kind of fissure, crack, gate, *rajadura*—a crack between the world is what I call it—the hole, the interfaces.

Q.Before we began taping, you remembered that people generally assume that you have read a lot of theory, since your books enact so many of the concepts poststructural theory has espoused. You must have read Foucault, you must have read Derrida, you must have read Irigaray or Cixous. You said that you hadn't read them before you wrote *Borderlands*, but that the ideas are "out there."

A.Yes, the ideas are out there because we are all people who are in more or less the same territory. We occupy the world of the academy and of the late twentieth century. We've read some of the same books, we've seen some of the same movies, we have similar ideas about relationships, whether we're French or born in the United States or raised here. In reflecting on what we know and on our experiences, we come up with these paradigms, concepts of what it is that life is about, about how interactions and power struggles work. Those theorists give it different terms than I do; a lot of my terms are in Spanish, like *conocimiento*. A lot of the concepts that I have about composition and postcoloniality are attempts to connect pre-Columbian histories and values and systems with the postcolonial twentieth century. A lot of times I will start with a cultural figure from the precolonial: *Coatlicue*, or *la Llorona*. Then I look at the experience in 1997 that Chicanos and Chicanas are going through, and I try to see a connection to what was going on then. I want to show a continuity, to show a progression. I try to give a term, to find a language for my ideas and my concepts that comes from the indigenous part of me rather than from the European part of me, so I come up with *Coatlicue*, and *la facultad*, and *la frontera*, and *Nepantla*—concepts that mean: "Here's a little nugget of a system of knowledge that is different from the Euro-American. This is my hit on it, but it's also a *mestizo/mestiza*, cognitive kind of perception, so therefore this ideology or this little nugget of knowledge is both indigenous and Western. It's a hybridity, a mixture, because I live in this liminal state in between worlds, in between realities, in between systems of knowledge, in between symbology systems." This liminal, borderland, terrain or passageway, this interface, is what I call *Nepantla*. All of the concepts that I have about composition, all of the concepts that I have about postcoloniality, come under this umbrella heading of *Nepantla*, which means *el lugar en medio*, the space in between, the middle ground. I first saw that word in Rosario Castellano's writings. When they dug up the streets of Mexico City to build the subway system, they found the *Templo Mayor*. In it they found the statue of *Coatlicue*, and they found all these artifacts, and they found murals on the walls, and one of the murals was *Nepantla*. There are also all these words that begin with *Nepantla* and end in other endings in *Nahuatl*. One of them is "between two oceans": that's the *Nepantla*. Whenever two things meet there's the *Nepantla*, so they have tons and tons of words with the root word *Nepantla*. *Borderlands* falls into that category, but *Borderlands* is just one project of this overall umbrella project that is my life's work, my life's writing. *Borderlands* is just one hit on it. And this new book that I'm working on now— on composition and on the process of writing, and on identity, and on knowledge, and on the construction of all of these things—is like a sequel to *Borderlands*. All of my books are parts of this project.

Q. And the book of short stories that you're working on, too.

A. Yes, and the process for my composing all these projects is very much Coyochauqui, the moon goddess that got dismembered. In composing, you take things apart and everything is fragmented, and then you struggle to put things together.

Q.Is there any sense of weaving in what comes after the tearing apart, from the language? I also think of weaving as a metaphor for what happens at some points in writing.

A.Yes, there is—a kind of weaving, a rearranging. Anyway, I'm enumerating the different stages of my writing process. And what's funny is that I started out just talking about writing, and then I branched off into other art forms: into musical composition, dances that get choreographed, film, video—all of these arts have elements in common. Even architecture and building construction have something in common with composition, even though in the construction of a building you have to have all the details first—where the electrical outlets have to be, where the windows are, what the dimensions are. Then you're allowed to be creative: you can manipulate things; you can move the light switch a little bit. But with writing, you can approach it from an outline, from something that's already framed for you; or you can start composing with a loosely held-together frame; or you can jump into it and start anywhere. You can start in the end and go to the beginning, or you can start in the middle and go both directions, toward the beginning and the end. The frames for all of these art forms vary a little bit, but a lot of the process of the composition is very similar.

Okay, so once I found that out, I started looking at how I create aspects of my identity. Identity is very much a fictive construction: you compose it of what's out there, what the culture gives you, and what you resist in the culture. This identity also has this kind of projection of your self into a future identity. You can say here's the image of Gloria, or here's the image of Andrea that I want to project in the next seven years, the kind of person that I'd like to be in the future; and then you start building that Andrea. You can start building that Andrea by saying, "I'm going to make more time for myself, I'm going to value solitude, I'm going to get rid of the clutter, I'm going to find out what my own goals are and what my agenda is, and go with that instead of what my mother, or my family, or the academy, or my husband wants, and these are the projects that I'm going to concentrate on." You reshape yourself. But first you get that self image in your head, and then you project that out into the world. When you look at it ten years later, you won't recognize yourself. When you go back home to your mom and to your brothers and sisters, you'll be an entirely different person, and they won't see how you came from there to here. So you keep creating your identity this way.

Then I took all of this knowledge a step further, to reality. I realized that if I can compose this text, and if I can compose my identity, then I can also compose reality out there. It all has to do with the angle of looking at things. Say all your life you've perceived Andrea as being this one kind of person, you've perceived an essay to be this one kind of composition, you've perceived the planet earth and the United Sates to be this kind of country and this kind of reality. Then you find out that you don't have to write the essay this way, that you don't have to be the Andrea that you've been all your life, and that if you see that shed and that sky and that sea and all that happens in it from this other angle, then you will see something else. You can recreate reality. But you're going to need some help, because it's all done in relationship with other people. When we are born we are taught by our culture that this is up, and this is down, and that's a piece of wood, and that's a no-no. To change the tree, the up and down, and the no-no, you have to get the rest of your peers to see things in this same way—that that's *not* a tree, and that's *not* a no-no. You know what I'm saying. It's all of us that created this physics, this quantum mechanics; now we all have to recreate something different. A scientist will be the first to give us an idea of this other universe, of this other atom; the writer will be the first to give us an idea of this other emotional experience, this other perception, this other angle. It has to be one of the members of the tribe to start making that aperture, that little hole, that crack. It has to be one of the members of the community to say, "Yeah, this is a different way of looking at reality." Then everybody else will say, "Yeah, why didn't I think of that? That's true." All of a sudden you'll have a congress, a consensual basis for this reality that you're observing. And once you have this consensual view of reality, along comes Anzaldúa, who says, "No, that's just the reality that your particular people—who are Indo-European, or Western, or Inuit, or whatever—that's just your gift. Here's a different way of looking at reality."

Q. When you were talking about your architect, it made me think about what you later said about the importance of other people and always having other people around you. When I think of the feminist architect that you worked with for the addition to your house, that person brought a lot to the project, but you were important to the project, too. And then the electricians and the plumbers .... Was it a deeply collaborative project?

A. Yes. They consulted with me, but they knew that I didn't have the know-how. They said, "What kind of space do you want to live in?" and I said, "Tall, a lot of opening, a lot of window space." And then they said, "Well, how tall?" Then there is the city code. You have to have certain amount of free territory in your lot; you can only build so many square feet. I was limited to that, so I said, "I'll go up." Then there are the neighbors. I had to get permission, because some of these windows overlook them. There's a public hearing if you build a two-story, because you're impinging on somebody else's space. So anyway, all of those people and the architect had their visions of what they wanted the space to be like, and I had mine, and I wanted them to co-create it with me. I didn't want it to be just me. There's always negotiating. The corner windows are two or three hundred dollars more expensive then the regular windows, and I said, "I can't afford that." But the architect was invested in having these corner windows— which had been my idea in the first place—so I said, "Well, this is your project, too, so we'll go with that." I wanted only one door, because I felt that French doors were not as secure, but then I talked to the carpenter, who said, "No, this glass is very durable." It's all very collaborative.

Q. I was just looking at your children's book; obviously you collaborated with the artist on that project, too.

A. Well, it wasn't quite a straight collaboration, because I did the text first and then I gave it to the artist. But now I am doing a project for a middle-school girl readership, and there I will be working with the artist. But I also think that there is no such thing as a single author. I write my texts, but I borrow the ideas and images from other people. Sometimes I forget that I've borrowed them. I might read some phrase from a poem or fiction, and I like the way it describes the cold. Years and years go by, and I do something similar with my description, but I've forgotten that I've gotten it somewhere else. Then I show my text in draft form to a lot of people for feedback: that's another level of co-creating with somebody. Then my readers do the same thing. They put all of their experience into the text and they change *Borderlands* into many different texts. It's different for every reader. It's not mine anymore.

Q.Does that feel okay to you? You don't feel possessive about your writing as your "property?"

A.No, I don't; I've always felt that way about writing. I do the composing, but it's taken from little mosaics of other people's lives, other people's perceptions. I take all of these pieces and rearrange them. When I'm writing I always have the company of the reader. Sometimes I'm writing with my friends in mind, and sometimes for people like you who teach writing. In writing, I'm just talking with you without your being here. This is where style comes in. Style is my relationship with you, how I decide what register of language to use, how much Spanglish, how much vernacular. It's all done in the company of others, while in solitude—which is a contradiction.

Q.Are there some stylists that have been really important to you?

A.Well, I know that thematically Julio Cortazar has influenced me. He was an Argentinean writer living in France who wrote *Hopscotch* and *End of the Game and Other Stories,* and he wrote a lot about these in-between places of reality impinging on each other. In terms of my feminist ideas, my gender liberation ideas, *Jane Eyre* influenced me. I read it thirteen times when I was growing up. I really like how this little girl is so assertive. I like her being able to support herself differently from gender roles that were assigned to women. In terms of style, I recently read a mystery by Ruth Rendell, *No Night is Too Long.* She writes popular stuff under the name Barbara Vine. She can really get into the rhythm of the lines, the words, the voice. I read Cormac McCarthy's *All the Pretty Horses.* I didn't finish the book, but I thought it had a style very similar to mine.

Q.You mentioned Toni Morrison. Have you read a lot of her work?

A.Yes, in the past I did. I think *Song of Solomon* was the last book of hers that I read. I stopped reading her a few years ago; I don't know why. I have her books, and I'm going to pick them up again.

Q.Have you read Borges?

A.Yes. I have his entire collected works.

Q.I was thinking about the story "The Aleph," and that certain spot where, if you lie down and you put your eye there, you can see everything.

A.Yes, when I talk about borders with my students, I use a visual of the Aleph.

Q.Didn't Borges write in both Spanish and English as you do?

A.I think he wrote mainly in Spanish, but was heavily influenced by English writers. He read Poe and Hawthorne and people like that.

Q.I picked up a book the other day called the *History of Reading*, by Alberto Manguel, who lived in Argentina for a time and who read to Borges for several years. And he would go there at night and Borges would say, "shall we have Kipling tonight, or shall we have Poe?" and he would read.

A.Style is a very difficult concept. Often I go to visuals to clarify my concepts, as I've said. For example, I think what's going on now at the turn of the century is exemplified by the *remolino*, the whirlwind, the vortex. North of the equator, the movement is clockwise, so all of our knowledge on this side moves clockwise. South of the equator, the movement is counter-clockwise. The rivers flow the other way here. As a *mestiza*, I'm living on the equator. Some of my culture, the indigenous and the Mexican culture, pulls me counter-clockwise. This comes with its own perception of being. And over here, in North America, all of the knowledge that I learned in school, all of the ways that I've learned to look at life, is pulling me the other way. I'm pulled in two different ways. I think that postcoloniality is situated right here. If you consider the counter-clockwise to be the colonized cultures and the clockwise to be the colonizer cultures, then there is this tension and you're trying to accommodate both of these cultures and still be comfortable. But it's a struggle to find this peace, this settlement. You have to change the clockwise move-ment to be counter-clockwise once in a while, and sometimes you have to change this counter-clockwise movement to move like the North. It's a state that's very unsettling. It's also the state you are in when you are trying to compose. Moving clockwise is every-thing that has been written: the literature, the norm, the genre laws. As a writer, you are trying to add to those genre laws, to that knowledge, to that literature, to that art. You have to go along with it in some ways, but to create some changes you have to go counter-clockwise. This is the struggle for a writer like me: how much can you get away with without losing the whole thing? All of these metaphors come around and around: to style, to compo-sition itself, to identity, to the creation of knowledge, and to the creation of experience.

Q.When I look at your writing, I think yours is a mixture of styles.

Have you seen other people that mix things up the way you do?

A. Well, other Chicanas were mixing Spanglish in poetry, but not in theory, not in academic writing. And I think of style as trying to recover a childhood place where you code switch. If I am fictionalizing a certain experience, I go back to the reality of the experience in my memory, and it takes place in both languages. So I get into that style. But I think that what I was trying to do by code-switching was to inject some of my history and some of my identity into this text that white people were going to read or black people were going to read or Native American people were going to read. I was trying to make them stop and think. Code-switching jerks the reader out of his world and makes her think, "Oh, this is my world, this is another world, this is her world where she does this, where it's possible to say words in Spanish." It's like taking the counter-clockwise and injecting it into the clockwise. I think that's why I started that. And now a lot of Chicanas are doing it.

Q. Think of the same thing about injecting, but injecting the discourse of lesbianism or alternative sexuality of any kind into traditional heterosexuality. It does the same thing. It insists that we go this way and it helps readers to inhabit other ways of being, other ways of knowing. Isn't that very important too?

A. And you know we live in the *remolino*, the vortex, the whirlwind; and in this time everything is very much confused: values, ideology, identity. The student is caught in her own little vortex. What I would like to do is what Carlos Castaneda was told to do by Don Juan the shaman: to stop the world. The world is this reality and the world is also the description we have of it in our heads. How do you stop that and say, "No, this other world exists, this other possibility, this other reality. You have to stop this world a little bit to get the other one in. So I would like to stop the *remolino* for just a second, the second that it takes the reader to say, "I didn't know that Chicano Spanish was the bastard language. And if Chicano Spanish is a bastard language, what registers of English are also bastards and not allowed into the academy?" Then they start looking at British English, Australian English, Canadian English, United States English. Then at all of the dialects and all of the registers: academic, formal, slang. And then maybe the reader will say, "I'm a redneck and this is my language, and maybe I should write about this language for this particular class." Just for that little second it stops them. Does this make sense to you? Or maybe I'm being too presumptuous and I don't really do that. Anyway, I think that writing has that faculty, but it has to be honest writing and it has to be writing the struggle.

Q. When bell hooks says that language is a place of struggle, I think that's what she means: you're struggling to get language out of the clockwise just for the second and into the counter-clockwise, and it's a terrible struggle. It goes on your whole life—if I understand her correctly. Did you have any teachers that . . .

A. Pointed me in this direction?

Q. Or that nurtured you in your writing, reading, and thinking?

A. I had a favorite teacher when I was in elementary school who influenced the way I look at history, at the teacher-student dynamic, and at power, domination and subordination. He would have students teach the class. I was a shy little Chicanita, but I was known as "the brain" because I had the best grades. So he would have me do stuff. I liked to help the other kids. I was his pet: I would grade the papers, and I ended up making up the tests. He would leave me in the classroom. He'd go outside for twenty minutes, and I would be like the little teacher. I learned a lot about power and about teaching.

Then, when I was in high school, they put me in the accelerated section. There were plus one, two, three, four sections and regular one, two, three, four sections. Chicanos were put in the one, two, three, four sections, and the whites were all in the plus, except for me and Danny—we were put in the plus. There were also some whites who were in the one, two, three, four. I was put in the "accelerated" level with Danny, but I had no interaction with the white kids because they looked down on me. I was with the white kids for English, Math, Science—for everything except Health, PE and Homeroom, which I had with Chicanos. One of the teachers that I had was really into building vocabulary. I remember opening dictionaries and encyclopedias and reading whole chunks. I loved to look at the meanings of words. The whole time I was very studious and very withdrawn from other people, very shy. That particular teacher said that I had a facility with words, but that I needed to be trained. But then she would ignore me and pay attention to the white kids, so it was like a put-down rather than praise. Then I had a teacher in college who felt one of the pieces I wrote should be published.

Then I went to grad school after I got my BA, and I had a teacher named James Sledd at the University of Texas. He was the first person ever to encourage me to talk about cultural stuff. I wrote an essay for him called "Growing up Chicana," which was the basis for the *Prieta* in *This Bridge Called My Back*. It was also the basis for a manuscript that I did on my memories, which I then took parts of and made into *Borderlands*. And now I have taken part of it and made it into this book of stories, and other segments of it are going into *la Llorona: Theorizing Identity, Knowledge, Composition*. All of that has its roots in the very first essay that I wrote for James Sledd called "Growing up Chicana." He encouraged me to talk about cultural things, and I used some Mexican words and some terms in Spanish. I had written some stories way back when I was working on my BA, and some when I was working on my MA. They all code-switched, but when I wrote for James Sledd, we were doing something different. We were trying to write formally: what we would call now theorizing; what was called then criticism. His encouragement was very important to me, and he was also very important to me as a role model. He was very much a maverick against the university; he was very much at odds, an outsider. From him I learned that an outsider is not just somebody of a different skin; it could be somebody who's white, who's usually an insider but who crosses back and forth between outsider and insider. So he was my model to think about insider/outsider, and then I had my whole life to think about *Nosotras*, us and them.

Q. Did you mention an undergraduate teacher who said that something you had written could be published?

A. Yes. This was at Texas Woman's College in Denton. But I couldn't afford to go to Denton. So then I had to get out for two years and work. I saved money for two years, and then I went to Pan American. I published the essay from my first year in a little Pan American quarterly. Few of the teachers encouraged me. When I was working on my MA, I would constantly be marked down on my papers for being too subjective, for not following the rhetoric of Aristotle and Cicero. You know, the model that people value, with the logical development of ideas. I would constantly get marked down. Across the board, all of the professors—in Comp Lit, in English Lit, in all of the classes that I took for my MA, and later on while working for a Ph.D. in Austin—marked me down.

Even the ones I took here at UC-Santa Cruz, teachers who were using my book as a textbook—when I turned in my papers, they would subtly want me to write the status-quo way, even though they would use my book as a model for how to do things differently.

So it was a great shock to me several years ago when the CCCC conference invited me to speak. The very same discipline, the very same teachers who had marked me down and had said that I was writing incorrectly, all of a sudden invited me to speak. Then I started getting requests for reprints in composition readers. That was a shock to me. Finding that composition people were reading me was a bigger shock than finding that anthropologists or that women's studies people were reading me. Just a few days ago I was sent a book, a textbook for students. One of the sections is on place, and they took a little segment of Chapter 7, "*La Conciencia de la Mestiza*," where I talk about the valley and returning to the valley. The students are supposed to take that little piece of writing, and write a letter saying what I wrote, assuming my place, signing the letter "Gloria Anzaldúa." I'll show you the book if you don't believe it. I don't know how the students are supposed to do this.

Q. English in colleges and in universities has traditionally been a gatekeeper, functioning to keep the gate closed. Only in the last twenty-five years or so have people in English, and mostly people in composition, said, "We don't want to do that anymore. If we are going to be gatekeepers, we want to be opening the gate." That is a very, very big change.

A. It was a big shock for me to find composition people picking me up, and only a slightly smaller shock to find Spanish and Portuguese modern language people putting my stuff in their readers. Because we Chicanas were not part of Latino writing. They just included Mexican, South American, and Central American writers, not Chicanas. They put Sandra Cisneros in there, they put me in there. I am now a Latina writer. Can you believe that?

Q. We have talked about some of these issues of unity, rationality, organization, and coherence; and of how we can make a space for intuition, emotion, and the body in writing and in the construction of knowledge—what Kenneth Burke calls the paralogical, to go along with the logical, and the logical has had a stranglehold on the teaching of writing. You have to start with *A* and you must end with Z. You can't start with Q.

A. I use "paralogical" in the forward to the encyclopedia, in talking about spirituality and reality. When I use these terms, sometimes I think I made them up. I know "paranormal," so I think "paralogical."

Q. Before our time is over, would you talk at least a little bit about activism and working for change? Because in your writing, it's very clear that you see writing and activism as related. I think that it's less clear how we engage others in doing that kind of activism.

A. Well, I think that a lot of the activism for writers and artists stems from trying to heal the wounds. You've been oppressed as a woman, or oppressed as a queer, or oppressed racially as a colonized person, and you want to deal with that oppression, with those wounds. Why did this happen to you? Why is it so hard? Who are these people that are oppressing you, and why do they have a license to oppress you? For me it started as a child. Children don't have any recourse. They can be abused by their parents. They don't have any rights. Society doesn't protect them. In my case, I was such a freak, such a strange little thing that I felt all of the ill winds that were blowing. I really felt them. I had a very low threshold of pain. The differences that I felt between me and other people were so excruciating. I felt like such a freak. I was trying to make meaning of my existence and my pain, and that in turn led me to writing. In writing I'm trying to write about these moments where I took things into my own hands and I said, "This is not the way things are supposed to be. Girl children are not supposed to be treated this way. Women are not supposed to be battered; they're not supposed to be second-class citizens. Chicanas shouldn't be treated in this way in society." I started grappling with those issues, and writing became a way of activism, a way of trying to make changes. But it wasn't enough just to sit and write and work on my computer. I had to connect the real-life, bodily experiences of people who were suffering because of some kind of oppression, or some kind of wound in their real lives, with what I was writing. It wasn't a disembodied kind of writing. And because I am a writer, voice—acquiring a voice, covering a voice, picking up a voice, creating a voice—was important. And then you run into this whole experience of unearthing, of discovering, of rediscovering, of recreating voices that have been silenced, voices that have been repressed, voices that have been made a secret. And not just for me, but for other Chicanas. Look at all these women who have certain realities that are similar to mine, but they don't really see them. But when they read a text by Toni Morrison or when they read *Borderlands,* they say, "Oh, that went on in my life, but I didn't have the words to articulate it. You articulated it for me, but it's really my experience." They see themselves in the text. Reading these other voices gives them permission to go out and acquire their own voices, to write in this way, to become an activist by using Spanglish, or by code-switching. And then they go out and they read the book to their little girls, or their neighbor's kids, or to their girlfriend, or to their boyfriend.

Q. It's like links in a chain or a circle that keeps expanding?

A. Yes. As with my children's book *la Llorona,* it's really very much a cultural story. All that these Chicanitos read is white stuff, and then along comes *la Llorona* and they say, "Yeah, my grandmother used to tell me stories like that." And it feels really good for them to be in a book. There's this little kid—six, seven, eight, nine, ten—who never sees himself represented, so unearthing and nurturing that voice is part of the activism work. That's why I try to do so many anthologies. That's why I promote women, especially women of color and lesbians of all colors, and why I'm on editorial boards for magazines: because I want to get their voices out there. I believe that says something about activism, because in the process of creating the composition, the work of art, the painting, the film, you're creating the culture. You're rewriting the culture, which is very much an activist kind of thing. So writers have something in common with all of these people doing grass roots organizing and acting in the community: it's all about rewriting culture. You don't want a culture that batters women and children. By the year 2005, fifty percent of the group that is going to be labeled "poverty stricken"—fifty percent of it—are going to be women and children. That's a whole new thing, women out of jobs, homeless children. It's a reality that we need to speak of. Twenty years ago, incest was not part of consensual reality. It was the writers who wrote about it, feminists who talked about it, who made films about it, and who did art about incest and child abuse, who changed reality. Before that, it was just a given. You beat your wife, that's part of it. Having abusive sex with your wife is not rape. Consensual reality has been redefined by these people rewriting a culture. Now it's part of culture that when you batter someone, you're supposed to be responsible. It's not something you can get away with unless you're a psychopath.

Q. What you just said makes me think of one of the things that's important about your work for postcolonial studies: your work goes beyond the deconstructive—which has been a large part of the very important work that postcolonial studies has done—to show what colonialism has done and been. But the kind of work that you're talking about creates a new reality. It goes beyond the deconstructing and the showing of old oppressions and hurts.

A. When you get into reading and writing the "other," into assuming some kind of authority for the "other"—whether you are the "other" or you are the subject—there's a community involved. And I think what you are saying is that postcolonial theorists sometimes forget what's going on here in the community, in the world that we inhabit.

Q. And so do teachers of writing, I hasten to add.

A. Yes. There's a responsibility that comes with invoking cultural and critical authority, and I think you could call that responsibility being open to activism and being responsible for your actions. No?

Q. I want to ask one other thing. Suppose you and I had a little child here, and we wanted to watch her grow up and be a writer. What would be your wildest dream for that little child in becoming a writer? What would you most hope for?

A. Well, I think what I would most hope for is probably not something that is possible. I would hope for her to have a peaceful community in all the different worlds, in all the different cultures, in all the different realities. I would hope for her to be a true *mestiza*, and I don't think it's possible right now because the powers that decide the laws of man are very much monolithical. It's not an equal kind of thing.

Q. Do you have any hopes that the situation might change in the future?

A. Yes, I do. I think we're drifting toward that. The distinction between the people with power and the people without power will get eased, so that the people without any agency now take on a little agency, and the people that were all-powerful now become a little powerless. There will be this kind of hybridity of equal parts, instead of a graft and a major tree. And I would like her to be able to explore the world and not to fear that she's going to be attacked, not to suffer being wounded. To live is to be in pain. To live is to struggle. Life hurts, but we can mitigate that hurt a little bit by having a society where the little girl child can pursue her interests and her dreams without being too much constrained by gender roles or racial law or the different epistemologies that say, "This is the way reality is." I don't know if that's ever going to happen. But I hope so. Sometimes I think so.

Works Cited

Anzaldúa, Gloria. *Borderlands/La Frontera: The New Mestiza*. San Francisco: Aunt Lute Books, 1987.

—, ed. *Making Face, Making Soul: Haciendo Caras: Creative and Critical Perspectives by Feminists of Color*. San Francisco: Aunt Lute Books, 1990.

Bickford, Susan. "In the Presence of Others: Arendt and Anzaldúa on the Paradox of Public Appearance." *Feminist Interpretations of Hannah Arendt*. Ed. Bonnie Honig. State College, PA: Penn State UP, 1995. 313-35.

Keating, AnnLouise. *Women Reading/Women Writing: Self-Invention in Paula Gunn Allen, Gloria Anzaldúa, and Audre Lorde*. Philadelphia: Temple UP, 1996.

Moraga, Cherrie and Gloria Anzaldúa. *This Bridge Called My Back: Writings by Radical Women of Color*. First published by Persephone Press, Watertown, MA, 1981. Second ed. New York: Kitchen Table: Women of Color Press, 1983.

Perry, Donna. *Backtalk: Women Writers Speak Out*. New Brunswick, NJ: Rutgers UP, 1993.

Michael Eric

Dyson

Race and the Public Intellectual:
A Conversation with
Michael Eric Dyson

SIDNEY I. DOBRIN

Recently, conversations regarding what role universities play in larger communities have become prolific. Some scholars have argued that the walls that divide academics from the "real world" are false and that the university is as much the real world as any other site. Yet others have adamantly sought ways to maintain and strengthen the protective walls of the ivory tower, insisting that what gets done in the academy is somehow more virtuous because it is cerebral. Michael Eric Dyson, the self-proclaimed "Hip-Hop Public Intellectual," has emerged as a vocal radical who seeks to bring the intellectual work of the academy to mass culture in ways that not only encourage political action, but that retain academic integrity at the same time. For Dyson, doing this involves getting one's hands dirty and taking one's work to sites outside the academy. He says, "A kind of geography of destiny is linked to whether you occupy the terrain of the academy specifically as an academic. We love to talk about transgressions intellectually, academically, but we don't want to do it physically or epistemologically."

Dyson is by trade a preacher and a teacher. His books and articles appear in scholarly forums, religious forums, and the popular press; and they address issues that range from critiques of rap music to critical readings of Malcolm X to cultural theory to the examination of religious values. His voice is heard by many in the academy and many more outside its walls. It is to this end that Dyson works. He is clear: "I want to speak to the academy in very powerful and interesting ways, but I don't want to be limited to the academy." For Dyson, what goes on outside of the academy is of tremendous consequence, and in the conversation that follows, he is adamant about our need to talk about how race and discussions of race affect people on both sides of the academic wall.

What many will find interesting about Dyson's relational view of the university and the outside world is that he sees great importance in the kinds of theoretical work that get done in the university. For Dyson, theory becomes the avenue by which important questions get asked; yet, he contends that those questions do not need to be asked in ways that deny non-academics access to the answers. At the forefront of Dyson's agenda is a push for academic and mass-cultural discussions to better inform one another. This gets done, he argues, through public intellectualism. For Dyson, the job of the public intellectual—the black public intellectual, in particular—is to be a "paid pest" whose function is to disrupt and intervene in conversations in ways that are disturbing and that force people to ask "why they frame the questions in the way that they do or why they make the analysis they do."

For Dyson, disrupting notions of race and multiculturalism helps us understanding how issues of race, gender, class, and culture get constructed. He is critical of the market multiculturalism that inhabits American universities, contending that the rough edges and discomforting moments of race and multiculturalism are smoothed over in the versions universities promote; they lack the raw vitality and danger that should be associated with issues of conflict. However, he makes plain that the ways in which multiculturalism and issues of race are safely broached in classrooms are critically important. Dyson is clear that he would rather see conflicts of race break out in safe contestations in classrooms than not be discussed at all, and that he would much rather see classroom approaches to race and multiculturalism than many of the violent ways in which race gets "debated" in the street. When he talks of the conflict of race and culture, his metaphors reflect this violence and his wish for race to break out in classrooms so that it "wounds our most cherished expectations" of the safety of classroom multiculturalism.

What compositionists will notice immediately about Dyson is his acute awareness of how language comes to the fore in matters of race. He is self-conscious of the language he uses and the ways in which he addresses different audiences. But he is also cognizant of how theoretical approaches to understanding discourse and writing affect the epistemological ways in which race, gender, class, and ideology get constructed. Dyson identifies this intellectual engagement with language as having powerful implications in redefining the relationship between the work that gets done in the academy and the lives of people outside of its borders. Dyson seeks to make the intellectual projects of the academy available to the masses in accessible ways in order to enact change and to reenvision how the world views race, class, gender, and the other constructs that shape our thinking about difference.

Q. In *Reflecting Black* you've written, "The desire for literacy has characterized the culture of African-Americans since their arrival here under the myriad brutalities of slavery. Although reading and writing were legally prohibited, black folk developed a resourceful oral tradition that had cultural precedence in African societies. . . . Black folk generated an oral tradition that expressed and reinforced their cultural values, social norms, and religious beliefs. . . . Even with the subsequent development of literate intellectual traditions, a resonant orality continues to shape and influence cultural expression." You are a prolific writer; your work appears in numerous popular and scholarly forums. How important has writing become in the tradition of black storytelling, in shaping and influencing black cultural expression? How do you think of writing in the larger scope of black narrative?

A. Writing has become extraordinarily important in terms of black storytelling and in shaping and influencing black cultural expression, especially because of the centrality of narrative. The narrativity of black experience—the ways in which stories shape self-understanding and mediate self-revelation racially—is enormously powerful in narrative forms, especially autobiographical narratives, which constitute the attempt of the race both to state and then to move forward to its goals as revealed in stories of "overcoming odds," "up from slavery," and "out of the ghetto." Narrativity is an extraordinarily important component of self-understanding and the way in which African-American peoples constitute their own identities, especially in this postmodern world. Writing *per se*—the capacity of people to reflect critically upon their experiences and then filter those experiences through the lens of their own written work—certainly shapes and changes self-expression in a way different from, say, oral expression. In other words, as Ali Masri, the Africanist, says, there is something extraordinarily conservative about the oral form because it only preserves that which people remember and deem necessary to integrate into the fabric of their collective memory, whereas the written form contests certain narrow limitations of the oral form because it situates the writer and the reader in a trans-historical moment that allows the articulation of an extraordinary convergence of con- tested identities and conflicting identities. For instance, when we're writing and we have a body of writing to appeal to and a body of writing against which we can contrast our own self- understanding—our own self-revelation and self-invention against what Foucault said, against what Ellison said, against what Baldwin said, against what slave narratives have been talking about for the last century and as we've recuperated them—it is an extraordinar- ily different moment because the narrative community there constitutes a wedge of interpretation that is provided by the writing, the very physical act of having the paper to refer to.

In regard to the creation of the self through narrative, it is much different when you have an oral community where people are relying upon memory, upon the texture of their memory, to mediate their own self-understanding. Orality provides a differ- ent lens than writing does; writing is textured, embodied—what Haraway calls *material density*. The physical reality of the writing itself has a kind of phenomenological and epistemological *weight* levied against this memory because you can refer *to* the text, whereas in the oral traditions, they certainly have a kind of genealogical effect: one passes one thing on from another (as opposed to a kind of Nietzschian or Foucauldian sense of genealogy). The oral reference provides a kind of artifice of invented memory that in one sense is *not* the same as in written work.

So I think that writing is very important, and it's very impor- tant in terms of the transition of African peoples from modernist to postmodernist forms. Writing is enormously important to try to figure out what the past is about, what the present is about in relationship to that past, and how writing itself becomes a bridge of communication and connection between previous cultures and contemporary ones—*and* a way of reinventing the very character and texture of experience in light of one's own writing. Writing is as much about revelation as it's about invention. When one is writing, one is literally *writing into* and *writing from*, and those poles of writing into and writing from—inscribing and re-inscribing—situate the writer in a kind of interpretive and performative moment that allows the writer to be the mediator, to mediate between these two poles of invention. Especially for African-American people who are preoccupied with literacy, who are preoccupied with the articulation of a self through narrative, writing becomes a most important avenue of both revealing and inventing the future of the race.

Writing becomes, in relationship to other narrative forms, a crucial aspect of connecting ourselves to an old debate about black intelligence, but it also becomes a way of unleashing and constituting different forms of self-understanding that are necessary if we're to move beyond the *mere* fixation on the oral and the *mere* fixation on the cinematic to talk about the legitimate concern of literate expression. Black people have been torn in two directions here. On the one hand, we've said, "That's about white folk and what they do; that's about mainstream society and culture; black folks' abilities to articulate self-identity and revelation and culture are about orality, so writing is not a central part of our project." On the other hand, others have said, "No, *only* when we begin to write with a certain level of mastery and with those narrative patriarchal codes in place will we be able to exemplify our own specific form of mastery and intelligence, and then we will be in one sense entering the modern world and able to, in a very powerful way, show that we are worthy of participation in this American project of democracy and that we're worthy bearers of culture." What's important to me is not to discard writing as a central project of African and African-American peoples. There have been all kinds of writings embedded in black culture from the get-go. One of the things we have to see is that it's a deeply racist moment to suggest that writing (as opposed to orality) is about a tradition external to African-American culture. I see myself as a writer first and foremost in that sense: an articulator of speech, an articulator of ideas and the way in which ideas are not only mediated through speech but constituted in very powerful ways through the very act of writing, the physical weight of writing, the intellectual and ontological self-revelation that is expressed in writing.

We then have to figure out a way to link writing to a very

powerful articulation of black culture, and this is where, for me, questions of authenticity come in. It's not "authentic" for black folk to write at a certain level; it's authentic for them to speak. It's not authentic for them to engage in intellectual performances; it's about the articulation of the self through the body. So all of these other narrative forms (cinema and forms of musical culture) have precedence in African-American culture because, as Hortense Spillers points out, these are the forms that were demanded during slavery. Slave masters didn't say, "Come and perform a trope for us; come and perform a metaphoric allegory." They said, "Come and perform a song for us, and come engage in physical activity." We have to refocus activity on black intellectual expression through narrative forms that become a way for black people to extend and investigate a tradition that we have neglected. The best of black cultural and literary scholars have begun to force us to rethink these issues in light of notions of multiple literacies and of the way in which most literacies are connected to certain forms of cultural expression within black society.

So, writing is central. As we move into this hypertext and cyberworld, and the way in which the forms of expression are mediated not through people's physical writing but through exchange via information systems, the recovery of writing becomes a kind of nostalgic project (already ironically at the end of the twentieth century) and also an articulation of the necessity of still having a mediating agent—that is, the *writer* not only standing in for a larger narrative community, but intervening with his or her own viewpoints about what constitutes authentic legitimate powerful black identity.

Q. You've begun to discuss technology, and in contemporary composition scholarship there has been a lot of conversation regarding how technology affects writers. But there hasn't been much written about how technology specifically affects African-American writers. There are some who see cyber-writing and publishing as closer to oral communication than traditional writing and publication. Do you see this as a potential advantage for blacks and others? That is, how do you see technology and writing being affected by or affecting matters of language and race?

A. There certainly are advantages to new technologies in terms of cultural expressivity for black people. There is the argument that black people are scared off by technology and that the fears are justified primarily because these technologies are controlled by white elites who have no interest in investing the requisite capital in expanding the information superhighway into the black ghetto or into black communities, in making sure it has an off-ramp into the inner-city. On the other hand, we need to examine whether these technical elites are reproducing narratives of technical proficiency that already stigmatize black people because of their ostensible exclusion from the regime of intelligence. New technologies can primarily increase the capacity for black people to become part of this larger "global" world—*global* with scare quotes because part of globalization is about the reproduction of narratives of mastery that allow the expansion of information in ways that I think are very problematic. In the sense of a global village, that international perspective that black people are talking about, this allows us to tap into that flow of information—here again, knowledge is mobility. It's good for African-American people and communities to be involved in this new technology. Yet, for black people the attempt to see ourselves related to technology is historically specific, involving the ways in which technologies have been deployed against black bodies, against black intelligences. The O. J. Simpson trial was an example of black people's resistance to certain forms of medical technology, feeling that it had been used against us in the past. The reason why so many people were willing to believe that O. J. was perhaps innocent—or at least not guilty—is that they thought of the Tuskegee experiment in which black folk had all kinds of medical/technological surveillance on their bodies. There's a kind of inbred hostility toward certain technologies, not because of their inherent capacity to do ill or good, but simply because of their social uses on black bodies. What we have to do is to uncouple the relationship between technological advance and racial repression, because there's a very strong tradition of that. Once black people find ways to intervene in those kinds of historically unjust and corrupt manifestations of technology, what we have to do is to seize the day if we're going to be part of a new world where technology has not only shaped the nature of writing, but where it has also shaped the capacity of people to interact with one another.

In a larger theoretical and philosophical sense, if we say oral communication is closer to technology than traditional writing and publication, then there are some arguments to be made on both sides. In one sense, that's absolutely right, because people have a kind of spontaneity with oral communication. If you're online and you're responding to a question being posed to you, there's a kind of textured dense immediacy and you respond spontaneously, whereas writing is about rewriting and reinvention. It's about taking an idea in certain linear forms and expressing a logic of inevitability that one either agrees or disagrees with, that one is able to revise in light of a rejection of that sentiment. If you're in a semiconscious state (as many writers are while they're writing) and you find that you don't like what you've written, you can revise it. However, in oral communication that is mediated through online technology, the possibility of that spontaneity is greater but the capacity to revise once one has committed oneself to a statement is limited when the other person immediately responds. In a written situation, there's a prefabricated consciousness that allows one to write, rewrite, revise, and then come at a multiple sense of understandings before one delivers what the definitive statement is that one believes. Now, in one sense, that's being interrupted by new technologies where one commits oneself with more immediacy. That's closer to oral communication where orality is seen as the kind of spontaneous articulation of beliefs. But there's a different sense of orality that I think is much more profound: the way in which the oral tradition itself has already weeded out alternative visions of a particular story to become that oral tradition. When we talk about oral tradition versus orality, oral tradition says that there's a much more conservative estimation of what can survive transmission from one generation to another. New technologies explode that kind of oral tradition. New technologies explode the capacity of a thousand people to reflect on a particular instance of articulation. For instance, say I make a statement online that I think Michael Jackson's hyperbaric chamber was a way of preserving what has already disappeared: his race as a signifier for his own identity. If you're online, you've got a hundred people who are going to argue with you, reaffirm it, give you alternative readings. That's a very powerful moment when indeed there's a communal sense of creating an idea. The very act of creativity is predicated on a kind of Lone Ranger trope for self-understanding and invention of the text. At least online there's a capacity for interaction with a whole range of narrative communicants who are able to shape, reshape, revise, or at least argue with you about what you think. Therefore, it's not simply what you think; it's about the interaction among members of that artificial community. In *that* sense, this new form bodes extraordinarily well for a range of black people.

In terms of language and race, this technology has the capacity to expand the boundaries of the American democratic experience into hyperspace in ways that are very positive. So, it's all for the good that black people are getting online, getting on e-mail, getting hooked up, because that expands our capacity to talk about issues of mobility, democracy, welfare reform, and the resources that can help us rethink how we can get connected around the globe, or even around this country. That's very powerful. On the other hand, to the degree to which African-American people are excluded from this process, there will be the rearticulation of the notion that technology and African-American identity are somehow not simply juxtaposed but contradictory, and a kind of reassertion of a horrible, horrible tradition in the Western world—especially in American culture—where scientific and techno-scientific processes have excluded black people and their lives have become the object of that techno-scientific culture and not the subject. One of the powerful things about this new technology is that it allows black people to extend their capacity for agency, to become subjects of that techno-scientific culture and not merely objects. So, I think that it shouldn't be just an uncritical celebration; it should be a kind of cautionary note about the ethical limits imposed upon techno-scientific culture.

Q. You briefly mentioned access. Would you speak to how class intersects with matters of race when we talk about technology?

A. There's no question that the folk who are getting online are more or less middle-class black folk or black folk who have access to traditional forms of literacy through traditional forms of education such as college. There have been many attempts to try to get some of this technology into the inner-city, and we're just now getting people to use computers in the inner-city in ways that people were doing twenty years ago in suburban America. Class intervenes powerfully in race in terms of techno-scientific culture precisely because those African-American people who get hooked up, who get wired, are those who already understand the nature of the game, and the nature of the game is about manipulation of information. It's about reproduction of identity through techno-scientific narratives that allow people not only to control and dominate information, but allow that information to enable them to accumulate capital. The connection between capital and technology is being obfuscated by this ostensible notion of the democratic exchange of information among participants, but we know that's not the case. What is really the case is that a specific class of people has had access to this technology. So in that sense, class and race work against many black and brown folk who really could take greater advantage of what's being offered online.

Q. You're very conscious of language. You seem to enjoy words, and you play with them when you write: You refer to your "color commentary" on BET about the O.J. case; you pun with phrases like "Crossing over Jordan" in reference to Michael Jordan and "what a difference a Dre makes." You've also written that it is clear that "language is crucial to understanding, perhaps solving, though at other times even intensifying, the quandaries of identity that vex most blacks." You argue that, "Black culture lives and dies by language." It's a big question to ask about the relationship between race and language—an inquiry that your work regularly explores in depth. But could you talk about how language affects your own coming to terms with race?

A. That's a very powerful question. There's an old Bible passage, somewhere in the Psalms: "I was conceived in sin and born in iniquity." I feel that I was born in language; I feel that there's a verbal womb, a rhetorical womb, that I was nurtured in. My mother, who was a highly intelligent black woman, appreciated literacy but was prevented from it because she was a female and the youngest of a family of five children born to a farmer in Alabama. From the very beginning I was bathed in the ethos of linguistic appreciation. My mother talked to us and read to us. And then I went to church; the church is a very important narrative community for me, very powerful—not only in terms of the norms it mediates in regard to the stances one should take politically and spiritually, but simply because of the resplendent resonances that were there in terms of language: hearing the power of articulations of black preachers, hearing the linguistic innovations of black singers, hearing the rhetorical dexterity of a revivalist who came to town to try to paint the picture of God dying on a cross and the differences that death made, not simply telling us about a theology of atonement, not simply talking to us (in dry, arcane, academized, theological language) about the dispensation of God. They wanted to paint a picture; they wanted us to feel it, to feel the kind of existential and ontological density of linguistic specificity. What I mean by "linguistic specificity" is that the language itself had a performative capacity, "performative" in the most enlarging and very powerful sense of that word. They not only were performing The Word from God, but they themselves, the words, were performing a kind of oracular and wisdom-tradition intervention upon our lives. That was extraordinarily important to me because I got a sense of the rhythms, the passions, the almost physical texture of language; I felt the very visceral dimensions of verbal articulation.

In elementary school, my fifth-grade teacher, Mrs. James (about whom I've written), had an extraordinary capacity to make black history come alive off the page, and she did so through teaching us painting and poetry. The poetry, especially, and writing our own stories was very important. Mrs. James encouraged us to see a direct connection between the capacities for invention and self-revelation from prior black generations and our own. She made the capacity to be a linguistic animal a very real and appealing one for us. She taught us that if we're really going to be powerful black people, intelligent black people, then we've got to do what other powerful, intelligent black people did: they wrote, they thought, they created.

As you say, I try to integrate a variety of perspectives about language in my own work now because I think that we should take note of what Derrida does with language and how he challenges straightforward traditional literary conceptions of language such as logocentrism. We've got to demythologize that through a kind of deconstructive practice that asks not simply, "What does it mean?" but, "How does it signify?" Multiple valences and a multiple convergence of meanings which contest in a linguistic space for logic have to be acknowledged as an index of the political economy of expressive culture, but so must its situatedness and embodiedness and embeddedness in a real political context where words make a difference about who we are and what we understand and to what uses those words will be put. I saw that operating in the black church in terms of spiritual and moral differences, and I've now taken that lesson seriously in the so-called secular arena. We have to take Derrida seriously; we have to take Foucault seriously when he talks about the insurrection of subjugating knowledges and the ways in which those knowledges make possible different articulative moments within African-American expressive culture and writing. Also, I think we've got to baptize them, as I've tried to argue. I think that the baptism of Derrida or Foucault or Guattari or Baudrillard or Deleuze doesn't mean that we have a narrow nation-state articulation of the logic of American democracy or nationalism—that is, make them show passports because we Americans demand that foreigners genuflect before the altar of American identity. No. It simply means that we have to take the lesson of shading and of creating a discursive frame that allows the particularities and resonances of *this* soil, of the American and, in my case, the African-American soil to dirty language, to dirty theory, to make more gritty the realities that so smoothly travel from European culture to American theory, especially as they are applied to African-American culture. Language is in itself a metaphor of the extraordinary capacity of identities to be shaped and reshaped, of the incredible convergences of different and simultaneous meanings of life that in some senses claim space within both our intellectual and moral worlds and the ways in which those of us who are writers, artists, and intellectuals have to appreciate the extraordinary power that language continues to have especially in minority communities and in oppressed communities where language becomes an index of one's own status. It becomes an index of one's own attempt to create oneself against the world and to say to the world, "I *do* exist." That's why, for me, instances of certain hip-hop culture have been incredibly important in mediating that reality, especially for young black men and women who have been marginalized, not only within the larger white society and mainstream culture, but who have been marginalized even within African-American culture. Those linguistic divisions in black society continue to index deeper class divisions that we have not paid sufficient attention to.

Q. In the preface to *Between God and Gangsta Rap*, you write, "The recycling of tired debates about racial and cultural authenticity abound. These debates have taken many forms in many different forums, but they all come down to the same question: how can we define the Real Black Person?" Obviously, there is also no Real

Black Writer, but do institutional, mass-read texts—such as multicultural readers—that depict a particular black experience attempt to construct a "Real Black Person" and a "Real Black Writer" in the name of diversity and tolerance?

A. Yes, and no. One of the hidden logics of multiculturalism is an attempt to elide or distort or at least obfuscate the incredible heterogeneity and the raucous diversity that is contained in black identity—or any minority identity. Multiculturalism is a concession to the need to package black identity for a larger world to consume, to mainstream the particularity and specificity of black identity. So in this case, multiculturalism is indivisible from the commodity fetishism and the consumptive realities of the American intellectual scene.

Q. Something like the Epcot version of culture.

A. There it is; that's exactly right! Multiculturalism at that level indexes the necessity or desire to cross over black culture in acceptable mainstream forms under the guise of accepting the reality that other voices must be heard. What's interesting about multiculturalism, however, is that there's a leveling effect in the sense that it says that there are interchangeable others that are being mobilized within the multicultural discourse. In other words, multiculturalism suggests that we have a relative equality of articulation within the space of American intellectual culture and that what we have to do is pay attention to equally objective and informative ways of understanding the world. I don't know if that's what was meant by all those struggles from Frederick Douglass to DuBois down from Sojourner Truth down to Angela Davis. That was meant in terms of appealing to certain literate and oral traditions within African-American culture to situate black life against the injustice and the economic inequality that was being perpetrated. Multiculturalism doesn't pay attention to the need to argue that these things are not all the same, that we're not all participating equally at the table. This is the problem. A person like Richard Rorty talks about conversation as if we all had equal access to the table, as if there were no filters in terms of class or race or gender as to who could get to the table to converse about differences.

To use the metaphor of conversation that Rorty got from Michael Oakeshott is to suggest that there is no political/economic analysis of who gets to sit at that table, who gets to participate in that dialogue about determining what is real and what's not real, what's important and what's not important, what's moral and what's immoral. I feel the same about a multiculturalism that argues that there is a kind of implicit equality of means by which people have access to the debate about what gets to constitute real knowledge. The reality is that it's radically unequal; it has tremendous marks of inequality. Those marks of inequality are marked in the very appropriation of marginalized minority discourses for the purposes of reproducing a hegemonic conception of what is real and authentic by using the name and the color of blackness to repress other dissident forms of blackness that challenge that narrow market multiculturalism that has been prevalent. In that sense, the Real Black Person is being put forth. Here the authentic African-American is being put forth, not only for the consumptive desires of a market multiculturalism that demands the Real Black, but also to exclude the capacity of other legitimate, powerful black voices to challenge that narrow hegemony and to suggest that there are alternative versions that need to be taken seriously. In that sense, I'm suspicious. It's a dubious project to have a kind of corporate multiculturalism that doesn't pay attention to the radical particularity and specific heterogeneities being produced on the African-American terrain.

The institutionalization of black identity through multiculturalism is at least as problematic to me as those people who are critical of gangsta rap and the way in which gangsta rap presents an authentic black person to the narrative as black-as-thug, or the ghetto as only about thugerian thanatopsies and not about black school teachers working against the odds, young black ghetto residents trying to master their algebra through a hail of bullets. The reduction to the Real Black Person—the tropes of authenticity and the narrow conceptions of what reality is about, this template of ontological essentialism that really obscures the radical complexity and heterogeneity of black identity—is deeply problematic. Market multiculturalism and corporate multicentrism are deeply problematic.

Q. Many people argue that the jargon-rich language of the academy is more obfuscating than illuminating for those outside of the specialized area of academic work. Yet, you write in *Between God and Gangsta Rap*, "The language of the academy is crucial because it allows me to communicate within a community of scholars whose work contributes to the intellectual strength of our culture. ... The language of the academy is most important to me because it provides a critical vocabulary to explore the complex features of American and African-American life. The language of the academy should never divorce itself from the politics of crisis, social problems, cultural circumstances, moral dilemmas, or intellectual questions of the world in which we live." You continue, "As a public intellectual, I am motivated to translate my religious, academic, and political ideas into a language that is accessible without being simplistic." How do you see the transition between academic discourse and more public discourses affecting your work? Are there problems of translation when moving between discourses?

A. I see the transition from the academic to the public as a self-conscious decision to intervene in debates and conversations that happen in public spheres (a different public sphere from the academy because I consider the academy a public sphere) and that have enormous consequence on everyday people's lives. The transition, however, is not smooth; the demands for rigorous debate within the academy are much different from those demands in the public sphere. There are enormous debates going on right now about the function of academized language. I'm not one who—for obvious reasons, self-interest being the primary one [laughter]—jumps on academics because they don't speak for a public audience or because they cannot speak in ways that are clear and articulate. Those are loaded terms: *clear, articulate.* As many other scholars—Henry Giroux, Donna Haraway—have all reminded us, language has multiple functions even within a limited context. To understand that is to acknowledge that there are a variety of fronts upon which we must launch our linguistic and rhetorical resistance against political destruction, against moral misery, and against narrow conceptions of what language does and how it functions. Being reared in a black church, being reared in a so-called minority linguistic community that had rich resources that were concealed and obscured for a variety of reasons, I think that I'm sensitive to the claim against academics and probably understand their defensiveness when they say, "We're writing for a specific audience." That's fine. If you write an article that will be read by a thousand people, and that those thousand people gain something from it, there's an exchange of information, there's an exchange of ideas, there's a sharpening of the debate, there's a deepening of the basis upon which we understand a particular intellectual subject. There's no reason to be apologetic for that because that's a very specific function within a larger academic enterprise that needs to be undertaken.

If, for instance, somebody writes an essay on a specific aspect of Foucault's appropriation of Benthamite conceptions of the prison that makes clear the relationship between Bentham and Foucault and also rearticulates our conceptions of the panopticon and how surveillance operates as it's extended into the black ghetto, that's all for the good—even if only a thousand people understand the language in which it's deployed and if only they get it. That means that some advance in understanding and exchange of information has gone on, and that's a legitimate enterprise. We don't have a problem with brain surgeons who speak languages that only twelve people can understand. If the man or woman can save your life, speak the jargon; do what you've got to do; operate! So, I don't have a problem with the similar kind of precise, rigorous uses of language that happen in academic circles. The problem arises when hostility is directed against those who are able to take the information, to take the knowledge, to take the profound rigor that is often suggested in such exercises and make them available to a broader audience.

Now, necessarily giving up something in terms of depth for breadth is inevitable. I've written for *Cultural Studies* and *Cultural Critique* and journals that four or five thousand people may read, and I've written for forums that a million and a half and two million people have read. We have to respect the genre. We, as academics, have a deep hostility to those who are public; those who are public intellectuals are viewed as sell-outs. We have our own version of the authentic academic and the authentic intellectual. Authenticity is quite interestingly debated, not only within African-American circles, but within academic circles where people have their narrow conception of what the authentic intellectual is. Interestingly enough, from the late '80s with Russell Jacoby's book on the last intellectual, this debate has been fiercely fought, and interestingly enough around the black public intellectual. I think some of that hostility may be racially coded, but a lot of that hostility is coded in terms of these rigid territorial disputes. A kind of geography of destiny is linked to whether you occupy the terrain of the academy specifically as an academic. We love to talk about transgressions intellectually, academically, but we don't want to do it physically or epistemologically.

Q. We resist the critique of being being in an ivory tower, but then we're the ones who insist on putting ourselves there.

A. That's right. We want to attack the ivory tower from the ivory tower. What's interesting is that these bullets are boomeranging. We celebrate transgression, we celebrate hybridity, we celebrate migration and mobility, but when people actually do these things, there's incredible resentment against those movements.

Q. In *Professional Correctness*, Stanley Fish argues that as academics we cannot be public intellectuals, and as public intellectuals we give up our roles as university scholars. In essence, he argues that Michael Eric Dyson cannot simultaneously be an academic and a public intellectual. Your critique of the university sees the academy as inseparable from the "real world" and that our roles in the university are as important as any other vocation outside of the academy. How do you respond to Fish's critique? As the university becomes more interdisciplinary, do you see (as Fish does) interdisciplinarity as a threat to universities or as having potential to intervene in public policy and the larger culture?

A. Stanley Fish is a really smart guy. I always listen carefully to what he says. Some of his criticisms are right on target, but on this point I dissent. He's right to challenge us to rethink the relationship between what we do and what we say. He's also forcing us, even more poignantly, to take seriously the idea that serving on a committee in the academy where you deploy Marxist language to demythologize class relationships is not the same as being involved in a labor dispute in the local AFL-CIO or talking about the interests of black workers on the line in Detroit. No question that he's absolutely right. But that doesn't mean, therefore, that the function of the intellectual deploying Marxist language to demythologize class relations is not, therefore, important. It's a different kind of importance. As a black person in the academy, I don't have the luxury of saying who's more real than the next person. I don't have the luxury of saying, "this is good and this is not good," precisely because we just got into the so-called mainstream academy. The real point is that there are multiple sites for intervention on behalf of political interests. In the Fishian cosmology, there's a radical bifurcation between the *real* world in which people operate with political interests at hand and deploy languages to defend those interests, and the academy, which is a different sphere of knowledge-production and consumption with different political interests. They both have a set of interests that need to be taken seriously. The academy is a public sphere; it is a deep and broad public sphere where interesting, important debates are happening. That's from the perspective of African-American people (or at least this particular black intellectual) who have been closed out from that debate for so long. Knowing that we were closed out means that we have understood that what was going on there was important. Charles Murray and Richard Herrnstein (although they were dealing with simplistic scientific theories about genetic inheritance of race, ideas that were deconstructed by people twenty years ago) sold 400,000 copies of their book. Now in one sense, we know most people didn't read that book; the very existence of that book was a phenomeno-logical weight to justify cultural prejudices about African-American intelligence. But what that also suggests is that black people understand that those debates have enormous consequence and significance upon African-American material interests. We already see the connection between the academy and the "real world," because the real world looks to the academy to justify its prejudices, to dress them up in scientific discourse that allows them to gain legitimacy and power. We have understood all along that even though twelve people may be reading that book, one of the twelve could end up being a congressman, or a policy maker, or the director of an institute that has the ability to determine resources for a whole lot of black people. We have to deconstruct and demythologize this radical bifurcation between the academy and the real world. Both are real worlds constituted equally by narratives of political interest that are being deployed to defend certain perspectives. Truth and politics are deeply united in ways that, I think, Fish is not paying sufficient attention to.

What's important about interdisciplinarity is that it threatens those people who have narrow political interests and who are trying to maintain and preserve their bailiwick. Fish gives elo-quent but quite problematic articulation to a narrower vision of the life of the mind than I would like. He cautions us about thinking that those of us who make Marxist or progressive analyses of forms of oppression are substituting this for real work. It is itself real work. It performs an intellectual function that is both daring, given the narrow hegemony of a conservative vision of the academy that prevails, and intellectually important to the concrete interests of people outside of the academy. Before I entered the academy, I worked in two factories, and I was a teen father working and hustling at two different jobs. People in Detroit University and Wayne State University who were trying to think about the relationship between labor and commodity and wage and alienation and other intellectual projects were very powerful and important in making substantive political interventions on behalf of those of us in that real movement and in forcing us to take seriously the life of the mind as a way to defend our interests and to be conscious of the fact that we had interests to be defended.

Interdisciplinarity is really an index of this postmodern moment when we take the multiplicity not only of ideals and knowledges, but when we get to ask questions about who gets to control knowledge, for what purposes is it being deployed, and whose interests are being protected by a narrow conception of the life of the mind that is rooted in academic disciplines that pay no attention to what other people in other intellectual enterprises are doing. What's important is that it is the most powerfully artificial conception of the life of the mind to segregate knowledge in terms of disciplines. It argues against the best, most powerful traditions of Western intellectual enterprise.

Q. In *Race Rules* you write, "The anointing of a few voices to represent The Race is an old, abiding problem. For much of our history, blacks have had to rely on spokespersons to express our views and air our grievances to a white majority that controlled access to everything from education to employment." You discuss who gets to be black public intellectuals, who chooses them, and why they receive the attention they do. In contemporary America, there are relatively few black intellectuals. This suggests that the intellectual/academic world—which is still made up primarily of middle-class Anglo males—has constructed methods of gatekeeping (for example, graduate school entrance requirements, hiring practices, tenure, publication, speaking engagements) that "select" particular leaders to serve as "representative" voices. More exactly, having only a few black intellectuals is a product of the kind of oppressive strategies of management and containment maintained by the academy. What does this say about the small numbers of black public and the possibility of the "radicalness" of public intellectuals such as yourself? Can you really be radical and effect change from the inside when the institution has, in fact, sanctioned your radicalness? After all, you are a high-profile, well-paid member of the academy.

A. Exactly right. No doubt about it. It's very difficult. I think that it's necessary to acknowledge not only the accuracy of the critique, and to extend the political efficacy of that accuracy by being self-critical. There's always a dimension of hubris in self-criticism because then you're pointing to how self-critical I can be and look how critically engaging I can be about my own position even as I consolidate my interest as a high-profile, well-paid black intellectual. I face that problem head on. It is very difficult. And you're absolutely right in terms of the sanctioning of the radicalism that we express: it is being deployed within a larger narrative of co-optation by the American academy that we criticize and from whose base we articulate our own conceptions of the world. So there's no doubt that it's very difficult, but I think it's inevitable in the sense that this is the present condition under which we live as we fight for change from within and certainly from without. There's no question that we have to begin to raise larger questions and to provoke a more profound analysis not only of our own subject positions but of our own professional positions within the hierarchy of privilege and visibility that we presently enjoy. What's very difficult is to figure out how we both criticize our own participation in the academy, in this regime of black intellectuals who have been anointed, and at the same time maintain enough visibility and influence to have our voices make a difference. In that one sense, it is a very difficult project. Also, we can ask questions about whom we refer to in our work. What is interesting to me is that when we read interviews with high-profile black intellectuals we get the same old names. There's a narrative reinscription of fame and a hierarchy of privilege established within the linguistic practices of black intellectuals so that if we keep hearing about the same novelist, the same intellectual, even though they are deserving of enormous mention and enormous merit, what happens is that we feel they are the only important voices out there. One of the most powerful things we can do as black intellectuals, especially those of us who are highly visible, is to talk about those intellectuals whose work is different from ours and whose work may challenge ours, and whose voices would not ordinarily be heard if we did not mention them.

Q. You're leading into my next question. You write, "We don't speak for The Race. We speak as representatives of the ideological strands of blackness, and for those kinships we possess outside of black communities, that we think most healthy. . . . We ain't messiahs." At the same time, though, you also write, "Equally worrisome, too many black public intellectuals hog the ball and refuse to pass it to others on their team. Many times I've been invited on a television program, a prestigious panel, or a national radio program because a white critic or intellectual recommended me. Later I often discover that another prominent black intellectual, when consulted, had conveniently forgotten to mention my name or that of other qualified black intellectuals. Ugly indeed." Do you think this is because those black public intellectuals who now have the spotlight actually do want to be anointed as spokesperson to represent "The Race"? Does the cult of celebrity, the protection of position as black intellectuals, work *against* a sort of "hand up for someone on the rung below" attitude?

A. There is no question that many of us black intellectuals do want to be the "head nigger in charge." We do want to be the most visible, or as I say in my book, the "hottest Negro in the country." There's no question that to attain a certain form of visibility in American culture as an intellectual is itself dizzying, and there is a kind of narcotic effect. When people like Oprah or Charlie Rose or Montel Williams call you up, or when you are invited to write op-eds for the *Washington Post* or the *New York Times,* or when you're referred to as one of the leading voices of your generation, or in my case as the leading young, black, Hip-Hop intellectual, that is very seductive. It's very powerfully entrapping. First, it invites us to read our own press. Second, it invites us to believe our own press. Third, it invites us to reproduce our own press— even if we consciously, through the rhetoric of humility, defer that to others or assign it to other onlookers or other sycophants who believe in the absolute integrity of our intellectual vision. There is no doubt that this is a temptation among intellectuals— especially among black intellectuals, given the small numbers of us who are able to survive and thrive—to be *the person*, or as Zora Neale Hurston said, "the Pet Negro." We have to constantly resist that temptation by constantly making forays into and interventions into those base communities that we say we represent or at least ostensibly speak for.

There is no question that one of the most dispiriting things that I've seen among black public intellectuals is a kind of vicious, cruel sniping, rhetorical attacks, and pettiness behind the scenes. Now this is not endemic to black culture. This is where I think Henry Kissinger is absolutely right, that the politics of the academy are so vicious because there is so little at stake. We are fighting for this small land. The topography of black intellectual space in the academy is so constricted that we are indeed fighting over a narrow terrain. The vicious consequence of those kinds of contestations is that they do not produce good benefits for the people that we claim we represent, or that we were put in place to represent. So, not only are there many who have a secret desire to be *the One*, we also prevent, by virtue of our fame and visibility, the kind of moral imperative that used to be "each one teach one, each one reach one," or lifting as we climb. There ain't much lifting as we climb, except lifting our own mobility, lifting our own stakes, lifting our own visibility. We are not lifting others, carrying those on our rhetorical, intellectual backs. The consequence is that it creates a hierarchy, a two- or three- or four-tiered system of black intellectuals.

Q. You're critically conscious of your role as black public intellectual. In *Race Rules* you offer a critical series of awards you call the "Envys." Your purpose is both to critique black public intellectuals and to answer critiques leveled by black public intellectuals. Though many of these critiques are unrelenting in their criticism, you don't leave yourself out of your own attack, and you award yourself "The Spike Lee/Terry McMillan Award for Shameless Self Promotion" for your lobbying for publicity for your work. Nonetheless, you are critical of how other black public intellectuals use the role of public intellectual and what they promote in that role. In light of your comments regarding the "lone black leader," and the "ugliness" of not nurturing other black intellectuals' careers, is such criticism helpful?

A. It can be construed as a kind of self-congratulatory self-flagellation in public that only reinforces the very visibility that I claim has unequally been cast on some intellectuals, including myself. I think I'm caught in a kind of endless night of the soul in being preoccupied with those levels of unfairness that prevent other worthy black intellectuals from coming to the fore. In that sense, my criticism can be construed in a negative way. The positive way in which it can be construed is in the ability of black intellectuals to take this tongue-in-cheek. Partly what I'm saying is "lighten up." This is not something that is going to ultimately change the world if we ourselves participate or do not participate in it. What I was trying to say in those tongue-in-cheek awards is that we talk about being critical, but let's bring some of that critical light upon ourselves. Let's cast that critical acumen upon ourselves, and, by doing so, let's raise questions about the nature of our work, about the real limits that our work has, and about the ways in which we are able to make interventions. We at least can be more conscious about the need to include others. The positive nature of my work can be that it will create a larger discourse space where people can say, "That was funny, but . . ." or they can say, "That wasn't so funny because these charges are on target because . . ." or they can say, "Well, even though Dyson is trying to promote himself *yet again*, what's important about his critique is that it does raise very powerful issues about the nature of the kind of work in which we give the voice of the Negro to a very few black people, while the masses of intellectuals and academicians have no access." That can be helpful if it produces the material effect of having people interrogate their own practices, of having people ask why there is a need to salute and anoint a few voices. What I want to raise out of this, if nothing else, is why it is that a few black people are anointed to determine what other black people receive. The very purpose of those of us who are so-called "radical black intellectuals" was to raise questions about gatekeepers, about the intellectual Booker T. Washingtons who were able to dole out punishment or reward based upon their understanding of the political efficacy of a particular work or a particular career. That is the kind of thing we have to interrogate relentlessly if we are to at least raise the possibility of other voices emerging.

Q.In April of 1996, *Harper's* published a conversation on race between Jorge Klor De Alva, Earl Shorris, and Cornel West. In this discussion, West argues that "when we talk about identity, it's really important to define it. Identity has to do with protection, association, and recognition. People protect their bodies, their labor, their communities, their way of life; in order to be associated with people who ascribe value to them, who take them seriously, who respect them; and for purposes of recognition, to be acknowledged, to feel as if one actually belongs to a group over time and space, we have to be very specific about what the credible options are for them at any given moment." De Alva later says, "All identities are up for grabs. But black intellectuals in the United States, unlike Latino intellectuals in the United States, have an enormous media space within which to shape the politics of naming and to affect the symbols and meanings associated with certain terms. Thus, practically overnight, they convinced the media that they were an ethnic group and shifted over to the model of African-American, hyphenated American, as opposed to being named by color. Knowing what we know about the negative aspects of naming, it would be better for all of us, regardless of color, if those who consider themselves, and are seen as, black intellectuals were to stop participating in the insidious one-drop-rule game of identifying themselves as black." You've written quite a bit about identity politics. How do you respond to this exchange between West and De Alva?

A. West is absolutely right in terms of protection, association, and recognition, especially as those three modes of response to the formation of identity have played themselves out within histori- cally constituted black communities. It is an implicit rebuttal of Paul Gilroy's notion that any notion of ethnic solidarity is itself to buy into a backwards view of black identity. Gilroy has been especially critical of black American intellectuals for what he considers to be their essentialist identities. Interestingly enough, those very black intellectuals in America have written powerfully about hybridity and about identity and about the need to talk about the transgressive potentials of black identity, of pulling into view what Stuart Hall calls postmodern identity. It's a very complex navigation of a variety of possibilities and subject positions within a narrative of recognition. So West's notion that it's protection, association, and recognition is about rooting it in a very specific context of how African-Americans have contested the erosion of their identities, the attack on their identities, and how identity politics at a certain level is a response to narrow, vicious stereotypes imposed on us from the outside.

Jorge's response about seeing black Americans' considering themselves black as a kind of surrender to this "one-drop rule" misses the point of history and the context of culture. History suggests that these are objective criteria—objective in the sense that they were socially constructed as the norm by which black people were judged. So even if black identity is up for grabs, it has a limit. It certainly is up for grabs, as I've argued in my work about the fluidity of these boundaries of black identity, but it has real historical and cultural and racial limitations. Jorge is expressing the bitter edge and a misled conception of this postmodern vision of black identity. Saying that black identity is much more fluid, that it has much more movable boundaries, that it is a moveable feast of self-reinvention is not to say that there are no bottom lines. As Elizabeth Alexander says, "Listen, I believe in de-essentialized, racialized politics; but there's got to be a bottom line." The bottom line is drawn by the material effects of the historically constituted notions of blackness both within African-American culture and outside of black culture. As the old saying goes, you can tell the policeman that race is a trope, but if he's beating your head and you're saying, "Listen, this is a historically constituted, socially constructed reality that has no basis beyond our agreement and consensus in American culture," that's cool, but your head is still being beaten. So the material consequences of the association of race with black identity, with black skin, has to be acknowledged as a serious consequence against which we must articulate our understanding.

In this exchange between West and Jorge, what West understands is the need to ground the politics of black identity in cultural specificity and in racial particularities that acknowledge the function of geography and of biology, even if we want to overcome and transgress against them. Jorge appeals to a language that is much more inviting in terms of interrogating blackness as a historically constituted and socially constructed reality, but he does not pay sufficient attention to how blackness signifies in multiple ways in the public sphere. One of the most powerful ways it signifies is as a descriptive term to name people of color who have historically been constituted as black, and whose identities are invested both in protecting that boundary of blackness and in raising questions about its limitations at the same time. So, I'd agree with West about the historical constitution and the social rooting of it, and with Jorge about the need to raise questions about those boundaries but to link them politically.

Q.Composition, like many intellectual disciplines, has been engaged
in its own version of the "theory wars." You are very careful in
your writing to acknowledge the importance of academic theories—particularly postmodernisms. You write, "At its best,
theory should help us unmask the barbarous practices associated
with some traditions of eloquent expression. But like a good
sermon or a well-tailored suit, theory shouldn't show its seams."
You write in *Between God and Gangsta Rap,* "With some adjust-
ments, I think theory may help to explain black culture." What
role do you see theory playing in race issues? And, would you
describe the "seamless" theory?

A.[laughter] Hey man, I just write about these things; I didn't expect
to get asked about them. Well, the role of theory in black culture
is multiple. First, theory should help us clarify what we take to be
concrete experience, the relationship between theory and practice. All practices are theorized and all theories are practiced at a
certain level, not necessarily in a particular logical or linear order.
The first function of theory is to make us understand that
practices have components of intellectual aspiration that are
sometimes obfuscated and often concealed. Second, theory
forces us to understand that black culture is much more difficult,
much more complex, much more multi-layered, and much more
combative, even within its own boundaries, than people have
given voice to. Theory is needed to name the different aspects
and components of that contested terrain. For instance, say that
Gates is trying to talk about the way in which signifying practices
name certain rhetorical devices that have been deployed within
black culture from Blues culture down to other literary expressions; that is very important. But what is also important is that
theory try to help us understand the difference between signifying
practices in Blues culture and signifying practices in Hip-Hop
culture. What is important is that the theorization of black culture
helps us comprehend elements that we historically have neglected,
elements that have always been there but that we have not
sufficiently paid attention to, and the ways in which our own
understandings of black culture are already theory laden. That is,
we never begin in a pre-theoretical density in terms of interpreting
black culture. We are already theorizing, even if we do not have
the official language of the academic proles to express that theory;
people who interpret black culture are already working with a

theoretical base. What theory does is ask that to become explicit. Theory asks this illusory pre-theoretical density to come out of the closet and to admit that it is already theoretical. Theory is always operating in terms of how people understand themselves in relationship to black culture.

For me a seamless theory is one that does not have to display the most blatant forms of jargon-ridden discourse to make its point. A seamless theory is the ability to express very powerfully, intelligently, and articulately an idea that is very complex but in ways that broader people beyond your discipline have access to. That, to me, is a theory that may have some jargon involved but that mostly does not rely on the old habits of thought that jargon signifies and that forces us to break new ground by saying it in ways that a geologist may understand as well as a literary theorist who has training in the field. The importance of that is that a person like myself who has written for these different audiences gives up something when doing either one. What that kind of writing has forced me to see is that if I'm going to write for an audience beyond my discipline, beyond my particular training, beyond the people who speak a similar language to me, I then have to write in ways that appeal broadly to people who are intelligent and who have the capacity not only to understand the language but to use it in ways that I may never have the opportunity to do. I want to reach them. The best, most politically efficacious use of theory is its capacity to show people things they did not know before in ways that they understand. That to me is a seamless theory, at least in terms of its linguistic practice.

Q. For many theorists, notions of disruption become critical in the critique of traditional power structures. You write of black public intellectuals that they are "leaders of a particular kind. We stir up trouble in broad daylight so that the pieties by which we live and the principles for which we die, both as a people and a nation, are subject to critical conversation." However, in many of your discussions of black political figures and movements you are also critical of how disruption gets used. For instance you juxtapose the militant disruptiveness of Malcolm X and the assimilative, non-disruptiveness of Colin Powell. Would you speak to the idea of disruption in the role of racial matters?

A. Disruption is a primary prerogative of those of us who are paid pests. I consider cultural critics and black intellectuals to be paid pests. We are trying to point not only to the emperor having no clothes, but to the imperialism that has a whole bunch of clothes and to what it is dressed up in. I think our function is to disrupt and intervene in conversations in ways that are disturbing, that in it's very disturbance forces people to ask why they frame the questions in the way that they do or why they make the analysis they do. Disruption is not simply a kind of orgasm for its own sake, a kind of intellectual anarchy that has no political efficacy. Disruption has a political goal: to force us to interrogate practices through a different lens or to see them differently in the same lens. For instance, race may be the lens that people use, but if they begin to see different aspects of race differently because of the questions we raise, that is a very important function. We do not always have to do away with the very lens through which people see, although that metaphor itself gives us a kind of ideological purchase that is very narrowly conservative. In some instances we have to shatter the whole lens. Not only do we have to shatter the lens, but we have to shatter the paradigm of the lens, the ocular-centrism by which we understand knowledge. As Martin James has written in *Downcast Eyes*, this ocular-centric metaphor misses the way in which the other metaphors of knowledge can operate. We have to talk about hearing; we have to talk about feeling. Partly what we do then as black intellectuals is to disrupt that ocular-centric metaphor whereby vision or blindness operates, and the lens is important to talk about how we experience visceral realities phenomenologically that have been downplayed through, say, anti-feminist discourse. What we have to do is create a string of metaphors that give us a different interventional possibility into the terrain of knowledge, politics and culture. That kind of disruption is very important in terms of race because of the way in which historically constituted black communities have had to argue with intellectual paradigms of injustice and because of the ways in which they have struggled against them in terms of their own bodies and movements. So, Marcus Garvey's movement, Martin Luther King, Jr.'s civil rights movement, A. Philip Randolph's movement are very important sites and terrains of contestation that imagine a different space than an intellectual argument about inequality. It is putting forth a very powerful rejection and rebuttal of both stereotype and inequality through the embodied articulation of black resistance.

But intellectually the disruption, too, is important in terms of racial matters where those of us who are called upon to think critically about race have to disrupt not only dominant paradigms but the ways in which we settle into our own resistant paradigms that themselves become new orthodoxies. Disruption is quite unsettling precisely because we can never be settled finally in a position from which we would defend certain visions or attack certain versions of black life for the rest of our intellectual lives. The kind of perennial, migratory possibilities, the kind of endless mobility, is what disruption is about. That's why it can never be settled in the hands of one set of intellectuals to talk about what black culture is about. That's why the very nature of disruption is a critical necessity for interrogating black practices and racial matters and has to always be changing hands. It is not that we can't have a long career in disruption or in interrogating race. It means that we have to have other voices that challenge us, even in our disruptive practices about what the function of our disruption is.

Q. There's a xeroxed poster on a colleague's door in my department of a photograph of an old, wooden sign that reads, "We Serve Whites Only. No Spanish or Mexicans." The sign was posted in 1949 to enforce the Jim Crow laws in San Antonio. On the copy, someone has written, "History is not just black and white." Though you make an effort to discuss races—particularly when you discuss issues of violence in terms of Latinas, Koreans, Asians, and so on—your work on race deals mostly (as most work on race does) with issues of black and white. Would you discuss the black and white depictions of race in America and speak to the (fewer than black) "other" race intellectuals?

A. If we are asking what it means if the narrative frame is black and white, it certainly buys into a very narrow conception, although a very real one, for Africans in the diasporate America. The black/ white disjunction was one that curtailed our own economic and social mobility, one that contained the potentiality for the destruction of our material interest, and one in which we have had to exist in a kind of symbiotic relationship. This is why the work of theorists like James Scott, who talks about infra-politics and everyday forms of resistance and how they get played out in African-American culture through the theorized relationship between the black and the white, is so important. How symbiotically have black people had to exist in relationship to white people? As Ralph Ellison said, we can't even imagine America without black Americans, although white Americans have not always taken that seriously. The black/white disjunction is a reflection of the existential, economic, and political realities that obtain for Africans in the diaspora and their relationship to the mainstream. That is why James Scott's work is important, because you figure out how to situate yourself as a degraded subject in relationship to the overarching object of both your interests and the need for survival—that is, the white majority. Much of black culture has been developed in response to maintaining, preserving, and surviving *vis-à-vis* this dominant, hegemonic Other and the survival techniques that had to be marshaled in the face of that. This is how these infra-politics are talked about by people like Robin Kelly in *Race Rebels,* in which he talks about black people on the bus in Birmingham and how, even though they were not involved explicitly in racial politics, they were involved nonetheless in powerful ways by refusing on that space of the bus certain racial meanings that were ascribed to them.

All this means is that the black/white bifurcation has been one of necessity and survival for African-American people in this country. The depictions of black/white among black and white people have been about overcoming barriers to get to know one another. White people must get to know more about black people. One of the necessities and strategies for survival is that black folk have had to know white folk. You have to know your enemy; you have to know whom you are dealing with. Was it Fanny Lou Hamer who said that the mistake that white folk made is that they put black people behind them and not in front of them? If they put black people in front of them, they could have surveilled them in a certain way. But since they put black people behind them, black people learned all the secrets and strategies of white folk and how to please them and how to "get over" on them. The black/white bifurcation has been about *knowing* white people; there's a kind of epistemology of friendship. If you know white people, you'll know better how to get along with them.

One of the real liabilities of simply seeing race in black and white is that we begin to miss how race is being constructed and has been constructed around a number of axes that go beyond the black/white divide. Even certain debates within black culture and white culture are geographical. For instance, the black/

Jewish conflict is a geographical one at a certain level. It is going to be happening much more powerfully in New York than in California. But in California the black/white divide is challenged by the black/brown divide or the black/Korean divide—not only in terms of black/Korean and black/Latino, but Latinos and whites and Latinos who are white, Hispanic as white and Hispanic as non-white, Hispanic as black and non-black. What it begins to introduce is that there is a racial millenialism that does not simply follow the axis of black/white but that follows many more axes that force us—should force us—to rethink how we understand the black/white divide. It does not mean that the divide is not important or that it has not been crucial even as an analogy for other minorities who have fought for inclusion in the larger circle of American identity and privilege. What it does suggest is that the black/white divide misses how we try to impose upon other minorities substitute black status as a minority.

Q. In the *Harper's* interview that I mentioned earlier, Klor De Alva claims that "with the exception of black-white relations, the racial perspective is not the critical one for most folks. The cultural perspective was, at one time, very sharply drawn, including the religious line between Catholics and Protestants, Jews and Protestants, Jews and Catholics, Jews and Christians. But in the course of the twentieth century, we have seen in the United States a phenomenon that we do not see anyplace else in the world—the capacity to blur the differences between these cultural groups, to construct them in such a way that they became insignificant and to fuse them into a new group called whites, which didn't exist before." If this is true, why has "difference" in America been reduced, at least publicly, to matters of color?

A. It's been reduced to matters of color, but it's more or less what's called "pigmintocracy." I talk about the difference between pigmintosis and pigmintification. Pigmintification means that you get adopted within the larger pigmintocracy, the regime of color that's associated with white skin. Within pigmintosis you get excluded from that regime of color. Color is so important because it was never a reference to itself. Color was a politically invested category that revealed our own prejudices and biases and the ways in which we distributed political and economic resources. Jorge is right that whiteness became a blurred distinction in America. It became a self-sufficient or all-sufficient, category that wiped out certain distinctions: German, Polish, Irish. But they did survive in terms of ethnic and religious practices within American culture; I don't think he's right there. Racialization in America is predicated on pigmintocracy—that is, the way in which goods are distributed according to one's own relationship to an ideal of color.

Color never was simply about skin tone. It was about the intellectual, ideological, and political dimensions of American culture that revealed our conflicts over issues of African versus European and American identity. If we are literalist about this color thing, we miss the way in which a pigmintocracy was predicated upon a whole range of conflicted political and economic and social meanings that were themselves being mediated through this notion of skin and pigment. Skin and pigment become the more visible index of a regime and hierarchy of privilege and status that was associated with a different understanding of species. What I think Jorge is overlooking here is that there was what some people call pseudo-speciation, the attempt to divorce black people from the quality and character of what it meant to be a human being. The other ethnic groups that came over to America did not get pseudo-speciated. They did not get written out of the dominant narrative text of humanity that included all white ethnics even if there was a hierarchy of visibility, influence, and privilege, whereas with black people there was an attempt to rule them out of the race.

Q. In the Preface to *Making Malcolm*, you discuss an uncomfortable incident that occurred in one of your classes when tension between students about racial divisions erupted. Where does race belong in the classroom?

A. Everywhere and nowhere. Race is an inevitable feature of the classroom; it is the ineluctable product of the racialization of American society. To expect that the classroom will somehow be exempt from the racialized meanings that are exploding in our culture is to have a sort of pedagogical naivete that is not only insular but is also destructive. Race belongs in the classroom where race belongs in society. I think about race in the sense that Foucault thinks about power. It's not simply about, as Weber conceives it, these structures of domination, these hierarchies in which we have power associated with certain positions. Power breaks out everywhere, Foucault reminds us, even among and between people who are themselves oppressed or marginalized. Race is a kind of fusion of these Weberian and Foucauldian perspectives. There certainly is a hierarchy of race where power is associated with being white and not black, white and not brown, white and not red. These are objective conditions of race that we would do well to heed.

On the other hand, race breaks out in all kinds of interesting and unfastidious ways. It breaks out in uncomfortable and disruptive ways. Race can always surprise us. Like a camel, it has the capacity to do greater injury when we attempt to coop it up as opposed to when we let it run free. A classroom is an artificial cage for the animal of race, and race breaks out everywhere. That is powerful and productive because it wounds our most cherished expectations of what I called earlier "market multiculturalism." In African-American studies classes like mine at Brown University, race breaks out in the most uncomfortable, but I think highly instructive, ways. In the conflict between this set of black men who thought they knew Malcolm and had earned their right and privilege to define Malcolm for the rest of us and to cage Malcolm up, not only did race break out but I think Malcolm did, too. The place of race in the classroom is precisely at the center of our conversations about a whole range not only of disciplines and professions but of issues and subject matters. It does not simply belong in a class on ethnic studies or African-American culture. Race belongs in a class on Aristotelian conceptions of inequality, Neo-Platonic philosophy, and on every American subject matter precisely because it is like what they call in logic the suppressed premise of so many syllogisms of American democracy. Race is part and parcel of the very fabric of the American intellectual project and also at the heart of the American project of democracy and self-discovery. We would be well-served to be more explicit about it and, therefore, to take it into account rather than to allow it to inform our debates from a distance. By informing our debates from a distance, we do not get a chance to theorize race, we do not get a chance to explore race, and we do not get a chance to demythologize racist power to hurt and harm us precisely because it is excluded from our explicit articulations.

Q.I'd like to pick up on your metaphor of the wild animal in the classroom and ask, have we made race safe? Have universities done to race what may have been done to some feminisms by saying that we can talk about these discourses in universities so long as this is what we discuss and this isn't? Have multicultural pedagogies taken the thorns out of race matters?

A. Yes, there is no question about it. But that is the risk we run for the kind of progress we want, and the kind of progress we want is that we would rather people talk about it in denuded contexts that deprive race of its real vigor, of its real fierceness, of its rhetorical ferocity than have fights in the streets. We would rather have that than the riots of 1992. We would rather have that than the situations in which black or white or Other people lose their lives contesting terrain that has become deeply racialized but not theorized around race. Yes, there are trade-offs. But with the kind of conscientious objection to the war of multiculturalism which is fought with rubber bullets rather than real ones, we certainly want to introduce (excuse this violent metaphor) sharper distinctions between where the blood is really being spilled on the outside of these debates. There is an advantage to that. There is no doubt about the articulation of the real divisions that race brings, the real conflicts that it introduces. And they have to be touched on in our debates in ways that make us uncomfortable with our ability to so smoothly dismiss the differences that race introduces without paying the consequences. We do not often pay the consequences in our own classrooms, in our faculty meetings, in the academy in general. That is why when we have racial representation by proxy, that is one thing. But when real gays and lesbians show up, when real black folks show up, when real Latinos show up, and they are not as nice and they are not as observant of the traditions of racial discourse as white liberals who set out twenty years ago, that creates real tension. I do not think we should gainsay those kinds of tensions. Those kinds of tensions are real, and they are instructive politically about the limits to which we are able to go in dealing with racial discourse— and, more importantly, not only racial discourse, but racial transformation. So, yes, we have done that, but at the same time I'd rather have that kind of discourse against which we must fight and that we have to deploy in service of defending a more radical, a more powerful, a more disruptive conception of multiculturalism than one in which the debates are handled in the street where bloodshed and violence are its only consequences.

Q. How do public intellectuals play into that then?

A. We either play the good role or the bad role. We play into it in the sense that we extend the capacity for people to feel safe by saying, "Well, I've listened to Michael Eric Dyson or Cornel West or bell hooks and now I feel that I've gotten my multicultural booster; I've got the multicultural vaccination that protects me, that gives me a vaccination against any form of racism." That is obviously not the case. So we get used as these vaccinations, and people feel that they are immune now to racist ideology and become much more problematic than those who have not been vaccinated, who do not give a damn about being vaccinated, who resist it and who in their own honest expression of their feelings talk quite frankly in ways that lead to more racial progress than those who feel that they have nothing to learn. We can end up perpetuating that by being used against our own will that way, but we can also disrupt it as public intellectuals by going on television shows and disagreeing with the common market version of multiculturalism by saying that it is much more complex, much deeper, and much more profound than that.

Q. What do you do then to keep race from being safe? What kinds of work—both public and academic—do you advocate?

A. What I do is preach. I stay in contact with people whose anger is much more meated and raw. When I visit prison—I have a brother who is serving life in prison for second-degree murder and who's converted to the Moorish Temple of Muslim Experience—and we talk about racial issues, he gives me a hell of an interesting perspective. Both of us came out of the ghetto of Detroit and are now living the proverbial difference of the professor and the prisoner. That reality of feeling the sharp edges of his own critique of people like me, and me specifically, delivers me from a kind of anesthetized, romanticized sphere where I'm somehow exempt from the very passions that I claim I want to represent in my work, and that I certainly do and hope to do.

Also, I try to get involved with union movements and with black churches, especially where black people are concerned about issues of race and how their anger and their conspiracy theories come together. Even if intellectually I want to avoid some of the conspiracy theories that they have or the resentments that they nurture, I understand and feel what drives them. It reminds me of where I was as a poor black kid in Detroit, a teen father who was hustling, who was thought of as one of these pathologized, nihilistic black kids. I try to bring that into the classroom by means of some of the subjects that I deal with and some of the issues of race that I try to confront.

Q. There is an interesting division that gets played out in discussions of race and discussions of postcolonial theories. Jenny Sharpe, in "Is the United States Postcolonial?: Transnationalism, Immigration, and Race," argues that "when used as a descriptive term for the United States, *postcolonial* does not name its past as a white settler colony or its emergence as a neocolonial power; rather, it designates the presence of racial minorities and Third World immigrants." She goes on to argue that "an understanding of 'the postcolonial condition' as racial exclusion offers an explanation for the past history of 'internal colonies' but not the present status of the United States as a neocolonial power." With the noted exception of bell hooks, who looks at African-American writers, Gloria Anzaldúa who works with Latina/Chicana literature and cultural experience, and a few scholars of indigenous North American populations, there are very few who address the fact that much of the scholarly work regarding issues particular to the United States are in fact issues of postcolonialism. At the same time, the kinds of academic attention that U.S. scholars give to postcolonial theory is being given to the writers and the cultures of, for instance, India, Sri Lanka, Pakistan, and so on, not to issues of the United States. What significance, if any, do you see in the academy's refusal to validate the postcolonial nature of both the writers and the writing that has been and continues to be produced in the United State by peoples of color?

A. This is a problem of avoidance. This is a problem of linguistic and rhetorical and ideological avoidance, of not acknowledging the degree to which this society's racist policies and practices are part of a deeper project of colonial and imperial expansion that happened on the backs of black peoples, red peoples, and other native, indigenous peoples. But now, even as those scholars of color begin to interrogate its practices, this discourse is put into a narrowly racialized frame that pays attention to black/white differences and so on without linking them to an international context of colonialism. When it does, it's only in regard to the presence of minorities in this country as opposed to its own practice. So, partly what we're dealing with here is the self-identity of America as a colonial practitioner and an imperial power. What that signifies is the ability of America to absorb and redistribute dissent and the nomenclature that would name that dissent in ways that are less harmful, so that for America to conceive of itself as a colonial power—not simply *vis-à-vis* racial minorities, but as the expansion of its imperialist tentacles throughout the world—has become so contradictory to its self-identity that people are discouraged from even talking about it in those terms.

What's also interesting is that during the '60s and '70s people like Bob Blouner at Berkeley and other people who were talking about internal colonial theories, who were talking about the metaphoric relationship between America and colonial powers, were discouraged from doing so because it was said to be a narrow essentialist conception of the relationship between black and white or that it really wasn't exactly expressive of the caste dimensions between black and white in this country that happened in other spaces and places. In other words, the closest that we got to any sense of America as a colonial power was this notion of internal colonialism, talking about the ghetto as an internal colonized space, drawing on Fanon and other Third World theories to explain indigenous practices within America but never as largely America's colonial power.

To talk about America as a colonial empire and as a beast is really to direct attention from the domestic projects of civil rights, which were dependent upon the *largesse* and *noblesse oblige* of white liberals, to make a go of our own state. This is why even Martin Luther King, Jr., when he began to talk about America as a colonial power *vis-à-vis* Vietnam, was criticized not simply by white conservatives but by black so-called progressives and liberals who were upset that he was pilfering from the resources of the domestic situation for the civil rights movement. His world view was of a piece and of a whole. What's interesting is that we've been discouraged from seeing America as a colonial and imperial power because of deference to a domestic conception of civil rights that was narrowly insular, that was concerned about the project of African-American freedom within the circumscribed limits and discourse of American rights as opposed to seeing American imperialism, directed against black bodies, as part of an international project of colonial containment that America was the supreme arbiter of. Partly, that expresses attention to domestic situations that people were worried about pilfering the moral energies of the black movement in deference to this larger international perspective that would then reroute our energies into expressions that would lose our specific interrogation of the terrain that we found ourselves on, which is an America dealing with civil rights. But the genius of Martin Luther King, Jr. and Malcolm X was that they saw the international perspective. America has coded debates about race in terms of domestic territory and terrain alone; we've obscured the international connection of America as an imperialist terrorist. The colonizing impulses of America were somehow safely contained within racial discourses when America would acknowledge its own containment of black people within its own culture as a buy off, as a way of purchasing scholars of colors' silence about its materialist expansion internationally. In other words, the degree to which we're able domestically to reassign privileges within the territorial domestic space obscures the degree to which we are these international colonizers.

Now, those who have—besides bell hooks and some others—are on the periphery of so-called intellectual life within black culture. These are people who are also going to talk about conspiracy theories. These are folk who are black nationalists, who are going talk about the expansion of the colonial project of American culture. So the high-falutin black public intellectuals don't really want to be associated with those black scholars on the margin who are willing to indict America for its imperialist expansion and its colonial project because those people are not seen to be at the heart of the project of rights and debates within African-American culture. So the irony of this is that America buys silence from black scholars and other scholars of minority standing by rearranging domestic space. The topography of colonial space within American society obscures the recognition of colonial expansion outside the United States. Our silence and recognition of the international expansion of American capital and power is bought precisely because America is willing to throw us a few bones inside. So our internal colonization, which is expressed by our ignorance of this international situation, is a paradox and an irony. I think that the explosion of the postcolonialist theory of Homi Bhabha and others and the resurgence of interest in Fanon forces us to have this international connection that people like Malcolm and other marginal scholars within African-American communities have invited us to see for quite a while.

Q. You write in "Benediction: Letter to My Wife Marcia" that "many black men and women believe that placing questions of gender at the heart of black culture is an act of racial betrayal, a destructive diversion of attention away from race as the defining issue of black life." You continue, "I don't think race is the complete story. There's too much evidence that being gay, or lesbian, or female, or working poor makes a big difference in shaping the role race plays in black people's lives." In *Reflecting Black* you write that "sex, race, and class have also caused considerable conflicts and tensions between groups who compete for limited forms of cultural legitimacy, visibility, and support." And, you write that you want to "help us to begin the process of open, honest communication about the differences within our race." I wonder about the critique that when race, class, gender, and culture get discussed in the same breath, that focus is denied to individual issues. You argue that race can't be looked at as displaced from class, gender, or culture—that it doesn't exist in a vacuum. Is this the same for gender? How would you respond to feminist theorists or class theorists who don't want gender or class swallowed up in discussions of race?

A. There are two things going on here simultaneously that we have to pay attention to. First, if we say that gender and race and class have their own intellectual integrity, that they have their own intellectual space from which they should be theorized, then I say "Amen." There are irreducible categories not only for social theorizing but for personal identity and for collective communal mobilization—no question about that. But if we suggest that they can somehow be divisible from each other, that questions of gender don't have any relationship to class or to sexuality and so on, that is not the way it happens, because people experience themselves simultaneously. We have to say that questions of gender are implicated in questions of class and race and vice versa and all around. We should have specificity of analysis; the particularity with which these problems or categories of analysis or modes of identity manifest themselves has to be recognized and taken seriously. I would be the first to suggest that we can't subsume one of these under the other. The subsumption of race under class is ridiculous. We saw this in the Communist Party in the '30s and '40s in this country; we see this in certain orthodox Marxist traditions where people want to subsume issues of race under class. They have their own intellectual integrity, intellectual vitality, and ideological portfolio that allows the political consequences to be interrogated under specific kinds of intellectual interventions and interrogations.

On the other hand, I think that these categories are fused more, that they are more bloody than that, that they bleed into one another in ways that we don't always pay attention to. I don't think we can divide them in as neat a way as we can intellectually, or theoretically. For instance, what do we do with a person who happens to be gay and poor and black, or a woman who's lesbian and poor and black and a single mother? They don't have the luxury of a kind of pre-theoretical interrogation of their identity so that they can assign the most merit based upon what part of their identity has more consequence. There's a whole range of identities that are competing for expression, that are being constituted in this one body. What I have to say to feminist theorists who would say, "I don't want gender to be subsumed by race" is "fine, but I want gender to be thought of in relationship to race." Otherwise, what we might end up having is, say, white feminists who pay no attention to the effect of race so that when they interrogate the O. J. Simpson case, they see Nicole's body as a white woman's body or a universal woman's body being somehow marginalized in regard to the discussions about race, that race trumps gender. But what about for black women who see race and gender operating simultaneously? They want to say to black men, "Listen, you're not paying attention to the ways in which black women's bodies have occupied a segregated rhetorical space within African-American popular and intellectual culture." They want to say to white women, "You don't understand the way in which race has privileged white women's bodies against black women's bodies, and how the discursive terrain that white feminism operates on has all but excluded the geography of black identity for African-American women." I think that there's a way of paying attention to ideological specificity and particularity while understanding that that's an intellectual intervention, while understanding existentially and phenomenologically that the intervention of, the fusion of, and the bleeding of these multiple identities into each other has to be acknowledged as well.

Q. You make clear your conviction that conversations on race frequently silence the voices of black women. You write, "I agree with critics who argue that the rhetoric of black male suffering is often cobbled together from a distortion of black female troubles. Thus, the very language of black male crisis erases black women's faces and bodies from the canvas of social suffering. It is simply not true that black men's hurts are more important than the social horrors black women face." Would you talk about the apparent rift between black women and black men in contemporary discussions of race and how we might productively proceed as academics concerned with both race and gender?

A. I think the rift has developed as a result of the long elaboration of a whole host of factors that have been in black culture and American society from the beginning of our pilgrimage on American soil. The rift between black men and women expresses the gendering of internal differences and dissension within black culture and the way in which the gendered manifestation of those tensions has a particularly lethal effect on our own communities. The rift between black men and women expresses the differential treatment accorded black men and black women in the political economy of slavery and how the extension and expansion of that political economy of difference manifests itself now in the material effects and on the intellectual self-understandings of black masculine and black female culture. Even more particularly, the rift is a remaking of a divide-and-conquer strategy that was ingeniously employed to undermine any sense of consensus or solidarity that might have provided black people a way out of the divisiveness that was introduced as a means to destroy their ability to come together and say, "We won't put up with this." We understand this now in our postmodernist, black space where tropes of unity and solidarity are highly questioned, and for good reason. The function of unity has to be interrogated for its ability to close out other voices and visions that need to challenge that dominant hegemonic position within black culture. That's all for the good. But one of the negative consequences of that, culturally speaking, is the inability of black men and women to embrace each other across the chasm of gender. That's an outgrowth of these political machinations to destroy any sense of unity and consensus among black people, to see their lives in the same boat.

What happens is that black men and women are often in the same bed, but at each other's throats. The rift between black men and women occurs precisely because black men have uncritically incorporated a narrow masculinist psychology as a kind of fundamental structure of our consciousness in terms of combating not only white racism but what we consider to be the unjust manifestations of that white racism in black culture. Usually what we see as the most powerful rhetorical device to deploy against that racism is to view black women as the carriers of some particular strain or virus of exemption from white racism. As the story goes, black women are exempt from white racism because they have it better than black men. You don't hear this only in terms of black men, you hear it in terms of black women. Black women are less threatening; black women don't threaten white men in the same way. There's no doubt that given that we live in a patriarchal culture in which these codes of masculinity operate to legitimate certain forms of masculine power, there is a specific dimension that black men occupy that certainly is a particular and special threat to white patriarchal power. There's no question that there's a hell of a difference in terms of specific manifestations of challenge from black men and black women. The underside of that argument is that it tends to privilege black masculine suffering over black women's suffering, as if they somehow almost inherently don't have the same kind of problems with white racism that black men have. And so you've got an internal resentment against black women. These things are at the back of the kind of collective imaginary of black masculine and black female identities being construed and constructed in the space of black American culture at the end of the century where racial millenialism is being refracted through the prism of this narrow patriarchal lens. That's why I understand black women's objections to the Million Man March; it looked like the warming up of the same old patriarchal leftovers and the feeding of them to women as the new meal of black masculine identity, and that was really clearly a problem.

The academy, then, can do several things. First, it can begin to interrogate how masculinity, like race, is an artificial social construction. It can articulate that there's no such thing as a necessarily black masculine experience that has to be felt or interpreted in a certain way. It can begin to interrogate masculine identity as a gender. White people didn't have a race, and men didn't have a gender. Now men have a gender, and black men have a gender. The obsession with masculinity in our culture is an index of that. So what academics can do is help us understand the social production of gender and how it's constructed. Second, the academy can help explain the obsession with masculinity in black culture and then begin to help map out a kind of cartography of masculinity and patriarchy that helps us understand why we are obsessed with it, why there are some good things about the obsession with masculinity, and why there are a whole lot of bad things about it. What we have to do as academics is to try to filter the good from the bad and to figure out how we can produce enabling understandings of masculinity and of gender. And third, we have to begin to leave it not just to feminist critics to theorize the negative impact of gender in black communities. Male critics and academics have to begin to think much more self-critically about the function of gender in American society and about the relationships among gender, race, and class. Perhaps if we begin to deconstruct and demythologize some of these narrowly masculinist patriarchal conceptions of gender and masculine identity, we could then move toward understanding and embracing different elements of our identities that could then be embraced in much more constructive ways.

Q. As a public intellectual, you invite criticism and seem to favor keeping your work and the work of other public intellectuals meaningful and effective through criticisms. In *Race Rules* you write, "We all slip. And our critics should be there to catch us." Are there any criticisms of your work that you'd like to address?

A. There have been some insightful criticisms of my work. For instance, people were quite interested in *Reflecting Black*. This book of cultural criticism was one of the first that tried to join both theoretical acuity with pop cultural expression and to try to take those two forms—interrogation and expression—seriously in the same text. But at the same time, there was a sacrifice of a certain sort of intellectual acuity. I think that there is a risk involved in trying to join and fuse genres. I wanted to take that risk because I don't want to have a limited audience. I want to speak to the academy in very powerful and interesting ways, but I don't want to be limited to the academy. I know people who limit themselves to the academy, and the academy becomes exaggerated in its importance in their lives. As a Christian who was taught to be suspicious of any form of idolatry, I don't want to make a fetish of critical consciousness. I don't want to make an idol of the capacity to intervene intellectually in the world and make that my entire life and the academy the shrine wherein I worship. At the same time, I want to have a mode of criticism that allows me to be mobile, to move from the academy to the street to the world. I want to be able to speak to that world, and I want to have a language that is clear—with all the problematic implications of clarity. I want to have the ability to be eloquent and clear and powerful and persuasive because I've got a point to make, and I have a point of view. That point of view is worth more to me than what rewards I can reap in the academy; it's about making a difference in the lives of people I meet and whose lives I intend to represent in my work, even if they disagree with much of what I say. Black poor people, black working-class people, black kids who are being demonized as nihilistic animals, black kids who are seen as somehow extraneous, unnecessary to America—I want to speak for and with them. I want to speak for intellectuals who feel that because they're theoretically dense and sophisticated that they have nothing to say. I want to talk about the need to read those books and to struggle with them; anything worth knowing is worth knowing in a very difficult way. I would say to that criticism, I may not do it as well as it needs to be done, but I don't think that the project of trying to fuse those two genres is itself indictable.

There are also more harsh criticisms by people like Adolph Reed. That kind of vitriolic criticism is a sort of vicious gangsta rap in the guise of the academy, not even having the integrity of gangsta rappers who import all forms of signification and tropes and metaphors that indicate that they are not literally true, that they are engaging in a kind of metaphysical realm and a metaphorical world that collides on occasion. They are really artificially invoking an arena of experience that even though real in the world, they themselves realize that they're removed from it; they are thinking about, rapping about, speaking about, something that they know they are once removed from. So they use *bitch* and *whore*; they use *gangsta* and *nigger* in all kinds of interesting ways. But there's a kind of literalism about Adolph Reed that is quite disturbing and destructive—or scholars of that ilk, such as Eric

Lott. What is interesting to me about Eric Lott is that he feels free as a white scholar to use words like *troglodyte* and *caveman* and *middlebrow imbecilism* in regard to a work. I think he's a very smart, sophisticated guy who knows the historic contingency of racial rhetoric and who knows the traditional content of racial rhetoric assigned to tropes and metaphors that analyze black people. I would have thought he would have been a bit more careful about associating that—not that he had to worry about some PC police that would rigidly restrict his rhetoric, but that he would be more cautious about the historical inferences of race in assigning certain tropes and metaphors to a person's work. That doesn't in any way take away from the legitimacy of his criticism of my work as not being leftist enough, that by being involved in the public sphere you have to sacrifice certain radical dimensions. This kind of more-leftist-than-thou criticism has a limit in a way: in itself, it becomes cannibalistic. Authors feed off one another to prove that they are more leftist than the next person, and yet the political consequences of that kind of work is only to enhance the scholar's position. It has no consequences on the material effects of the lives of people that they claim they speak for more powerfully than a person like myself: poor black people, poor working-class white people, working-class people, and so on, or even radicals and progressives.

I think I've learned much from people who have taken issue with my work, who have said that there are certain sacrifices that one makes when one moves from the academy into the public sphere, and I think that's absolutely right. But my answer would be: then, you've got to do work for the academy that is important and that is integral to the perpetuation and production of scholarly, academic work; but you've also got to do work that is accountable to a public, that also stands in need of the rich traditions of intellectual reflection that we can bring to bear upon those subjects. And my own mediating position between the academy and the public sphere may never diminish the tension that I feel in terms of traversing those terrains and going back and forth. I hope I won't lose that tension, because I think that tension in some ways informs and gives my work a certain moral authority and hopefully an intellectual integrity that, if not always right, at least is always intending to reflect those tensions in ways that help both the academy and the so-called public sphere. The public sphere needs the intellectual acuity of the academic world. The academic world needs the doses of material consequences and political effects that the public sphere can bring about. That's what I intend to do in my work: to bridge the gulf, to fuse the genres, to swerve between the genres, and to do something really powerful in asking questions about how we can move beyond narrow disciplinary boundaries and narrow divisions between the "real" and the represented and get to the heart of the matter, which is to use powerfully clear work and to serve as a political interest that can be morally defended.

Ernesto

Laclau

Hegemony and the Future of Democracy: Ernesto Laclau's Political Philosophy

Lynn Worsham and Gary A. Olson

For political philosopher Ernesto Laclau, social theory must become more strategic if it is to provide a productive analysis of the complexity of contemporary society. Grasping this complexity requires a discourse combining traditions of thought that begin from different starting points but that all converge on political analysis. Thus, as Laclau points out in the interview below, he seeks to deepen the project of radical democracy by operating deconstructively within Marxist categories in order to present an analysis that goes beyond Marxism but that "nourished itself from Marxism as one its roots." It is toward the goal of developing a strategy for the left that he has devoted himself, first in *Hegemony and Socialist Strategy* (coauthored with Chantal Mouffe) and more recently in *Emancipation(s)* and *New Reflections on the Revolution of Our Time*.

In a bold theoretical project that has undergone development and revision over the last decade, Laclau has maintained that "hegemony" must be the key concept in political analysis; it is the precondition of any kind of strategic thinking. Working to extend Gramsci's elaboration of the concept of hegemony, Laclau sees hegemony not as the imposition of a pregiven set of ideas but as "something that emerges from the political interaction of groups"; it is not simply the domination by an elite, but instead is a *process* of ongoing struggle that constitutes the social. Hegemonic struggle requires the identification of what Laclau calls "floating signifiers," those signifiers that are open to continual contestation and articulation to radically different political projects. "Democracy," in his view, is a key example of a floating signifier—its meaning essentially ambiguous as a consequence of its history and widespread circulation. To hegemonize a content for "democracy" would require a fixing (always provisional) of its meaning. Indeed, the open nature of the social and the very possibility of hegemonic struggle stem from the impossibility of total fixity. As Laclau reminds us, it is "urgent" that progressive intellectuals understand the logic of hegemony and the nature of hegemonic struggle (which the neoconservative right has mastered so well in recent years), and that they develop their own hegemonic strategies.

Central to developing these strategies is the "expansion of rhetoric and rhetorical argumentation." The process of argumentation has to operate at a "plurality of levels," and social theory has to "advance in the direction of generalized rhetorics." In part, this means that intellectuals must not undervalue their own potential influence on social policy. Although "high theory" and other "intellectual developments" have produced and can continue to produce real effects in the world, Laclau believes that intellectuals must also write to more popular audiences in more accessible prose. It is important to note, though, that in speaking of rhetoric, rhetorical argumentation, and persuasion, Laclau means much more than "rational demonstration." He believes that we must deconstruct the simple opposition persuasion/force and remember that the logic of persuasion always carries within it an element of force—not necessarily physical force, but force in the sense that persuasion is "less than purely rational demonstration." Persuasion, in other words, is not a process of moving someone logically and step-by-step from one belief to another. Rather, persuasion becomes possible when new elements enter into the given situation that cannot be accommodated by the old view. At this point, the new view may forcefully displace the old view by introducing a principle of coherence and intelligibility into the situation. But the new view must have its vocal advocates, those who understand this nonliberal view of persuasion and the possibilities it offers for mining the vast resources of incoherence, contradiction, and outrage present in contemporary society.

Clearly, then, when Laclau speaks of social and political theory he always seems to have in mind practical results in the real world. For him, "the possibility of a free society depends on the existence of relations of power," and understanding and using these relations is key to creating productive alliances, new hegemonies. The formation of alliances is particularly important to this effort because it is "only on the basis of large varieties of social demands of oppressed groups that success in this hegemonic offensive becomes possible." In fact, he warns that there is a danger in any group becoming too preoccupied with the "particularity" of its own struggle because it then may fail to enter into relations of solidarity with other groups so as to engage in "wider struggles at the level of society." Such narrow actions are certain to have "no hegemonic consequences."

This understanding of hegemonic struggle as an ongoing and never-ending process offers a cogent critique of the liberal dream of a fully reconciled society from which "all antagonism and power relations would have been eliminated." Laclau argues compellingly that the "paradox of freedom" is that "in order to have freedom you have to institute the other of freedom, which is power." That is, there is no such thing as unrestricted freedom because that would mean logically the same thing as "a complete lack of freedom." Laclau explains, "You can only free some things by unfreeing some others, and in this sense power and hegemony are constitutive of social relations."

Laclau believes that literacy is an important element of the kind of revolutionary struggle he describes. He defines literacy in its widest sense and indeed in an entirely political sense. Literacy begins to be possible in a situation in which there is a proliferation of discourses opposed to oppression. In situations of oppression, the oppressed do not immediately or necessarily recognize themselves as such, but once discourses of liberation begin to proliferate and circulate, oppression can then become a question. For Laclau, a literate culture is a "culture of questions," and it is the ethical and political obligation of educators and progressive intellectuals to create such a culture, one that is democratic to the extent that the possibility of unlimited questioning exists.

Laclau's theoretical project is informed by postmodern discourses but does not surrender to postmodernism completely. His work offers a critique, on the one hand, of the postmodern position that privileges pure contextualism (what he calls "particularism") and the celebration of the logic of difference and diversity, and, on the other hand, of the Enlightenment position that privileges universalism and seeks to transcend all particularism through the ideal of consensus. He attempts to forge a third way, a dialectic that historicizes the relational interdependence of the universal and particular. This effort is motivated by two urgent questions, posed most pointedly in the preface to *Emancipation(s)*: How is the unity of the community to be grasped when we must start from social and cultural particularisms? Does this starting point exclude any identification with more universal human values? Keenly aware that the recent focus on cultural difference represents a potential deepening of democratic struggle, Laclau is equally aware that the making of political identities involves linking particular interests to wider, more universal social aims. The process through which this articulation occurs is called hegemonic struggle.

Compositionists concerned with the radical pedagogy of Paulo Freire are likely to be especially interested in the political theory of Laclau. The work of both theorists emerges from a Marxist and Gramscian perspective and attempts to analyze relations of power and domination and revitalize radical thought. Both writers exhibit a deep empathy for the oppressed, and both offer strategies for confronting systems of power and domination. In many ways, Laclau's work might be seen as a kind of extension of some of Freire's central concepts. Perhaps we can find in Laclau ways to deepen and enrich the kind of critical literacy so central to much of our own scholarship.

Q. The field of rhetoric and composition is devoted to the study of the practice of writing and its consequences. Do you think of yourself as a writer? What role has writing played in the development of your thought?

A. Well, I suppose I can say I am a writer in some sense. The point is that "writing" is not a unified category; it can refer to many different types of writing. I see myself these days as a theoretical writer: the way that I try to operate is basically through the production of theory. That has not always been the case. For instance, when I was in Argentina I worked for several years as the editor of a left-wing weekly, so there I was engaged in some form of journalism.

Q. In Richard Rorty's "liberal utopia," persuasion replaces force as a principal social arrangement. In your critique of Rorty, you demonstrate that not only is it impossible to oppose persuasion and force but that "persuasion is one form of force." You add, however, that persuasion cannot simply be reduced to force. Would you elaborate on the relationship of persuasion to force?

A. In the first place, the category of persuasion as used by Rorty has played the function of, let's say, reducing the epistemological ambitions of a dialogical exchange. For instance, take the case of Habermas. Habermas maintained that finally a dialogical situation would be able, at least as an ideal point of arrival, to conclude in a situation in which one and only one position is maintained by people engaged in the dialogue. Rorty does not believe that. He believes in the purely conversational nature of the agreement that people reach, and that is why persuasion is a category that is as important for him as it is. Now, what I was trying to do in the piece to which you refer is to deepen this logic of persuasion and to find out whether in persuasion, which is the opposite of force for Rorty, there is not an element of force so that one can deconstruct the opposition persuasion/force. What I think I have shown in that piece is that persuasion, precisely because it never presents an argument that should be accepted algorithmically, involves, if you will, an element of force. For example, if you think of the quasi-logical arguments of Chaim Perelman and his analysis of how persuasion operates, you see that an element of force necessarily has to be included. You persuade by something less than a rational type of demonstration. What is this something less? There you can have many possible answers, and all of them would be valued depending on the situation. For instance, you can provoke the sympathy of the listener. You can, on the other hand, present the argument so forcefully that you intimidate the listener, and you know the whole range of these possibilities.

Now, there is one point that for me is particularly important because it leads to central questions in the theory of hegemony: it is that when you are confronted with a situation in which there is no clear answer but in which an answer is needed nonetheless, the fact that some answer is provided becomes more important than its concrete content. That is an element of force—force not in the sense of physical force, but force in the sense that it is less than purely rational demonstration; purely rational demonstration would absolutely collapse the difference between the *ontic* character of the response and the ontological character of being a response. My argument is that in any dialogical situation these two dimensions never collapse, and that is what leads to the deconstruction of the pure alternative force/persuasion. This concept in another sense—for instance, in the Anglo-American discussion—has been very useful when we come to the notion of decision. A distinction is made between the cause of a decision and the motive of a decision, the cause being what provoked the decision. I think there is nothing more complicated than distinguishing between cause and motive, precisely because a motive is never totally algorithmically grounded. We have to play around the deconstruction of this stark opposition in which traditional rationalistic discourse is grounded.

Q. We'd like to follow up on this subject. Throughout your work, you insist that "hegemony" must be the key concept of political analysis. You say that hegemony is not the imposition of a pregiven set of ideas and practices but "something that emerges from the political interaction of groups." That is, hegemony is not a simple matter of forceful domination by an elite but, rather, is a process of ongoing struggle that constitutes the social. In *Emancipation(s)* you at times seem to suggest an identification between hegemony and persuasion, and at other times you assert that the internal logic of the hegemonic operation *underlies* the process of persuasion, which seems to suggest a distance or difference between the two. Exactly how do you perceive the relationship of persuasion and hegemony?

A. We can start from the point where we ended in the previous answer. The question of hegemony is linked to a situation in which something is missing and a particular content takes up the representation of that missing element. For instance, there's a very good example that I used in one of my pieces. In the immediate post-war period in Italy, people used to say that the Fascists had succeeded in carrying out the revolution in which the Communists had failed. Obviously, this is nonsense because a Fascist revolution and a Communist revolution from the point of view of their content would have been completely different. So, what created the acceptability of such an assertion? Simply the fact that revolution for people meant the realization that the Italian state had to be founded again, that the type of political organization which had emerged from the *Risorgimento* was in tatters and that as a result some radical refoundation of the Italian state was needed. In the political semantics of the time, this is what was meant by revolution. It has a purely negative content because revolution means the fullness of society which is lacking. When people are in a situation of radical disorder, people need some kind of order, and the nature of the particular order is secondary. This relationship in which a certain particular content assumes the function of a universal fullness which is totally incommensurate with it is exactly what I call a hegemonic relationship. As you see, the dimension of force is present there, and the dimension of persuasion has to be present there as well, in the sense that I mentioned before. If we had a dialogical situation in which we reached, at least as a regulative idea, a point in which between the *ontic* and the ontological dimensions there would be no difference, in which there would be a complete overlapping, then in that case there would be nothing to hegemonize because this absent fullness of the community could be given by one and only one political content. But there is no overlapping there between particularity and universal function; in that case the relation is going to be hegemonic because there is always going to be a precarious taking up of this universal function by the particularity of social forces.

Let me give you another example. In the classical Marxist conception, the moment of universality was the moment of simplification of the social structure under capitalism. Universality was a category coming from Hegelian philosophy. For Hegel, the universal class was bureaucracy. Marx said that bureaucracy—that is, the state—is not the moment of the universal of the community but is an instrument of the ruling class, so it is also a moment of particularity. So, how do you reach the moment of universality if you have only the dispersion of concrete interests in civil society? The answer was that this is only possible if there is something going on at the level of civil society by which the moment of universality will emerge there. This was the emergence of the proletariat, which through the increasing simplification of the social structure under capitalism would represent the point of view of the totality of the community and, from this point of view, universality. Now, when society did not advance in that direction, the result was the proliferation of differences in civil society. And what happened with the moment of universality? The answer to that is hegemony. This was exactly the problem of Gramsci. Gramsci develops hegemony theoretically up to a certain point. I think these two dimensions—universality and particularity, which I think we will discuss later—come together through these particular mechanisms.

Q. Literacy theorists associated with what is often called "liberatory learning" contend that literacy is a key element in the emancipation of oppressed groups. Many feminists agree; for example, Donna Haraway commented in a recent *JAC* interview that "you can't talk about the history of contemporary liberation struggles without talking about . . . literacy projects." What do you believe is the role of literacy projects in struggles against oppression?

A. As far as I understand the concept, the question of the role of a literacy project conceived in the broad sense would be close to what Foucault called a "proliferation of discourses." In a situation in which emancipatory struggles start, there is always a whole transformation at the discursive level: you know how to handle a set of situations to which you didn't have access before. So discourses against oppression (if we understand by that the notion of literacy in its widest sense) are absolutely essential for any struggle against oppression. And here I would like to add something. In general, situations of oppression are not situations in which the oppressed immediately recognize themselves as such. They are situations in which in some sense the identity of the oppressed breaks up and in which precisely these tools of liberation struggle—discourses—are not present. At the moment in which they start being present, we are in a situation in which oppression begins to be radically a question and in which different outcomes are possible. For example, in many areas of the Third World, you do not find class interests in the classical sense because class interests were conceived as constituted around positions in the production process. What you find in many places in the Third World is that people don't have a precise insertion in the production process because there is a wide situation of social marginality. When you have a situation of social marginality, the idea of an interest given by your objective insertion in the relations of production simply does not work.

I remember, for instance, that in the 1930s in the middle of the world economic crisis, Trotsky wrote that if unemployment were to continue at the present level, we would no longer be able to conceive the unemployed in terms of the Marxian category of an industrial reserve army; and if this were so, the whole Marxian theory of the classes would have to be rethought because the category of classes would not embrace everything that had to be embraced in order to conceptualize oppression. In this situation, you often find that populist discourses emerge. Many times at the level of national politics people start acquiring a sense of identity, and you find that they have to reconstruct at the political level through these discourses (which would be new forms of literacy in the broad sense that we are defining it) an identity which does not emerge spontaneously at the level of civil society. This is why I think there was a shift in my conception about this matter. When Chantal Mouffe and I wrote *Hegemony and Socialist Strategy*, we were still arguing that the moment of the dislocation of social relations, the moment which constitutes the limit of the objectivity of social relations, is given by antagonism. Later on I came to think that this was not enough because constructing a social dislocation—an antagonism—is already a discursive response. You construct the Other who dislocates your identity as an enemy, but there are alternative forms. For instance, people can say that this is the expression of the wrath of God, that this is an expression of our sins and that we have to prepare for the day of atonement. So, there is already a discursive organization in constructing somebody as an enemy which involves a whole technology of power in the mobilization of the oppressed. That is why in *New Reflections* I have insisted on the primary character of dislocation rather than antagonism.

Q. You also say in *New Reflections* that "There is democracy as long as there is the possibility of unlimited questioning." And in the "Politics and the Limits of Modernity," you write, "The sense of an intellectual intervention emerges only when it is possible to reconstitute the system of questions that it seeks to answer." Your focus on questioning should be of particular interest to liberatory teachers, whose pedagogical problem arguably is to teach students to recognize and ask questions that produce an intellectual intervention in a given historico-discursive formation. The question of course is *how* to do this, how to convey to students the sense of the vital importance of questions and questioning.

A. Paulo Freire would have good answers to this question, but I'm not really the person to answer it. However, what I would like to elaborate on for a moment is the strong distinction—question and answer. The point is: is there any question that is not already in some sense an answer to what it is posing? I think questions do not operate as purely neutral, leaving the field of the answer entirely open; rather, questions operate in the sense of narrowing the field of the answer. So questioning is already the first step in the organization of a discursive field. If we are speaking about literacy in the wide sense, as in the previous question, in that case, to create a culture of questions is absolutely important and is perhaps what distinguishes a dogmatic education or a dogmatic approach to any kind of social practice from a position which is not dogmatic, which is open. It cannot be totally open because in that case there would be no questions either. But it cannot be entirely closed either. So, I would see the whole complex of the relationship question/answer as a continuum in which there are different levels of closedness. This is important for democratic theory because questions can close a certain field, but they can also constitute a community which poses itself a set of problems while at the same time maintaining relatively open the fields of the answers. A community in which there is no community of questions is not a community at all.

Q. You have defined *hegemony* as a "logic of articulation" and *articulation* as "a *political construction* from dissimilar elements." You've also said that "articulation cannot just be conceived as the linkage of dissimilar and fully constituted elements." For instance, your own work takes "the best fragments" of Marxist theory and links them with useful elements from postmodern theory to intervene productively in the present theoretical and political situation. As a discursive practice, articulation is of potential use to those of us who study the liberatory possibilities of literacy and writing. What do you see as the role of the concept of articulation for a theory of writing?

A. Articulation is a category which started being important for this type of analysis only with Althusserianism. Before that we had only heard of articulated lorries. It became a theoretically relevant question precisely because Althusser was trying to think a combination of elements that according to classical Marxist theory were uncombinable because they belong to different stages of social evolution. For instance, the notion of the articulation of the modes of production became very much in use in the 1960s in order to define situations in the Third World where you have an incorporation into a world economy of modes of production which were not capitalist and which, however, were integrated within the structure of world capitalism. The way I have developed the notion of articulation in relation to hegemony is the following: as you very well point out here, we cannot conceive of articulation as the linkage of similar and fully constituted elements, precisely because if the elements were fully constituted, the articulation would not play any kind of a grounding role. If you want to conceive of articulation, you can go for instance to the Saussurian model. In the Saussurian model, as far as language is a system of difference, this means, on the one hand, that the social totality in some sense is presupposed by the signifying totality, let's say. The signifying totality is presupposed by any single act of signification but at the same time is exposed to new elements because new elements are going to produce a new articulation of everything that was within the structure. So, articulation in this sense became the basic category of social analysis as far as all social practices are signifying practices. When I say that I take the best fragments of Marxist theory, what I'm saying is that by these fragments' entering into articulatory practices with other elements, they are transforming their nature. There is a set of categories that still can be there but which, however, play a completely different role than they play in classical Marxism. Now, when you ask me about the concept of articulation in a theory of writing, what are you aiming at?

Q. We are curious about the potential for using, either explicitly or implicitly, the concept of articulation in teaching students to think through writing, to think in the process of writing. There is an unfolding of thought in the process of writing. Thinking and writing are quite interconnected, and you're in many ways talking about a way of thinking. So, we're interested in the possibilities of using the concept of articulation to describe how we go about putting together elements of different theories, different discourses, to then produce some kind of intellectual intervention. This is particularly relevant, for example, in trying to help graduate students become good thinkers so that they can produce first-rate work that is not just a simple recombination of other people's ideas, but that is the kind of combination that actually produces a significant intellectual intervention.

A. I wonder if the most relevant concept for that purpose would not be inscription. That is, any writing is a process of inscription. By "inscription" I mean a process in which through putting two things together, the nature of these two things is in some way modified. For instance, you were speaking about graduate students. I have long experience as a Ph.D. supervisor. One of the most difficult problems that I have found is that students sometimes establish a radical separation between case study and theoretical framework. With such separation you are in a situation in which the theoretical chapter could be identical in all the dissertations and the case study is the only thing that changes from one to the other, which means that the two things have not been articulated at all. Coming back to the Saussurian example that I was giving before, if language is by definition a system of difference and by extension any signifying structure is like that, then the incorporation of new elements has to modify all the elements of the whole. In theoretical discourses, this means that there is no case study which should not modify the theory as well. If articulation is defined in this sense, the conclusion is that through each case study—in fact, the ideology of the case study has to be broken—the theory itself has to be in some sense modified, modified not in the sense of putting it outside, but modified simply in showing theoretical aspects through a new light; and at the same time, the case study (which is comparatively more easy) can be inscribed within a theory. The moment of inscription operates in two ways. My experience is that this is one of the most difficult things for graduate students to learn how to do. But it makes the whole difference between a purely scholarly exercise—scholarly in the bad sense of the term, of simply showing that you have understood a theory in an effort to be able to competently apply it to some case—and to enter into a process in which the theory illuminates the case and the case illuminates the theory. I think that the whole distinction between empirical and theoretical research has to be put, from this point of view, into question. And from this point of view, the category of articulation can help us think about the matter.

Q. Your work is a critique on the one hand of the postmodern position that privileges pure contextualism (what you call "particularism") and that historicizes the concept of the universal, and on the other hand, of the Enlightenment position that privileges universalism and seeks to transcend all particularisms. You attempt to forge a third way, a dialectic that demonstrates the relational interdependence of the universal and the particular. What are the theoretical and political exigencies that compel you to make this move?

A. In the first place, I think that pure particularism is impossible because each pure particularity has to define itself by its differences with other particularities, and the system of these particularities necessarily reconstructs a certain universality—and the worst form of universality, universality conceived as a ground. This is the first theoretical difficulty. A political difficulty is that I don't think pure particularism can do the job because what would be the particularism of a certain community? If this community is a particular one, this means that it does not overlap exactly with the global community conceived as a whole. In that case, it's going to experience a set of pressures from outside itself. If you have national, racial, ethnic, or cultural minorities, one of their requests in order to assert their particularism would be the right of these communities to assert their identity. If you assert the right of a whole community to defend its own identity, what you are asserting is a principle that is not quite context bound.

There is a strong tendency toward contextualization in contemporary politics and in contemporary theory, but the consequence of this movement toward contextualization is that there is a different movement, a movement toward decontextualization. For instance, a discourse of rights is going to be a decontextualizing discourse because as far as it is not a purely xenophobic discourse it will have to assert itself in terms of some universality. Now, what is wrong with the idea of universality in the classical sense? That it gave to universality a content which can be specified in absolutely positive terms—man is a rational animal, and so on—and in this sense it gave to it a content which in the last analysis was always particular and was associated with the tradition of a certain culture. For example, democracy as it was conceived from the eighteenth century on was based on a discourse of equalization. The universalism of the French Revolution led in that direction. Marxism—because Marx thought, as I said before, that there was an increasing homogenization of social structure—tended to move toward a discourse of universality that was incompatible with difference, which in fact eliminated differences. Today, the problem of democracy is the opposite. Once you have a society in which you have a multiplicity of cultures, demands, interests, and so on, how do you combine them in a way that is compatible with the defense of their particularity? This is the problem of democracy today, so in some sense we are in the antipodes of the classical theory of democracy.

Now, what I have tried to do, especially in the essays collected in *Emancipation(s)*, is to rescue a notion of universality which is not restricted to an a priori given content and which is given by the notion of hegemony. I used the notion of empty signifier (which is developed especially in the essay I like most in that volume, "Why Do Empty Signifiers Matter to Politics?") to try to develop precisely this argument. If we go back to what I was saying before about hegemony, you can immediately see the connection. If the systematicity of the system—the totality, what would constitute the moment of universalization—is something which is both impossible and necessary, it will need to have access in some way to representation. But the means of representation are going to be constitutively inadequate because they can only be specific particularities. Now, with hegemony, the relationship by which at some point a certain particularity assumes this function of universal representation involves a moment of universality, a universality, however, deprived of any kind of positive content—this is the difference with the Habermasian notion of universality. But my argument is that this leads to a more radical kind of democratic politics, because if the moment of universality had a content given a priori once and for all, no dialogical process would be possible; things would have been decided from the very beginning. If, on the other hand, this element of universality is going to be necessary but does not have a content of its own and it's only given in a transient way by the particular social force, in that case hegemonic rearticulations are always possible, and this incompletion of society is what keeps the possibility of a democratic exchange constantly open.

Q. The body of your work suggests the possibility of deepening the project of radical democracy through its articulation with poststructuralism, specifically deconstruction. How might deconstruction become central to a theory of politics? We can anticipate how you might answer given what you've just said about the particular and universal.

A. I think that deconstruction is basically a theory about the decision taken in an undecidable terrain. For instance, in *Speech and Phenomena* Derrida shows in what way the articulation between knowledge and meaning in Husserl does not lead necessarily to the subordination of meaning to knowledge. Husserl, in fact, emancipates the two dimensions and shows that they can go in completely different directions. Once you have a radical undecidablity in the relationship between these two dimensions, he says, Husserl makes an ethico-theoretical decision, which is to subordinate one to the other in a new sense. But the contingency of these decisions always remains there. For instance, he says that Joyce took exactly the opposite direction from Husserl. If you have undecidability in this radical sense, and, on the other hand, you have the need for a decision (for instance, Derrida insists in his later works that there is an urgency in a decision; I would say that a decision is something one has to make too soon), in that sense, the decision is going to produce some kind of articulation between two elements which is not required at the level of the structure. This is very close to hegemonic articulation in the sense that I was referring to before.

Q. You've said that your preference is for a "liberal-democratic-socialist society," and you often differentiate your vision of a radical democracy from both classical liberal democracy and from the neoconservative effort to redeploy liberal political theory for its own ends. What are the crucial differences between your radicalized notion of democracy and these others?

A. The classical liberal notion of democracy was limited to a particular sphere: the sphere of citizenship, the public space of citizenship. Liberals say that in the private sphere people can be as different from each other as they want but that they are equal within the public sphere. Because there is in classical liberalism an assertion of both equality at one level and inequality at another level, the degree of democratization to which this theory can reach is a limited one. That is why I insist on the notion of democratic revolution, which is based on some of the points that Claude Lefort developed but that Tocqueville formulated originally. The argument of Tocqueville was that once people accept the principle of equality in some sphere, they will not accept being equal in one sphere and unequal in a different one; they will try to be equal in all spheres. My notion of democratic revolution is based in the expansion of this logic of equality from the public sphere of citizenship to different spheres—for instance, in socialist discourses in the nineteenth century to the economic sphere, and in this century to the equality between sexes, people of different sexual orientations, races, ethnic groups, and so on. Once you assert the principle of equality in all its dimensions, you are erasing the distinction between a public sphere and a private sphere. For example, some women say that "the personal is political"; what they are saying is that the logic of equality expands to a sphere from which it had been originally excluded. Well, classical liberal thought is very much based on this differentiation between public and private spaces and in that sense cannot advance very much in the direction of radical democracy. The neoconservative offensive is even clearer from this point of view: in the private sphere, only individuals can exist. But in the neoconservative offensive, the logic of equality plays practically no role at all. So this would basically be the difference between the two notions of democracy.

Q. In an attempt to devise an anti-foundational epistemology, many postmodern thinkers have focused on knowledge as radically contingent, local, and contextualized. Many rhetorical theorists, in fact, are fully committed to a neopragmatic notion that all knowledge is radically contextual and, thus, rhetorical. You caution, however, that this approach does not fully consider the limitations of "context" itself. How might we continue to understand the centrality of context while remaining aware of its limitations?

A. Let me say first that I would agree that knowledge is radically contingent, local, and contextualized; so I would accept that view. The difficulty, however, starts when one tries to define what a context is. Derrida is right in saying that defining the limits of context is one of the most difficult things you can do. The point is that in spite of the contextual specificity of every context there are logics of relative universalization operating within them. For instance, I spoke earlier about the discourses of rights. If you have discourses about human rights, in a very ultimate sense, these are contextual rights because they depend on people believing a set of key things about human beings which since the eighteenth century have been expanding more and more. So you have a very very radical and generalized context. This is obviously not the localized context people are thinking about when they make certain radically postmodern types of assertions. If contexts have within themselves this tendency toward decontextualization through universalization, in an ultimate ontological sense, context is always dominant but its dimensions are changing all the time. I think that what we have is simply a relative universalization of values. The point is that in the current debate the whole discussion has gone in the direction of putting into question the essentialist notion of universality, of asserting pure contextualized particularity. But for the reason I've mentioned, this is not without any difficulties either. So, I think we have to operate on the two levels: to accept radical contextualization, but to show how in any context there is something going beyond the context itself. Here, what I've called "the logic of equivalence" is very important in order to universalize some values. For instance, you can say that women had to fight for their rights as women, Chicanos had to fight for their rights as Chicanos, and so on. But can they fight for their rights without entering into some equivalential logic which puts their struggle together with the struggle of other people and in this sense produces a certain relative universalization of value? I don't think this is possible. They have to operate at the same level—at the level of contextualization on the one hand and at the level of this weakened form of the universalization of values on the other. What I deny to classical universalism is its assertion, not this relative and weakened universalization through equivalence. What I deny is that there is something which is universal per se and which does not depend on contextual interaction in order to create its relative universalities.

Q. Since the early 1980s, the concept of "the social" has become increasingly central to composition scholarship as theorists have interrogated the connections between rhetoric and epistemology. The social is also an important element in your own thinking. For example, you distinguish your view of the social from what might be called a common-sense definition of society, "an ensemble of *physically* existing agents who live within a given territory." Such an unnuanced perspective is not uncommon in composition theory. How might we in composition more productively think the social, especially in relation to the political?

A. Let me answer the point concerning the relationship between the social and the political, and you can draw your own conclusions about composition. The notion of the social in my work has been presented in terms of two counterpositions. One is the relationship between the social and the political, the other the distinction between the social and society. Let's start with this last distinction. I understand "society" to mean simply the possibility of closure of all social meaning around a matrix which can explain all its partial processes. That would be, for instance, the position of classical structuralism. On the other hand, if one takes a more poststructuralist position—the impossibility of closing any context and among them the societal context as a unified whole—what you have are marginal processes which constantly disrupt meaning and do not lead to the closure of society around a single matrix. When we have the social defined in this sense as something which creates meaning but which makes closure impossible, I tended to speak of "the social" instead of "society." That was an early distinction. For example, that is precisely the argument which is being presented in the article on the impossibility of society.

I think the second distinction—the distinction between the social and the political—is more relevant. And that is connectedwith the distinction between sedimentation and reactivation, a distinction that comes from Husserl. Husserl said that the original acts of the production of meaning by a transcendental subject are acts which in social practice become repetitious and forget the moment of their original institution. For him, reactivation was to go back to this original institution through which sedimented meaning was constituted. The difference is that for Husserl this moment of reactivation consists in going back to an original institution which constituted the object and which had a positive content and character. The way I am presenting the argument is that we live in a world of sedimented social practices. The moment of reactivation consists not in going to an original founding moment, as in Husserl, but to an original contingent decision through which the social was instituted. This moment of the institution of the social through contingent decisions is what I call "the political."

In some sense, we are living in a world in which "the social" explains eighty percent of our social practices, while there are areas of undecidability in which acts of institution of a political nature are required. For example, if you live in a period of relative social stability, you are going to have that the social expands at the expense of the political. If you are living in an organic crisis period, in the Gramscian sense, obviously many more areas of social life are susceptible to political construction. The way I see the history of social theory is that up to the end of the seventeenth century the threatened European communities which had emerged from the wars of religion were very conscious of the problem of the political nature of the social link. For instance, Hobbes would be a typical example. And so, political philosophy occupied a central role. In contrast, what happened from the eighteenth century onward was an increasing confidence of society in its ability of self-regulation. From the invisible hand of Adam Smith to sociology in the nineteenth century, there is a progressive abandonment of the perspective of political analysis, of political philosophy, and an increasing sociologization of the categories of social analysis. I think that today we are in some sense returning to a consideration of the political nature of the social precisely because people have less confidence in the mechanism of self-reproduction. For example, in conditions of globalization you always need to produce political forms of rearticulation in order to make society work to some extent. So, probably today we are in a process in which the political is returning—to use an expression of Chantal's—to occupy a more central role in the understanding of social mechanisms.

Q. In "Community and Its Paradoxes," you state, "I am very much in favour of reintroducing the dimension of violence within reform. A world in which reform takes place without violence is not a world in which I would like to live." In fact, you claim that "the existence of violence and antagonisms is the very condition of a free society." In what ways is violence constitutive of the social? What limitations, if any, would you place on the use of violence?

A. This is related to an argument that I present in *New Reflections* in my letter to Aletta Norval. The argument that I pose is essentially that the possibility of a free society depends on the existence of relations of power. The argument is approximately the following. What is taking a decision? Taking a decision can follow either of two mechanisms. If I have to take a decision, I am confronted with a set of alternatives, but the determination of which is the best alternative is an algorithmic one; in that case, there is one and only one possible choice between the alternatives. In that case, I am not deciding anything; the structure has taken the decision for me. So, in what case do I really have a choice? It is when the field of decision is indeterminate. That is, the decision can be mine only in so far as the structure does not determine which is the good solution. But this means that taking a decision is to some extent to operate arbitrarily. Now, when we pass from individual to collective decisions, one group of people will prefer one decision, and another group will prefer a different one. The result of this is that as there is no ultimate algorithm which can arbitrate between them, the mechanism by which one decision is imposed at the expense of the others is going to involve power in some sense, even in the limited sense of winning an election. People will have things imposed on them that they do not want. In this sense, taking decisions and establishing relations of power necessarily go together. I would argue that this is not bad. This is violence, power, but it's not bad. Why? Because the other alternative would be that all decisions are algorithmic, and in that case we would have no freedom at all. The only thing we would have is the Spinozian freedom of being conscious of necessity. And I would not like to live in that society because it is a society from which freedom would have been totally eliminated. This is the paradox of freedom: in order to have freedom you have to institute the other of freedom, which is power. You can destroy some forms of power, but the destruction of these forms of power would involve establishing new relations of power of a different kind.

In what sense would unrestricted freedom be possible? My answer is that it is not possible because unrestricted freedom would be the same thing as a complete lack of freedom. You can only free some things by unfreeing some others, and in this sense power and hegemony are constitutive of social relations. At some point, for instance, you want to free women from oppression, but freeing women from oppression will mean establishing relations of power over people who oppose this process of freedom. The whole argument is against the idea of a reconciled society from which all antagonism and power relations would have been eliminated.

Q. Would you not put limitations on the violence that is constitutive of freedom?

A. I think I would put limitations on it, but I cannot determine these limitations except by conceiving a certain context. In some contexts I would be perfectly happy to incur an act of terrorism to destroy a very oppressive regime; in other contexts, no. The terrorism that the resistance in France used in the Second World War—destroying railway stations, for example—is a kind of terrorism in a particular context that I'm perfectly prepared to subscribe to. So the problem of the limitation of violence cannot be solved on the basis of a blueprint determining in a rationalistic way what kind of violence is good and what is bad. That depends.

Q. One could argue that the debate about multiculturalism in the U.S. is stalled precisely by a politics of recognition and an imperative to celebrate difference. You assert in "Subject of Politics, Politics of the Subject" that a politics of pure difference is "the route to self-apartheid." What do you see as the dangers of the construction of political identities exclusively through a logic of difference?

A. I want to stress this point: the danger implicit in any kind of social relation—in any kind of antagonistic struggle, let's say—is that if only the particularity of the struggle is recognized without entering into relations of solidarity with other groups and engaging in wider struggles at the level of society, then the group will be totally enclosed in its particularized demands and its actions will have no hegemonic consequences at the wider level. Let me give you an example. There were some discussions in Britain after the Labour Party victory about how black people should operate in relation to the Labour victory. There were some positions arguing that from the point of view of black interests it is the same thing whether the conservatives or Labour had won the election. Labour had made very few pronouncements in defense of black demands. Some people argued in those terms; other people within the black communities argued in a way more sympathetic to a Labour victory. Now, what would be a position of pure particularism? A position of pure particularism would be to say that our interests to be defended are exclusively black ones and that the libertarian spirit which for a few weeks dominated British society after the election is something from which we have to keep totally apart. Now, what is relevant is the whole distinction—that, for instance, Gramsci made—between a corporative defense of an interest and a hegemonic attitude. A hegemonic policy is one which tries to present particular interests as necessary to carry out a wider social aim.

To explain this point, I used in one of my works the example of Mary Wollstonecraft. The rights of man and citizens excluded women, but her attitude was not to say that because the rights of man and citizens are purely male interests, we won't have anything to do with them. She says, instead, that if the rights of man and citizens are not extended to women, there is an internal limitation which prevents the extension of the democratic revolution in a variety of dimensions. As another example, the defense of black interests in America took place following the Second World War on a very comprehensive basis. The blacks had a discourse which was not a purely particularized discourse, but a discourse which defended civil liberties, civil rights in a much wider sense, in spite of the fact that the reaction of the white establishment, even the liberal white establishment, to the assertion of these rights was rather timid—to put it mildly, no? I remember a black activist of the 1930s (I don't remember his name) who said something like, "The most sympathetic president that I have found to black causes in America was Franklin Roosevelt, and all the concessions I got from him were at gunpoint."

So, these two dimensions are constantly present. I'm very much in favor of multiculturalism. In fact, I think multiculturalism has been one of the great developments in American politics over the last decades. What I'm concerned about, however, is to find the means by which pure particularism can be overcome by a more comprehensive type of discourse. I'm not saying that pure particularism is necessarily predominating, but definitely it is a danger which is potentially there, as it is in any group that starts having at the same time to assert its own identity and to inscribe its own identity in wider causes at the level of national politics.

Q. In your Preface to Slavoj Zizek's *The Sublime Object of Ideology*, you suggest that "the Lacanian concept of enjoyment, *jouissance*, . . . enables us to understand the logic of exclusion operating in discourses such a racism." This is a provocative statement, one that alludes to what might be at work affectively in the perpetuation of racist practices. Would you further describe the relationship you see between *jouissance* and racism?

A. I'm simply summarizing an argument of Zizek's. What it basically comes down to is the fact that enjoyment is very much linked to the practice of exclusion. For example, if I am in a situation in which I feel vulnerable, weak, I project onto some particular Other the source of my own limitations—the Black, the Jew, the Bosnian, whatever group that can be seen as the symbol of what is lacking in my situation. The whole structure of enjoyment, which certainly is more complicated in Lacan than that, turns around this double relationship in which the Other is the negative mirror of my own lack. This is approximately what the argument is about.

Q. In a recent *JAC* interview, African-American feminist bell hooks suggests that if we are ever to understand the dynamics of race so as to move toward a truly anti-racist society, whites are going to have to begin to interrogate "whiteness." What she is suggesting is the necessity of understanding the *relational* character of racial identities. Given your interest in the making of political identities, what steps do you recommend we take to initiate such an interrogation?

A. I'm very much in agreement with bell hooks' assertion. When one is thinking about black identities or white identities, one is not thinking two separate things; one is thinking in discourses which constitute whiteness through the exclusion of blackness and through the exclusion of many other things. Because whiteness is a comprehensive category, you will exclude homosexuals and many others who function in your discourse as the Other. In that case, it is not possible to destabilize this form of discrimination without at the same time destablizing the category of whiteness which constitutes the hard core of positivity against which these discourses operate. So, I agree very much with that assertion because otherwise we would have the simplistic idea that you can simply incorporate rights or the defense of a set of groups without modifying the very identity of the groups which have represented the point of view of the oppressor. It is not simply a matter of extending to other groups something which belongs to the dominant group; it's that the process of this extension destablizes the very categories of the dominant groups as such.

Q. You occasionally refer to the work of Homi Bhabha and particularly his notion of hybridization. Do you find the work of postcolonial theorists generally useful in your efforts to theorize the discursive conditions of possibility for the emergence of new political identities? It seems related to what you were just saying.

A. Yes, very much so. I find the work not only of Homi but also of Gayatri Spivak to be very relevant to this point of view. The category of hybridization shows its potential precisely by pointing out those fields of ambiguity that I was describing before. What does hybridization mean? Simply that I cannot enclose myself in a pure identity of the oppressed. What I was saying before about the oppressor also relates to the identity of the oppressed. The oppressed also constitute their identity by denying the identity of the oppressor. But the process of advancing the claims against a system of oppression destablizes both the identity of the oppressor and the identity of the oppressed. And here is where hybridization becomes necessary, becomes important. In the process of advancing its claims, the oppressed will have to negotiate within institutions, for instance. Once you negotiate within institutions, you are going to find the very ambiguities which are inherent in any institutional struggle. The more successful a group is in asserting its claim, the more this success will involve participating in a variety of institutions' relations of power and so on, which are going to put into question the original demand. At the same time, these institutions have a structure of their own. This structure can among other things produce a co-optation of the original group, so that there is a limitation of the radicalism of the original demands. On the other hand, if they continue in a purely anti-institutional struggle, they do not advance hegemonically in society at all. All kinds of hegemonic struggle always take place by negotiating between these two mutual impossibilities. Each one of these two logics of social action, if it is taken unilaterally, leads to social immobility, either by a pure segregationism in a purely anti-institutional struggle or through integration into institutions. It is only by combining the two in a pragmatic way that some kind of global advances of particular causes are made possible.

But here also the system of alliances is important because it is only on the basis of large varieties of social demands of oppressed groups that success in this hegemonic offensive becomes possible. For instance, I heard in America some years ago people saying that liberalism as a system is absolutely dead; no radical democratic struggle is possible within a liberal framework. This, I think, is pure defeatism because, in that case, if you don't want to influence institutions to change, what is the meaning of organizing a march in Washington in order to defend the right to choose and so on? You are constantly trying to modify liberal institutions by operating within the framework of these liberal institutions. I understand a discourse that is an *alternative* to operating within a liberal framework—for example, if somebody says I have a Leninist theory about the seizure of power—because in that case all your logic of political action is different. But if you don't have any kind of alternative logic and you operate in a purely ad hoc way without broad hegemonic objectives in mind, probably your action is going to be limited as well. So, here I think it is necessary to differentiate between liberalism—in the sense that I spoke about earlier, as different from a project of radical democracy—and operating within an institutional liberal framework, because what is at issue is to radicalize liberalism beyond the limits which were established by classical liberalism.

Q. In *New Reflections on the Revolution of Our Time* you state, "Destroying the hierarchies on which sexual or racial discrimination is based will, at some point, always require the construction of other exclusions for collective identities to be able to emerge." Certainly you don't mean to suggest that the struggle against racism and sexism is futile. How then, are we to decide which exclusions are to be accepted, tolerated, and viewed as supportive of a radical democratic project?

A. My answer would be the same as my earlier answer about contextualization. Definitely, if you are struggling against racism and sexism, you are going to exclude from your project some people who are defending, for instance, traditional values; you are going to exclude the moral majority, the Ku Klux Klan, and similar groups. So asserting a radical democratic project will include these types of exclusion. For example, you might exclude people who defend "the right to life" while you are defending certain values, but this is in the nature of social antagonism. Now, what groups have to be excluded from a radical democratic project depends on how a society is structured. How a project of this kind will advance in a country like Argentina or Italy or America is going to be completely different. For instance, I don't know to what extent the advancement of democratic causes in many countries of the Islamic world would involve the same type of exclusion that we would have in an American context today. Certainly, the relationship between democratic demands and

Islamism presents a very complicated set of issues because many causes that we would recognize as valid in the Islamic context— for example, in the struggle against the Iranian regime—will have to accept at the same time the Islamic constitution of subjects in many other respects with distinctions and causes that we would not accept in the Anglo-Saxon world today.

Q. But apart from the particular context, there's no sort of mechanism for how to determine what's to be tolerated?

A. Only the kind of relative universalized value that I was speaking about earlier. Today, for instance, discourses about national self-determination are discourses which have won an almost universal acceptance from the international point of view, so there you have a certain universality of values which on the basis of being put in equivalential exchange acquire this status. I'm not saying that everything is rigidly contextual from society to society, but the instances of the creation of hegemonic fronts around the radicalization of democracy in particular historical contexts are going to be different from each other. However, I think the argument has to go more and more in the direction of having as many universal values, conceived in this particular sense, as possible. But we cannot go beyond that. Even some of *them* are complicated. For instance, what about the right of national self-determination? What if a country is committing genocide inside its limits? Has the international community the right to intervene or not? You see how contextualized even a principle like that is?

Q. In "Power and Representation," you discuss the complex dynamics of political representation, saying that "the identity of the represented is transformed and enlarged through the process of representation." You also say that the "representative *inscribes* an interest in a complex reality different from that in which the interest was originally formulated and, in doing so, he or she constructs and transforms that interest." Given this view of the transformative nature of representation, what are the consequences for a truly workable representative democracy?

A. The argument is more or less the following: why is a relation of representation needed in the first place? Simply because a decision affecting your own interests is going to be taken in a place from which you are materially absent. In that case, it's inherent in the nature of any representation that the process is going to be a two-way process. Let's take a simple case that I once used in a talk. Let's suppose that you have farmers in a locality and that the only thing the farmers are concerned about is the maintenance of a tax against the import of agricultural products. Let's say they choose a representative to parliament. The representative to parliament cannot simply go and say, "I represent the farmers and so I'll vote in that direction." He or she has to construct an argument to convince other sectors different from the farmers. The representative will have to speak about the effects on industry, the national interest, and so on. This type of discourse cannot be simply derived from the interest of the farmers; it has to articulate the interest of the farmers to other things going on in the national community. So, in some sense, by producing a discourse of articulation the representative is having an effect on the represented themselves because at the end of the process the represented will have a more complex identity, a political identity more incorporated into the national community, than at the starting point when the represented had a very narrow interest. (Of course, there are cases in which the representative can betray the represented, but these are banal, no?) When this process takes place, there is a circulation of discourses in this community by which a certain universality is created because at the end of the day the farmers of these localities will have not only a discourse about taxes on agricultural products but will have a discourse about the development of the national economy, threats, and so on which will transform them into a more complex political people. In this sense, the process is a two-way process from represented to representative and from representative to represented; but, at the same time, the identity of both is constantly changing in the process.

Now, there *are* situations—for instance, cases of total marginality—in which people are totally dispossessed of any identification with an interest and the discourse of the representative is very important at the beginning in order to give them some sense of identity that they otherwise lack. But I'd say that this overwhelming influence of the representative is the most democratic thing that can happen in that particular context because thanks to those new discourses, these masses are launched into political action and mobilization, and in the process of this incorporation they develop more complex discourses of their own. The whole Gramscian notion of the organic intellectual was based exactly on this notion.

Q. In *Deconstruction and Pragmatism* you say that both in advanced industrial societies and in Third World countries the fragmentation of social identities leads to a situation "in which the most difficult thing is how to constitute an *interest* and a *will* to be represented in the political system." The task of political leaders "consists, quite frequently, of providing the marginalized masses with a *language* out of which it becomes possible for them to reconstitute a political identity and a political will." Given, as you say, that "the relation representative/represented has to be privileged as the very condition of a democratic participation and mobilization," how does a member of a dominant group undertake the work of representing members of a minority group in an ethical and politically progressive way?

A. Personally, I don't think this representing is done by a member of the dominant group.

Q. Not at all?

A. No, unless there is a split in the dominant group, something like that. For instance, if you have a dominant group in the south of Italy which is very closely connected to the Mafia, and you have a local lawyer who starts agitating against the Mafia and trying to mobilize the unions and a variety of other groups, the discourse of this mobilization is probably produced, initially at least, by this lawyer. But this lawyer is not part of the dominant group; he or she is somebody who is trying to confront the dominant group. What *can* happen, however (and this is probably the central meaning of your question), is that if you have totally unarticulated masses whose level of political discursivity is low in this situation of marginalization, the task of starting to organize them can be initiated not only by progressive politicians but also by the church, by reactionary politicians, by fascists—and this actually happens all the time. But this is exactly where hegemonic struggle lies. The reason why there is this struggle between groups operating in that direction is that this original lack cannot a priori be identified with any positive content. For instance, in the south of Italy communist lawyers played this role of mass organization in the first decades after the Second World War simply by saying, "Well, here the working classes are weak, so we cannot base the party on union activity as in the north. But here we can make sure that the premises of the party and the unions, even if they are weak, are the rallying points of a set of struggles—struggle against the Mafia, struggle for school cooperatives, and so on." In that sense, they articulated a variety of causes, but this was a hegemonic decision that was in no way predetermined to be taken by the communists. In some other localities, Christian democratic lawyers played a similar organizing role.

Q. Compositionists often deploy the terms *subject* and *subject position* but tend to make these terms synonymous. You provide us with a more nuanced political vocabulary by making a distinction between the two. At stake in this distinction is the possibility of social agency. How might we rethink these categories?

A. In *Hegemony and Socialist Strategy*, Chantal and I reduce—I think incorrectly—the problem of the subject to the problem of subject position. The problem of subject positions can be retrieved by a structuralist discourse very easily because you can say that subject positions are objective positions within the structure and that what you have to do is to describe the structure as a comprehensive whole; in that case, the problem of the subject is reduced to positioning it within the structure. For example, the notion of interpellation in the Althusserian approach led to some extent to the idea that we recruit subjects into the structure in this way. That is the point where Slavoj Zizek criticized our position in one of the first reviews of *Hegemony and Socialist Strategy*. It was published in a journal of the Lacanians in Paris. It was a very positive, favorable, and interesting review, but the criticism was that we were confusing subject with subject position, while subject in the Lacanian sense would always be the subject of the lack—that is, not a point within the structure, but a point of a lack from which the logic of identification starts. This later became very important for how I developed my argument about empty signifiers. If the only thing we had was subject position, the very logic of identification, which involves the place of lack (the failure of the fullness), would have been unthinkable. So, today I distinguish between subject and subject positions in this sense. Subject positions are part of the symbolic, but the realm of subjectivity is not exhausted in the symbolic; otherwise, we would have simple identity and no process of identification. This is the main change that has taken place.

Q. We'd like to ask a related question. Throughout your discussions of the constitution of subjectivity, you shift the focus from "identity" to "acts of identification." At one point you say that we cannot "give clear criteria for choosing that with which to identify." This move from "identity" to "identification" is part of the anti-essentialist mode of theorizing that you're committed to. What's striking about this view of subjectivity is that it seems to suggest that essentialism and identity politics should be reconceived as an effort to provide both the content and the criteria for choosing (perhaps more accurately, for regulating) acts of identification. Do you agree?

A. Obviously, identity politics today is a very wide field. I don't think one can say that identity politics and essentialism, for example, are the same kind of thing. Identity politics has helped very much to expand the notion of subjectivity, and in this sense it has also helped to break with essentialism in many directions. There can be, however, a form of identity politics that tends to be a rigid essentialism, and any kind of identity can lead to that—working class identity could lead to that; liberalism in terms of individualism could lead to that—so there is no discourse which is immune to essentializing tendencies. But first I would like to put into question the rationalism of the notion of "criteria for choosing" because it's not that somebody constitutes one's own identity by choosing this or that. Identity construction is a far more complicated process, and anybody familiar with psychoanalytic literature knows the set of things that are involved in it. What I would try to say are two things. First, the distinction between identity and identification is central. If one could have identity without requiring acts of identification, one would be entirely at the symbolic level, in Lacanian terms, and the dimension of the real, which is absolutely central and which requires constant acts of reidentification, would not be possible. Second, acts of identification—when they take place—are not acts in which people choose to be this or that because of some set of reasons. The process is much less automatic than that. What I have is an original lack. This original lack requires acts of identification. These acts of identification depend on many things—among other things, availability. For example, I mentioned earlier that if you lack fullness, a discourse which attempts to fill this lack, if it is the only available discourse which tries these functions, will tend to be accepted, and when the identificatory acts have taken place it is very difficult to move away from them. But as far as the question is concerned, I would say yes. If we have an essentialism which tries to provide a priori both the content and the criteria of choosing, that would be something which would be incompatible with the notion of identification that I'm developing. But I want to stress that this affects not only identity politics but any kind of politics.

Q. Your work on hegemony suggests that it is *urgent* for progressive intellectuals—who must operate in the vacuum created by the collapse of Marxism and the redrawing of geo-political arrangements—to understand the logic of hegemony and develop our own hegemonic strategies. What shape would you like to see these strategies take?

A. I see the development of a theory of hegemony as a precondition for any kind of strategic thinking, having to combine various tasks, all of which would involve the expansion of rhetoric and rhetorical argumentation. In the first place, I see that we need to have some sort of combination of what I would call various branches, various kinds of poststructuralist theory—and not only poststructuralism; for instance, the Wittgensteinian approach is very important to this matter. Deconstruction provides us with a discourse concerning the deepening of the logic of undecidability, which, for the reasons I mentioned earlier, becomes central. Lacanian theory provides us with a logic of the lack, the logic of the signifier, which is also a discourse of enormous importance. I am very much against attempts of simply opposing deconstruction to Lacanian theory. The two can be productively combined in a variety of ways. And I think that the whole conception of a microphysics of power can be complementary to this effort. One should not dismiss the work of Foucault (or, for the matter, of Deleuze and Guattari) too easily, as some people tend to do. So what we have is a very complicated discourse which has to combine traditions of thought that began from very different starting points but that are all converging on political analysis. And the analysis of the complexity of present day society has to go together with an analysis of the proliferation of the places of enunciation. For instance, if a study in terms of places of enunciation were made, we would see that the transformation of politics over the last thirty or forty or fifty years—let's say, since the end of the Second World War—has multiplied the places from which politically consequential enunciation is possible. This is linked, at the same time, to the disintegration of classical forms of social aggregation.

Once you have this multiplication of the places of enunciation, you also have a proliferation of rhetorical devices; given that we are dealing with a process of argumentation and that this process of argumentation has to operate at a plurality of levels, we are in a situation in which social theory has to advance in the direction of generalized rhetorics. This means, also, that thought has to be more strategic; it has to emphasize the strategic dimension to some extent (but only to some extent) at the expense of the structural dimensions. A structural analysis tries to define matrixes of the constitution of all possible variations of meaning, while strategic thought tries to see constant displacements of meaning in a regulated way, but the very regulation is something that is submitted to the very process of a displacement. So, this is to some extent the kind of theoretical activity toward which the possibility of formulating a theory of politics oriented in a radical sense has to move.

Q. To so many people in the U.S., this will be counterintuitive because we are taught to think of freedom as a state we achieve, just as we are taught to desire a harmonious society where power is equally distributed or eliminated altogether. Specifically how do we effect such a monumental conceptual change in people's thinking about freedom?

A. Writing, giving talks. Academics are also part of the real world and their influence should not be undervalued. There are many intermediate areas—some forms of journalism, some other forms of the circulation of ideas—in which it is important to engage oneself. Also, intellectual developments themselves have produced a set of historical effects—the development of Milton Friedman's theory, for example—without which the history of the last few years would have been different. Thatcherism, for example, would not have developed the way it did. I think it is important that intellectuals not only produce high theory but that they also write in ways that are accessible to a wider public. It's very important to develop this intermediate area of discourse. In fact, many people are writing in these ways. This is not to say that abstract theory doesn't have its own role to play, but it's not the only kind of discourse to which we have to devote our time.

Q. Because you are attempting to think a unique radical project, one that avoids the debilitating particularism of postmodern thought and the idealistic universalism of Habermasian and other liberal projects, many theorists are likely to misunderstand or take issue with your work. Are there any specific misunderstandings that you'd like to address at this time?

A. Well, there have been several misunderstandings: some of them are just quizzical; some of them are more important. Among the quizzical ones, let me just mention one. I wrote an article about the impossibility of society, meaning that society cannot be sutured in certain ways. A few years later, Margaret Thatcher said that society does not exist, meaning obviously something completely different, meaning that for her only individuals exist. Some people in a certainly not innocent way tried to confuse the two statements. For example, Terry Eagleton wrote in his book on ideology about the theory of the nonexistence of society developed by Margaret Thatcher and Ernesto Laclau.

Apart from such malevolent attempts at conflation, there are other misunderstandings that are more important. First, from the Marxian side. I've never tried to simply put aside Marxism as something that had to be abandoned. What I tried to do is to operate deconstructively within Marxian categories in order to present a discourse which certainly goes beyond Marxism but which nourished itself from Marxism as one of its roots. Now, many orthodox people didn't take that lightly, and they accused me of being some kind of renegade. Another misunderstanding—one that is perhaps more important—is that my intermediate position (which is not intermediate actually but is something which tries to go beyond the two extremes) concerning universalism and particularism has also presented some difficulty. For instance, people coming from the Habermasian camp thought that my discourse should be identified with pure particularism, which is not the case. And some people have seen the attempt to introduce this universalistic function, in the way I have described, as an attempt to criticize the discourses of the new social movements, which is the last thing I was trying to do because, as I said, for me multiculturalism is one absolutely progressive phenomenon.

Finally, there is a discussion going on—but here I do not know if these are misunderstandings or simply ambiguities in my analysis—that has produced very different readings. For example, Slavoj Zizek has always insisted that I was developing a basically Lacanian approach without formally using Lacanian language. He insisted that the categories of antagonism and hegemony were a rediscovery of the Lacanian "real." There are other theoretical approaches which on the contrary are very positive about my work, but they don't like the Lacanian appropriation. This is probably a debate that is going to go on in the near future. I have received some pieces that try to enter into this argument, and I simply reserve my final opinion for when I can read all this literature.

Chantal

Mouffe

Rethinking Political Community: Chantal Mouffe's Liberal Socialism

LYNN WORSHAM AND GARY A. OLSON

Like her sometime collaborator, Ernesto Laclau, Chantal Mouffe is devoted to the project of deepening and extending democratic revolution. Crucial to this project is the work of radical intellectuals whose task is to develop vocabularies that give insight to people's experiences so that they may struggle more effectively to transform relations of subordination and oppression. What Mouffe finds missing today, however, is precisely an effort to create the necessary languages of political analysis and action: "There is a real lack of imagination on the point of view of left-thinking intellectuals in creating new vocabularies which will make possible a radical democratic hegemony." Aware that new vocabularies cannot consist simply of different words that better fit the world but must also include new practices and institutions, Mouffe is nevertheless principally concerned with developing a post-Marxist political theory, one that gives Marxism its "theoretical dignity" by revising it to address the needs of the contemporary situation. Poststructuralism and liberal-democratic political thought are the unlikely agents enlisted to accomplish a revision that leaves none of the constituent vocabularies unchanged. And it is through this revision, which she calls liberal socialism, that Mouffe hopes to advance us toward radical democracy as a new form of political community.

Central to this new vocabulary are the liberal-democratic principles of liberty and equality for all. Turning the tables on recent challenges to Marxism that are focused on the absence, in current geopolitical arrangements, of "actually existing Marxism," Mouffe observes that the problem with "*really existing* liberal democracies is not their ideals; their ideals are wonderful. The problem is that those ideals are not put into practice in those societies." The problem, in short, is to take liberal ideals seriously, including what Mouffe calls "the axiological principle of pluralism." This requires a return to a sense of "the political" and a politics that recognizes "the impossibility of a completely harmonious society." What this means, of course, is that antagonism, conflict, and exclusion are inevitable and unavoidable, and that pluralism can never be "total" (totally inclusive); it can only be "limited."

Given this sense of "the political," and in light of recent neoconservative and neoliberal efforts to use liberal discourse to restore a hierarchic society, Mouffe argues in the following interview that the task of the left is to create a sense of political community by establishing social division (and political frontiers) on a new basis. Toward this end, she offers an important set of distinctions: between antagonism and agonism, and between enemy and adversary. Mouffe explains: "'Antagonism' is a relation between enemies; they want to destroy each other. 'Agonism' is a relation among adversaries." The difference between enemies and adversaries is that "you respect the right of the opponent to defend his or her point of view." Stated somewhat more pointedly, the difference is that respect for difference is put into practice as the principle of action in a democratic political community. Here Mouffe departs from the liberal tradition to suggest that a struggle among adversaries is a struggle to establish a different hegemony, a transformation in the relations of power, rather than a substitution of one elite by another that leaves power relations substantially unchanged. The aim of radical democratic politics is transformative—to create institutions in which conflict does not take the form of an antagonism between enemies that want to destroy one another but instead takes the form of agonism. The category of the enemy does not disappear, as Mouffe goes on to explain in *The Return of the Political*. It remains pertinent as a way of identifying "those who do not accept the democratic 'rules of the game' and who thereby exclude themselves from the political community."

Important to the constitution of political community and to the formation of a radical democratic hegemony is the creation of what Mouffe calls a "chain of equivalence" among different struggles (for example, feminism, gay rights, and anti-racism). A chain of equivalence does not form in terms of a common essence shared by different groups but through determining the adversary, the "them" to which "we" are opposed. Mouffe argues compellingly that democratic objectives are not going to be realized through essentialist (and separatist) forms of identity politics that merely seek to recognize and celebrate difference. The danger of this kind of identity politics is that it does not recognize the importance of creating a chain of equivalence among different struggles. Politics in this form is, in her view, "the last avatar of liberal ideology and interest-group pluralism." The only way in which things are going to change, Mouffe argues, is "by shaping a very strong chain of equivalence among different struggles."

Clearly, rhetoric, argumentation, and the concept of consensus are crucial to the constitution of collective identities and to the functioning of the kind of democratic political community, or *societas*, that she envisions. *Societas* names a bond that links citizens ("friends" and "adversaries") together but that leaves room for dissensus. It is a bond created by common values (for example, liberty and equality), although the definition or interpretation of those values is always in contestation. For Mouffe, there can be no "rational consensus," which, in principle, means a totally inclusive consensus. Consensus is always based on exclusion, on an excluded element or interpretation. However, as Mouffe points out, "The recognition that any form of consensus, any particular order, cannot exist without some form of exclusion should not be used in order to justify the presence of exclusion." A radical democratic society is one in which every form and basis of exclusion is continually put in question.

Thus, where there is consensus there is exclusion, and where there is exclusion there is the operation of power and hegemonic struggle. *Hegemony* is perhaps the pivotal term in Mouffe's vocabulary. A concept she developed with Laclau in *Hegemony and Socialist Strategy*, hegemony represents a radicalization of the notion of *process*, of political process. Hegemony is not simply the domination by one group or idea over another; it is a process of ongoing struggle that constitutes and transforms society. It is through hegemonic struggle that political frontiers are drawn and redrawn and political communities are made and unmade. While the left has apparently lost an understanding of the logic of hegemony, the neoconservative and neoliberal new right has gained a hegemonic role in defining the terms of political discourse. What we are seeing,

Mouffe opines, is an "abandonment by left-wing parties of what should be their task, which is to provide an alternative to neoliberal [and neoconservative] discourse."

A particularly rich resource for shaping a radical democratic hegemony that could challenge the new right can be found in the often overlooked role that passions and affects play in politics. Whereas other political theorists maintain that people act in politics to maximize their interests, or act according to reason and rationality, Mouffe suggests that political passions—for example, outrage, anger, empathy, and sympathy—are a basis for constructing a collective form of identification. She asks a searching question: "What makes people crystallize into a 'we,' a 'we' which is to act politically?" Neoconservatives have been particularly effective in mobilizing people's passions toward non-democratic ends. "The real issue for democratic politics," Mouffe says, "is how we can mobilize those passions toward democratic designs." A good question indeed.

Q. As you know, the field of rhetoric and composition is devoted to the study of the practice of writing, broadly conceived. Having written several books and articles, you've certainly had occasion to reflect on the process of writing. Do you think of yourself as a writer?

A. Well, I certainly would like to think of myself as a writer, and in a certain sense I do. In fact, before studying philosophy and losing some of my writing skill, I very much wanted to be a writer. That's what I dreamed of when I was an adolescent. There are two obstacles preventing me from becoming the kind of writer that I would like. The first is precisely the fact that I do philosophy. I know that some people (I'm thinking of Derrida) can do both. Engaging in some kind of argument through my philosophy very much describes my style of writing. I used to write much better before. But probably the most serious obstacle is the question of language. I can think of myself as a writer when I write in French, but not when I write in English. I can write in English and in Spanish (I'm basically trilingual), but when I write in English, I write in a very different way: I'm much more matter of fact, I stick to the argument, and there are lots of things concerning style that I can't really do in English. Unfortunately, from the point of view of writing, I write more and more in English. I used to write in French and then have my articles translated into English, but of course that's not very convenient. Now, if I'm writing for an English journal, I write in English; if I'm writing for a French journal, I write in French. And I realize there's a big difference. When I write in French, I can write in a much nicer way, and there are lots of things that I can say in French that I can't say in English. So, when I'm writing in English, I don't think, unfortunately, that I'm much of a writer.

Q. You have coauthored an important book with Ernesto Laclau and have collaborated with him on other scholarly projects. Do you see collaborative work as a *political* choice, perhaps especially appropriate in the context of U.S. and European universities which privilege a model of intellectual work that is highly individualistic?

A. In the abstract, I'm in favor of collaborative work; but to be absolutely honest, when Ernesto and I decided to write a book together, it was not at all for any political reason that we thought it was good to do collaborative work. In a sense, I wouldn't even say it was a choice. We felt that we *had* to do it. It was important to us because we felt that we were both interested in the same kind of problems and that our two approaches needed to complement each other. In a sense, I felt that what I wanted to say I could not really say on my own, and I think Ernesto felt the same. We felt that by putting our two skills and points of view together we could make an argument that neither of us would have been able to make alone. I must say, though, that many of my feminist friends were against our collaboration. They said, "Be careful in writing with a man. You will see that he's going to receive most of the credit, especially given the order of your names." They were really saying that I should not do it, but I felt that it was not a choice, that we were compelled to do it. So I don't want to say that we made a political choice. It wasn't like that.

Q. In a theoretical development that parallels and coincides with Ernesto Laclau's recent work, you claim that "the reformulation of the democratic project in terms of radical democracy requires giving up the abstract Enlightenment universalism of an undifferentiated human nature," and you seek "a new kind of articulation between the universal and the particular." You offer an alternative model of rationality and knowledge based on the Aristotelian concept of *phronesis*, characterizing it as a more adequate way to "grasp the kind of relation existing between the universal and particular in the sphere of human action." In what ways is *phronesis* a more useful way to think this relationship?

A. I wouldn't put it quite as you have, that I offer an alternative model based on the Aristotelian concept of *phronesis*. It's true that in many of my writings I argue in favor of this model of *phronesis* as being more adequate, but it's always in the context of a particular debate that has been taking place in political philosophy among the so-called neo-Kantian thinkers and the neo-Aristotelians. As you know, there have been opposing schools of thought on this question: people like John Rawls and Jürgen Habermas on the Kantian side; people like Alasdair MacIntyre or Bernard Williams on the neo-Aristotelian side. My sympathies and affinities go toward the neo-Aristotelian in that precise debate. So, when I was intervening in that debate, I was intervening by saying that I think this model of *phronesis*, that practical reason understood not in the Kantian sense but in the Aristotelian sense, is more adequate for thinking about questions of morality, ethics, and politics. But when I'm thinking of an alternative model, and if I'm thinking of where I would locate myself, I certainly don't consider myself a neo-Aristotelian, even though if I have to choose between the Kantian and the neo-Aristotelian in this debate I would take the side of the neo-Aristotelian.

What I've been trying to do recently could be described as more inscribed within a Wittgensteinian approach. I find the late Wittgenstein more interesting, and this is where I find more insight for developing my project of a non-rationalistic conception of politics. Much of my work recently is an attempt to try to develop those ideas for the study of politics. Wittgenstein never developed his work in terms of its meaning for politics, but I think that it can be very usefully appropriated for political philosophy. Of course, there are some affinities here with Aristotelian *phronesis*. It's the question of practices. I think it's very important to be able to think in terms of practices because that's where I find the articulation between the universal and the particular made in a much more adequate way. Another instance of applying abstract principles to the particular, one that's very important, is Wittgenstein's analysis of a rule. He says a rule is not an abstract that you apply to a practice; a rule can only exist in its practical implementation. That's what I find to be the best approach to thinking about the articulation between the particular and the universal. I find Wittgenstein much more useful because it's very difficult to completely separate the Aristotelian conception of *phronesis* from the whole metaphysical system of Aristotle. I disagree, for instance, with MacIntyre when he proposes a return to Aristotle. I think that we *cannot* return to Aristotle today. Of course, there are insights in Aristotle that are important and that we can develop, but I think that Wittgenstein takes us a step further. So I would define myself as a Wittgensteinian but not as an Aristotelian.

Q. You say in *The Return of the Political* that "To defend political liberalism and pluralism within a perspective which is not rationalist, we have to see parliament not as the place where one accedes to truth, but as the place where it ought to be possible to reach agreement on a reasonable solution through argument and persuasion, while being aware that such agreement can never be definitive and that it should always be open to challenge. Hence the importance of re-creating, in politics, the connection with the great tradition of rhetoric, as suggested by Chaim Perelman." In what ways is this rhetorical model different from consensus-based models that have been criticized as being exclusionary, silencing minority viewpoints?

A. First, we should realize that there are different possible readings of Perelman. For instance, the Habermasians read him in a way that puts much more emphasis on the possibility of an inclusive consensus than I do. Everything hinges on the way one understands what Perelman means by "universal audience." The Habermasians believe that such an audience potentially exists and that we can speak to it. In my reading, this is not Perelman's view. What he says is that there are some disciplines like philosophy that by their very nature—what Wittgenstein would call their "grammar"—need to address themselves to the universal audience *as if there were such a thing*. But I think that Perelman makes it clear that there are always different conflicting conceptions of this universal audience and that therefore there cannot be such a thing. If one accepts this interpretation, Perelman's conception of consensus has to be envisaged in a different way, one that does not conflict with the view I'm advocating.

It's not that I'm opposed to the idea of consensus, but what needs to be put into question is the nature of consensus because I think that every consensus is by nature exclusionary. There can never be a completely inclusive consensus. I would say that the very condition of the possibility for consensus is at the same time the condition of the impossibility of consensus without exclusion. We can find this same idea in Derrida, but Foucault is the one who made it very clear. It's important to realize that in order to have consensus there must be something which is excluded. So the question is not to say that therefore we're not going to seek consensus. That's where I would differ with Lyotard. I think we need in politics to establish consensus on the condition that we recognize that consensus can never be "rational." What I'm against is the idea of "rational" consensus because when you posit that idea, it means that you imagine a situation in which those exclusions, so to speak, disappear, in which we are unable to realize that this consensus which you claim to be rational is linked with exclusion. And rhetoric is important here. But it must be understood that this is the way in which we are going to try to reach some kind of reasonable agreement—"reasonable" meaning that in certain circumstances this is how a political community, on the basis of a certain principle or something it values, is going to *decide* what is acceptable; but this process can never coincide with "rational" consensus. It is always based on a form of exclusion.

So, to come back to Perelman, when we are going to try to establish this form of consensus—in fact, to define what the common good is, because that's what is at stake in politics—we can't do without this dimension on the condition that we recognize that there is no such thing as a *universel auditoire* or the common good and that it's always a question of hegemony. What is going to be defined at the moment as the common good is always a certain definition that excludes other definitions. Nevertheless, this movement to want a definition of the common good, to want a definition of a kind of consensus that I want to call "reasonable" in order to differentiate it from "the rational," is necessary to democratic politics.

Q. One of the striking things about the essays collected in *The Return of the Political* is the way you work with other political theories to develop the elements of your theory of radical democracy. For example, in the opening essay you write, "My objective is to work with [Carl] Schmitt, against Schmitt, and to use his insights in order to strengthen liberal democracy against his critiques." Would you tell us about your style of doing theory—of working "with," "against," and "beyond"—and the way in which it seems to discursively enact some of your key concepts: antagonism, the friend/adversary relation, and articulation, to name three?

A. It's interesting that you point to the analogy between my concepts, the ones I take to be important, and my style of doing theory because it's true that when I'm writing I always need to think in terms of somebody I'm arguing against. I can't just sit and try to develop an idea if it's not in relation to somebody arguing something different. I've got a very adversarial way of arguing. And of course there are certain similarities here with my own conception of agonistic pluralism, my whole idea about what it is to argue in the field of politics. There are two points basically. One is probably something that is more an individual way of doing theory in that not everybody would necessarily work in this way: my way of doing theory is very political because the aim of my theoretical work is political. When I'm doing theory, it's always because I want in a sense to intervene in politics, so I think that's the reason why I can't really set my argument if it's not in terms of what we could be doing differently. That's important for my way of thinking. I don't think I could ever write something if it's not in terms of what I am arguing against.

Now, the reference to Carl Schmitt makes me want to say something more about that. I think that there is something here that is more specific than this general way of arguing in terms of adversarial relations. I've often been asked by people, "Why are you interested in authors who approach the democratic condition so differently from you politically?" Schmitt is probably the most extreme case, but I'm very interested in Michael Oakeshott and in other conservative thinkers. I find that conservative thinkers are more sensitive than liberals like Habermas to a certain dimension which I want to bring to the fore: the critique of rationalism. Both Schmitt and Oakeshott and many conservatives are against rationalism. They are also more aware (certainly, Schmitt is) of a dimension of what I call "the political": the impossibility of a completely harmonious society. Of course, once that's said, they derive from this the completely opposite conclusion from the one I'm deriving. In part, that's why I find somebody like Schmitt such a challenge. In a sense, he's my favorite adversary because I start from quite a few premises that I share with Schmitt, and at some point I take the opposite direction. I think I'll always feel that it's either Schmitt or me who is right. For Schmitt, the type of pluralism I am advocating is absolutely impossible. His whole project is to put into question the very possibility of pluralism, precisely because if one takes seriously the question of the political, one cannot be a pluralist. My aim is precisely the opposite: to criticize the liberal for *not* taking serious advantage of the political and to try to reformulate a liberal democratic theory that would be *both* pluralist *and* political. That's why I think Schmitt is so important and why I'm working *with* him, in the sense of having some points at which I agree with him, but *against* him because we are coming from those common points to argue exactly opposite points of view and to derive opposite consequences. So, I obviously have a very specific adversarial relation with Schmitt.

Q. In "Post-Marxism Without Apologies," you and your coauthor identify yourselves with post-Marxism in an effort to "give to Marxism its theoretical dignity," which as you say "can only proceed from recognition of [Marxism's] limitations and of its historicality. Only through such recognition will Marx's work remain present in our tradition and our political culture." What would you say to Marxists such as Teresa Ebert who contend that we must return to Marx and to a classical Marxism in order to rebuild the left?

A. I must say that I find it very difficult to understand how some people can contend that we should return to Marx and to classical Marxism in order to rebuild the left. It seems to imply that nothing really important and new has been happening in the world since Marx, that all the answers were given in Marx and that what has been wrong is that Marx has not been well understood or well applied, and that by coming back to Marx they seem to imply that they are going to find a solution. For me Marx is a very important point of reference. One of the problems with much of what is going on today is the belief that one can get rid of Marx. Sometimes I'm amazed by the fact that some people speak or write as if Marx never existed. I find that very problematic. It's really an impoverishment of our way of thinking about politics to say, "Well, Marx was wrong." So this is certainly something I find terribly problematic. But I find just as problematic the idea that Marx was right and that we've got to go back to Marx. It's as if in physics some people were to say we've got to go back to Newton. I think that Marx is a very important point of reference, but if we want to be faithful to the spirit of Marx we should remember that Marx after all was the first one to say, "I'm not a Marxist" and that he was against this kind of mechanistic application of his code. So this is very important if one wants to be faithful to the teaching of Marx.

As an example, take the notion of antagonism. Marx was really the first to develop this notion, so I certainly don't want to get rid of him. I think that too much of liberal theory and democratic theory today is postulated on an exclusion of antagonism. My problem with Marx is that he reduced the question of antagonism to class antagonism. He certainly did not apply this notion to other social relations where antagonism can also exist— for example, the questions of race and gender. So what we need to do is to widen this notion of antagonism in order to make it much more productive for understanding the new forms of antagonism which have emerged. This is not going *back* to Marx; it is being faithful to Marx by developing his ideas in completely new and different situations. Of course, we define ourselves as post-Marxist but insist very much on the fact that it's "post" but it's also "Marxist." It's not a rejection of that tradition, but it's a tradition that can only be defended by developing it, not by coming back to "the truth" that was given one-hundred years ago to one single individual.

Q. In your efforts to deepen the democratic revolution, you seek to radicalize the idea of pluralism because, as you argue, it is at the heart of modern democracy. You also say that it is necessary to recognize the limits of pluralism. The liberal ideal of pluralism has a hold on a great many people. Would you discuss why it's necessary to move from a "total pluralism" to a more politically democratic and limited version?

A. Here, I think I need to make a series of distinctions because the term *pluralism* is so differently understood and is used in so many different ways that in order to specify what I mean I need to give a few explanations. First, we need to be able to see the difference between what could be called the empirical fact of pluralism and what I call the axiological principle of pluralism. For instance, when I say that the idea of pluralism is at the heart of modern democracy, I'm referring to pluralism as an axiological principle—contrary to John Rawls, for instance, who constantly speaks of "the fact" of pluralism, by which he means simply the existence of a plurality of conceptions of the good. That's not the way I speak of it. *Of course* there is the fact of pluralism, but from that fact nothing derives. From the fact of pluralism, one could just as well derive an authoritarian politics as a democratic one. In a sense, this is Thomas Hobbes' position; he is also very aware of the fact of pluralism, but from that he argues that the only form of order to impose is an authoritarian order. So, no things derive necessarily from the fact of plurality.

I think what's important in what I call modern democracy— and I present this as being a transformation of "regime," in the sense of a new symbolic ordering of social relations—is the acceptance of pluralism *and* of conflict (which in my view derives from pluralism), a recognition that we are going to try to create a society in which conflict is not repressed and which is going to make room for dissensus. That's the type of pluralism that comes from the liberal tradition. I value the liberal tradition because I think that this idea of pluralism cannot be derived from democracy. It's important to realize that in modern democracy we've got an articulation between two different traditions: the democratic one of popular sovereignty, and the liberal one of individual liberty. When I think of pluralism, I think of the idea of individual liberty in John Stuart Mill; that's what I think of as the liberal tradition. If we take pluralism to be this recognition of individual liberty, the kind of society in which we are not going to try to impose a single conception of the good life on everybody but in which we are going to allow for conflict about what the good life is, then this is incompatible with "total plurality." I could make the same kind of argument here that I made before with the question of consensus: the condition of the possibility for this kind of pluralism is at the same time the condition of the impossibility for a total pluralism. Total pluralism would mean that we are going to allow people who are *against* pluralism to have an equal say. In that case, of course, you are not going to be able to have a pluralist society.

Let me give you an example of this: a few years ago during the Rushdie affair in Britain there was a small but vocal group of fundamentalist Muslims who argued that in the name of pluralism they should be given the right to kill Rushdie legally. They were saying to the British state, "This is what our religion tells us to do, and if you are really pluralist, if you want to recognize *all* our differences, you should allow us to kill Rushdie and not go to jail." I remember that some liberals were in fact quite worried about this argument. They were saying, "They do have a point. If we are pluralists, we should take those demands into account." Of course, the British state did not allow them to do it, so the state was accused by those fundamentalist Muslims of not being liberal pluralists but liberal fundamentalists. They were saying, "The values that you impose are the values of liberalism; you are not really pluralists." Of course, in a sense they were right, but I think there is no way to escape this. If you want a pluralist society in which there is going to be the possibility for people to express a form of dissensus, then you need to create some kind of consensus on the value of pluralism, of pluralism as an axiological principle. This means that certain people who want to establish a theocratic kind of society are not going to be able to; their voice is not going to be accepted. So in order to have a pluralist society, you cannot have total pluralism because total pluralism would mean that the enemies of pluralism are going to be able to destroy the basis of that society.

Q. Much of your recent work attempts to reformulate the concept of citizenship for a radical and plural democracy. In this effort, you seek to draw on and at the same time transcend two models: the model offered by liberalism and the model offered by civic republicanism. Both of these models inform, either implicitly or explicitly, much composition theory, where the idea of creating an informed, educated citizenry is a goal of many compositionists who see the classroom as the ideal forum for democratic education. Unfortunately, a common view has been of a citizenry composed of an aggregate of autonomous individuals who can band together to pursue self-interest or a sense of the public good. In what ways might compositionists better understand citizenship as a political identity and an articulating principle?

A. What I've been trying to put forward is what I call an agonistic conception of citizenship. In considering the idea of citizenship, I criticize the liberal tradition of interest-group pluralism because for them there is no such thing as citizenship. Of course, they are citizens but they are defined by the position of rights that they are going to exercise against the state. So I don't think they could probably be called "citizens" in the meaning of this term in the civic republican tradition, for instance. I've been arguing that it's very important to reintroduce this idea of citizenship which was present in the civic republican tradition: citizenship is an identification, a principle of action. The problem with the civic republican tradition was that in the way that it had been formulated there was no room for pluralism. It postulated that there is a common good and common moral values that we all need to share in order to be good citizens. To be a good citizen is to identify with this common good and with these new shared moral values. I find this an interesting corrective to the disappearance of the idea of the common good and of this feeling of being part of a political community which has been erased from the liberal discourse, but we cannot really accept such a conception, for if we're going to be faithful to the value of pluralism, we need to make room for dissension about the common good and for different understandings of citizenship.

There is not only one position on what it means to be a good citizen. For instance, I speak of what it means to be a radical democratic citizen, which is different from being a neoliberal citizen, or a neoconservative citizen, or even a social democratic citizen. It's important to recognize that in a liberal democratic society, there must be some kind of consensus, but a consensus about the main values that make us members of this political community. At the same time, we must recognize that those values—which are liberty and equality for all, which for me are the basic ethical-political principles that inform human coexistence in a liberal democratic society—only exist in their interpretation, and those interpretations will always be in conflict. Take liberty. What is liberty? There is not one rational understanding of liberty. There are many different understandings, and they are all in competition. Take equality; it's the same. What is equality? There will always be struggle about what equality is. And the "all"? Who belongs to the "all"? This is another term which has been an object of contestation for a long time, and it always will be.

So I think that the consensus needed in a liberal democratic society will always be what I call a conflictual consensus. We agree on what makes us citizens, what links us together, what certain values link us; but when it comes to *defining* those values, to *interpreting* them, there will always be competition. That's what I call an agonistic conception of citizenship. A conception of citizenship is a certain understanding of what those definitions are, a certain interpretation of those values. There must be room for different interpretations of citizenship. We should not teach people that in order to be a good citizen you must act according to the common good; there is no such thing as "the" common good, even though it's an horizon that we cannot do without. Politics must always think in terms of the common good, but we will always define the common good in different ways, and that's what is missing from the civic republican conception. They believe there is a common good and that we should try to find it. Of course, the liberals just say there is no common good. But you cannot completely eliminate the notion of the common good either—otherwise you are in a pure politics of interest groups, and I think that's not good for democratic politics. So, I want to maintain reference to the common good but to pluralize it and make it a contested issue. That's what I call an agonistic conception of citizenship.

Q. So is the common good a kind of floating empty signifier to you?

A. Yes, yes. In fact, it would be a signifier in the way in which Ernesto defines it, a kind of horizon of meaning, something we will always be trying to define. And, of course, it relates to hegemony. A group is hegemonic when it has been able to define what the common good is. A conception of the common good is always a hegemonic definition, meaning that it will need to exclude other understandings of the common good. I think it's very important that radical democrats not pretend that they've got some kind of rational privilege in the way in which they are defining the common good. If, as I very much hope, at some point the definition of the common good that will become common sense and that will be accepted by everybody as natural were to become the radical democratic one, this doesn't mean that we will have therefore reached a rational consensus. It will mean that the other definitions have been displaced, but they are not going to disappear. They can always come back, so we constantly need to fight in order to maintain this hegemony. That's why I think, for instance, it's very dangerous to think in the way that Habermas does: that there is an evolution in which there are kinds of thresholds of democracy and of morality where once these thresholds are reached, in principle there cannot be any setback. It's always going to be a struggle. We can never take them for granted. I think, for instance, that women are very much aware of the fact that rights can be won *and* lost. It's not that because we have won one fight we are therefore forever free. We have got to be vigilant with respect to rights because they can be won and lost. This struggle for hegemony and for defining the common good will always go on. There is no point at which it is impossible to lose these rights because we have somehow coincided with rationality.

Q. In composition studies, two terms in particular tend to function as floating signifiers, categories that are essentially ambiguous, open to debate and struggle: the "intellectual" and "democracy." Both of these terms circulate in the disciplinary discourse quite freely and serve as warrants for diverse claims and diverging political projects; consequently, they provide an opening for the field to be articulated to a neoconservative political agenda. For those of us who want to see composition, and education in general, move decisively in the direction of a radical democracy, what do you see as the role of the intellectual in promoting the radical project of democracy?

A. It depends on what we understand by "move decisively." If we mean decisively in the sense that it's something that cannot be overturned, I don't think there is ever the possibility of moving in that way; but if by that we mean strong progress in that direction, this is different. I see intellectuals as the ones who elaborate and provide the vocabularies that then can be appropriated by people in order to give some thought to their experience so that they can transform their relations of subordination and oppression. For instance, in radical democracy it's important to formulate conceptions of equality and liberty in order to allow for a new common sense about equality and liberty to be defined. At this precise moment, the task of the intellectual is particularly crucial. We are facing a big deficit of these kinds of new vocabularies, and we are at a moment in which the hegemony of neoliberal discourse is so strong that it seems as if there is no alternative. Unfortunately—and I am speaking of Western Europe—many socialist parties seem to have been convinced of that. What's happening with Tony Blair in Britain is very much the acceptance of the dominant discourse of neoliberalism and of Thatcherism and the redefinition of the objective of the left *within* those parameters. There seems to be no alternative vocabulary. There seems to be no other way to think about this issue, and this is linked to the crisis of social democracy, the crisis of the communist model. Those are vocabularies that do not have any purchase on people's struggles, so the only kind of political language present today is neoliberalism.

There's a real lack of imagination on the point of view of left-thinking intellectuals in creating new vocabularies which will make possible a radical democratic hegemony. If we think, for instance, of what has been happening with neoliberalism, this neoliberal hegemony has been a long time in the making. In fact, there have been people like Friedrich Hayek and Milton Friedman since the 1940s; when there was a stronger social democratic hegemony, they were completely marginalized. They were in fact as marginalized in a sense as we radical democrats are today. Nevertheless, they organized themselves, they created the Mont Pelerin Society, and they slowly began to develop ideas that at some point in the '70s came to be appropriated by movements like Thatcherism and like Reaganism in America in order to give a new form to the political experience and to create new forms of subjectivities. What is missing today is an effort by radical democratic forces to begin to elaborate alternative vocabularies in order to undermine the hegemony of neoliberalism. When I say "vocabularies," of course, I'm not speaking only in terms of linguistics; it also means thinking about what kind of institutions and what kind of practices could be the ones in which new forms of citizenship could exist and what form of grassroots democracy could be conducive to the establishment of this kind of radical democratic hegemony. That's basically what intellectuals should be doing in my view.

Q. In *The Return of the Political*, your notion of politics begins with a view that the criterion of the political is the friend/enemy relation. This perspective makes antagonism and conflict central to politics. In fact, you say it is illusory to believe that antagonisms could ever be eliminated. This view flies in the face of the more comforting belief that political action will eventually lead to the end of politics and the institution of a society free of conflict. What you offer instead is *agonistic pluralism*—a view of the creation and maintenance of a radical and plural democratic order based on a distinction between "enemy" and "adversary." Would you elaborate on the distinction between enemy and adversary and discuss its importance to the formation of your concept of political community, or what you call *societas*?

A. I've already touched on some of these issues when I was talking about the question of pluralism, the question of consensus, and the question of agonistic citizenship. What I will insist on is the importance of the distinctions I'm making between "antagonism" and "agonism," "enemy" and "adversary." "Antagonism" is a relation between enemies; they want to destroy each other. "Agonism" is a relation among adversaries. I mean "adversaries" not at all in the sense in which this word is often used by liberal thinkers. The term *adversary* is a very common term not only in politics but in ordinary discourse. But what most liberal thinkers mean when they speak of the adversary is what should more properly be called an "opponent" or a "competitor," in the sense that what they want to do is occupy the place of the other. It's a struggle which is seen not in terms of hegemony but is as if I were in a neutral terrain and what I want to do is to push those people who are in power from this place so that I can occupy their place without transforming the relations of power. This is the way in which the struggle among adversaries is thought by liberal theorists, and it's usually seen as a struggle among elites, a question of replacing one elite with another. Unfortunately, that's also the way that the new socialist parties in Europe are thinking about politics: it's to push the conservatives out in order to occupy their place but not at all to establish a new hegemonic form in transforming the relations of power. Because of globalization and neoliberal dominance, they believe that the only thing they can do is to occupy the place of the other and do things a little bit differently.

When I speak of adversary, I'm not thinking at all like that. Struggle among adversaries is a struggle in order to establish a different hegemony. The difference is that you respect the right of the opponent to defend his or her point of view. It is an agonistic struggle among different understandings of citizenship. It is not the Jacobin model in which you want to destroy the other in order to establish your point of view and then not allow the other the possibility of coming back democratically. That's the struggle among enemies—the complete destruction of the other. In the struggle among adversaries, you respect the right of the other to have a different understanding of what citizenship is. You in fact are considered part of the political community because you have got the same reverence for the values of liberty and equality. The point is that you've got a different understanding of those values and of course you want to fight for the establishment of a new hegemony.

So I would say that the antagonistic dimension doesn't completely disappear because there is this question of the transformation of relations of power, but it is, so to speak, domesticated. In fact, I have argued that the main aim of democratic politics is to transform an antagonism into an agonism. Probably, "transforming" is not exactly the right word because once antagonism has emerged, it's very difficult to transform it into agonism. A better way to put it is that it is an effort to create the institution that would make it less likely for antagonism to emerge by providing the possibility for this to take the form of agonism. It is very important for democratic politics to recognize that there is an ever-present possibility of antagonism but that democratic politics is a type of institution in which this is not going to take the form of a struggle between enemies but between adversaries because that is what makes possible the recognition that we are part of a democratic political community. When I speak of *societas*, that is what I have in mind, this bond that links citizens together but which leaves room for dissensus. It is a bond created by common values, but those common values, as I said before when I was speaking about agonistic citizenship, are formed by a consensus that is always conflictual. What I call a *societas* is a modern democratic political community linked together precisely on that basis, not by a substantive idea of the common good because that would be a consensus which does not leave room for dissensus. We need consensus, but it needs to be consensus which makes room for different understandings of values. That's what I think *societas* is.

Q. You propose that the elaboration of a non-individualistic conception of the individual is one of the most pressing tasks necessary for movement in the direction of a radical and plural democracy. Toward this end, you suggest that the social agent is constituted by an ensemble of subject positions which are constructed by a diversity of discourses, among which there is no necessary relation but rather "the constant subversion and overdetermination of one by the others." Through this view you attempt to account for the possibility of agency as well as for such totalizing effects as the social relations of gender, race, and class. First, would you tell us how this conception of the individual does not easily slide back into the very individualistic conception of subjectivity that you seek to displace, and, would you also elaborate on what seems to be a very useful distinction between agency and subject position?

A. Well, I must confess that I can't really answer about the distinction between agency and subject position because I don't really understand what this distinction could be. I've always had a problem with this idea of agency. It's as if they have put two different problematics together that don't fit. There is no place to introduce this category of agency, which to me belongs to a completely different semantic world than what I am trying to put forward with the idea of subject position. I can't see what in this notion of agency would be different from subject position. Probably, what people want to insist on when they speak of agency is that you are going to be an actor. But, of course, this is what I try to express by the question of "identification," the fact that on the basis of different subject positions, suddenly there is some kind of crystallization into an identification and that is what will make people act. If your identification is along class lines or gender lines, then you will act accordingly. It's that move toward action. But I would try to think of that in terms of identification, which is made possible by the crystallization of a subject position.

But the more general issue here is my view on whether the individual does not slide back into an individualistic conception of subjectivity. What I'm criticizing when I speak of an individualistic conception is basically the liberal idea that is dominant in liberal political philosophy—which, by the way has been highly criticized by the communitarians—that an individual's rights exist so to speak out of the blue, that first you are a fully fledged individual, and then you enter into different social relations. This idea definitely needs to be criticized because epistemologically it doesn't make any sense. The work of Charles Taylor is important in that respect. He has shown how this liberal idea of the individual is a very specific historical position; it never existed before. And the work of people like Jean-Pierre Vernant and Pierre Vidal-Naquet has recently shown that this is a completely different conception of the person. So what we take to be "the" individual is really a result of anhistorical and discursive construction. Of course, it is a construction that should be valued and defended, so I don't want to reject this idea. In fact, it's very much the product of what I've insisted is an important part of modern liberal democracy: the idea of pluralism as individual liberty. I think that this is to be defended, but it needs to be expressed in non-individualistic ways, as precisely a product of inscription in certain types of practices—which, by the way, is important because it also makes you realize that you cannot take this individual for granted, that if you don't reproduce those practices which make possible this individuality, and this form of democratic individuality, you might lose it. I would say, without being unduly pessimistic, that in many areas we are in danger of losing this form of individuality because of the many practices of homogenization which don't make possible the re-creation of those forms of democratic individuality. If you take those forms of the individual for granted, as being given, then you don't feel the need to constantly create the practices by which those forms are made possible.

Q. One could argue that the debate about multiculturalism in the U.S. is stalled precisely by a politics of recognition and an imperative to celebrate difference. What do you see as the dangers of the construction of political identities exclusively through a logic of difference?

A. The main danger from the point of view of radical democratic politics is that we can only judge this according to what your political objective is. If we are committed to radical democratic politics, many forms of identity politics are dangerous because they go against the recognition of the importance of creating what I call a "chain of equivalence" among different struggles. They tend to put into question, as being something that will go against their demands, the very idea that they should link their struggle with other struggles. Even if we recognize why, in certain circumstances, people are driven to react in separatist ways, it is ultimately very negative politically because this certainly is not the way in which democratic objectives are going to be realized. Particularly in the current situation with this strong hegemony of neoliberalism, the only way in which things are going to be able to change is by shaping a very strong chain of equivalence among different struggles. Those forms of identity politics in fact go against the very idea of this chain of equivalence. I would say that they are basically the last avatar of liberal ideology and interest-group pluralism. It's a new form of interest group pluralism which is defined in another way, not so much in terms of interest groups but more in terms of community identities—but it's exactly the same kind of model. Having all those different groups goes against the very idea of the importance of creating this unity because these groups would see unity as undermining their struggle. At the moment when a kind of hegemonic form of politics is more necessary than ever if we are really going to be able to fight the dominant hegemony, those forms of the celebration of differences are developing a kind of politics that makes it much more difficult to do that. That's my main problem with it.

Q. In *Hegemony and Socialist Strategy*, you argue that the new social movements—feminism, gay rights, anti-racism, and so on—do not necessarily have a progressive character and that "it is therefore an error to think, as many do, that they spontaneously take their place in the context of left-wing politics." You go on to say that "There is no *unique* privileged position. . . . All struggles, whether those of workers or other political subjects, left to themselves, have a partial character and can be articulated to very different discourses." We wonder if there are not situations in which political identity and agency *are* produced almost spontaneously and by necessity. For example, consider the four-hundred-year long ordeal of American slavery and the subsequent history of economic and political disenfranchisement (bell hooks calls it "terrorism"). If "position" is discursively produced by historical events, would African Americans *not* have an oppositional consciousness and a certain epistemic privilege vis à vis U.S. race relations?

A. I do not really see how any group can have epistemic privilege. The case of African Americans could in fact be seen as a good example of my thesis that there is no social movement that will necessarily have a progressive character. But one needs to distinguish what I call "oppositional consciousness." There, yes, I can see why, given the history of slavery and political disenfranchisement, African Americans would have an oppositional consciousness, but for me that doesn't bestow any kind of epistemic privilege. Moreover, this kind of consciousness can be articulated in many different ways. There are ways in which this consciousness could be articulated in a way that is not progressive. I don't think that Farrakhan's movement is progressive from the point of view of democracy. I can understand perfectly well why in certain circumstances an African American would be attracted to that movement. So it's not at all a question of blaming, and there are many reasons that explain why this phenomenon can operate. But once that's said, this can't be seen as a movement of a progressive character. The same argument can be made for the question of feminism. There are many many different ways in which feminism can be articulated, and some of them are not progressive in the least. The same can be said for the gay movement. We don't have to believe that every form of reaction against gay oppression is progressive. You could have a form of gay politics that is very sexist or against women, for instance, if it comes from male gays, or one that is not progressive from the point of view of anti-racism. You can have groups that are obviously oppressed but who react against those forms of oppression in a way that can't be called progressive. And I think this is true for every type of group. There is no form of oppression which automatically leads to reacting in a progressive way. That's why there is always the possibility for a potentially democratic movement to be neutralized and recuperated by right-wing politics.

Q. You say in "Politics and the Limits of Liberalism" that "No state or political order, even a liberal one, can exist without some forms of exclusion." Your argument is that "it is very important to recognize those forms of exclusion for what they are and the violence that they signify, instead of concealing them under the veil of rationality." This seems to suggest that *full* participation in the political order is impossible. If so, and if violence and exclusion are structurally inevitable, on what basis do minorities—or any excluded group, for that matter—contest and seek to overturn their systematic exclusion? That is, how can minorities claim that the violence done to them is unjustified and intolerable?

A. The recognition that any form of consensus, any particular order, cannot exist without some form of exclusion should not be used in order to justify the presence of exclusion. People could argue, "Since we will never have a completely integrated society, why should we bother to fight at all?" But there's absolutely no reason to make that argument. We can at the same time recognize that there will always be some forms of exclusion, but nevertheless fight in order to make those forms of exclusion as minimal as possible. In fact, that is specifically the radical democratic understanding of citizenship: knowing that we are not going to realize a fully inclusive society. A radical democratic society should be a society in which exclusion should constantly be contestable because we should constantly wonder if those demands which have been excluded at a given moment should not now be included—knowing that you can never reach the point in which *all* demands are included. There are demands which by their very inclusion, for instance, will undermine some gains and some rights, so there will always be exclusion. The question is to constantly try to problematize those exclusions.

The second question is about how groups are going to fight to overturn exclusion. There are two points here that I want to make. One is that it's basically a question of hegemony. That's why the concept of hegemony is so important; it allows us to understand that what is considered legitimate and illegitimate, just and unjust, at a given moment is always the result of certain relations of power. You can always transform them. Take the case of feminism or the struggle against racism. Those were forms of exclusion that not that long ago were seen as based on nature. It was natural because *of course* blacks were inferior and women were inferior. But these are things that can be transformed—even those things that are presented as a question of nature. There is always a terrain for intervention. That's why, in general, a poststructuralist or deconstructionist view is important; it impedes the naturalizing of some forms of exclusion and makes it all a question of the struggle for power and hegemony.

There is another point I want to make which I've been working on recently and which is linked to what I see, paradoxically, as the positive aspect of liberal universalistic discourse. The articulation between liberalism and democracy that I was talking about before is a very conflictual one. Carl Schmitt (but also other theorists) speaks of the basic contradiction between liberalism and democracy. I think he's wrong. It's not a contradiction. I've been trying to present it as a tension. There is a tension because the logic of democracy, which is the logic of popular sovereignty, goes against the universalistic logic of pluralism. In order to have a democracy—a working democracy—you need to have a *demos*. You need to have a *demos* for citizens to be able to exercise their right of citizenship. To have a *demos* means that you need to have a "we" and that some people need to be excluded from that "we." This is an effect of the democratic project because in order for a democratic society to exist, for democratic citizens to be able to express their sovereignty, you need to have the *demos* and the *demos* needs to have people who are not part of the *demos*. That's the logic of exclusion. On the other hand, I think that it is important that this logic of democracy be articulated with the liberal discourse of human rights, of universality. This discourse goes in the opposite direction. It goes toward what we could call a logic of universal inclusion, which of course is impossible because if it were realized it would in fact undermine the possibility of democracy. But I think that it can also be seen as an important polemical instrument to problematize the exclusions which are needed by democracy. It's a way to subvert the need for closure. I think that democracy as popular sovereignty implies a moment of closure. Of course, there are many different understandings of liberalism, and here I'm basically thinking of what can be called ethical-political liberalism—the discourse of human rights, let's say. This can never be realized. Citizenship by itself means specific citizenship. But the discourse of liberalism in its universality allows us to subvert the necessary closure that is inscribed in the very idea of democracy.

Again, let me give an example: it's clear that most of the struggles for inclusion that have been fought by women and by blacks have used the universalistic discourse of "all men are equal": if "all," why not women; if all, why not blacks? I think that rhetorically the power of liberal discourse is very important, and I see human rights as a very important rhetorical device in order to interrupt and challenge the necessary closure inherent in the democratic project. There's a very productive tension between the two. But if we had only the liberal logic of universalism, it would mean the very disintegration of the political community and of self-government. On the other side, if we had the pure logic of democracy without this universalistic human rights discourse, we could find ourselves in a situation in which it would be too easy to justify those exclusions, to justify that one group of immigrants, for example, should not be given rights. So I think that this link between democracy and liberal democratic discourse is not a tension that we should try to overcome because it is in this space of tension that we can really create a pluralistic democracy. For me it's not at all something that must be seen as a bad thing; it's precisely the most positive feature of a liberal democratic society.

Q. What forms of violence—real and symbolic—are acceptable? Where do you draw the line?

A. There's absolutely no way in which one could draw the line from an abstract point of view. It's always a question of what's acceptable in *which* circumstances and by *whom*. I don't think that there is some answer that could be given for everybody and for all societies, even for liberal democratic societies. It very much depends on which positions you take, which view of citizenship you are going to defend in the agonistic contestation among notions of citizenship, because obviously the answer to that is going to be different according to the circumstances. Obviously, there are forms of violence which are perfectly justified in order to put an end to a dictatorship. I'm very much worried about the ultra anti-violence movement because violence is not necessarily bad. Violence in some cases might be absolutely necessary in order for a democratic society to emerge. This is a line that we need to draw, but we need to draw it always in different circumstances and there is no answer to where it should be drawn.

Q. In *Hegemony and Socialist Strategy* you and Ernesto Laclau differentiate among "subordination," "oppression," and "domination." Focusing specifically on subordination and oppression, you state that a relation of subordination is one in which an agent is subjected to the decisions of another. A relation of subordination becomes a relation of oppression once it is constituted as a site of antagonism and conflict. For those who are committed to identifying the discursive conditions for the emergence of social agency and collective action, the problem, you say, is to explain how relations of subordination become relations of oppression. This distinction offers a rich vocabulary for analyzing and intervening in prevailing social conditions. Yet, the distinction between subordination and oppression seems to be less central to your later work, where *subordination* is the apparent term of choice. Given the centrality of "antagonism" to your theory of politics, do you no longer find the distinction between subordination and oppression useful or valid for the political analysis of social relations?

A. I still find this distinction valid, and probably the reason why you feel that it has become less central in my later work is that I have been developing a kind of theory which is more linked with an analysis of the relations of subordination and is not so much concerned with the emergence of struggles against those relations of subordination. But in a different context—for instance, if I were interested in understanding the dynamics of a certain political movement—I probably would speak more of oppression and less of subordination. So it is not that I've abandoned the distinction or that I find it less interesting; it's more that given the type of theory I was developing, I was more concerned with the relations of subordination. I'm sure that in certain contexts I will still use the question of oppression. I must say that sometimes in speech one does not always tend to be so rigorous with one's terms, so probably in this very interview I've sometimes used the term *oppression* when in fact I should have used *subordination*, but I still think that the distinction between these terms is important.

Q. In the closing pages of *Hegemony and Socialist Strategy*, you and Ernesto Laclau argue persuasively that the neoconservative and neoliberal new right has taken on a hegemonic character which "seeks a profound transformation of the terms of political discourse" and which, "under the cover of the defence of 'individual liberty' would legitimize inequalities and restore hierarchical relations which the struggles of previous decades had destroyed." In that book and in your recent work, you propose a hegemonic strategy for the left that does not renounce liberal-democratic ideology but deepens and expands it in the direction of a radical and plural democracy. In the face of a neoconservative effort to restore a hierarchic society, you say that the hegemonic task of the left is to establish social division on a new basis. What new social divisions do you believe might be most productive in moving us toward radical democracy?

A. Well, I'm a bit puzzled about this. I don't remember that we argue exactly in those terms, saying that the hegemonic task of the left is to establish "social division" on a new basis. In fact, if we did say that, I'm not quite sure what we meant. If we used the term "social division," I certainly would not use the term today.

But what we had in mind, and what I still would use today, is the notion of "political frontiers," which I think is quite different. The question of social division is not something that we establish; the social division is there. But the hegemonic task of the left is certainly to establish political frontiers on a new basis. If we are going to formulate the question in that way—what new types of political frontiers could be more productive in moving us toward a radical democracy—that is something which I can see as having real meaning. I think one of the important tasks today is the redrawing of the frontier between left and right, not only in terms of radical democracy, but in terms of the very definition between left and right. One of the problems I see—and this is linked to what we were discussing before in terms of the hegemony of neoliberalism, the fact that the socialist practitioners see themselves more as competitors than as adversaries with respect to the practice of the right—is that there's been a real blurring of the frontier between left and right, which unfortunately has been received as progress. It is viewed that the more societies move toward some kind politics of the center, the more democratic they become. In France, for instance, one of the main themes of the socialists is that they've abandoned the Jacobin imaginary and now there is some kind of politics of the center, more of a consensus between left and right. In Britain, Tony Blair speaks of what he calls "the radical middle," again thinking that the politics of the center is what is needed. And lots of people have been arguing that the left/right distinction is something that is archaic, obsolete, and something that must be abandoned. I think that's very problematic. Of course, this is connected to my whole idea about politics being about adversaries and agonism. And one can see the reasons why this has happened. Certainly, the collapse of communism is one important reason. The main political frontier which had existed since the end of the Second World War, which was linked in terms of democracy versus communism, has collapsed. People are arguing that now there is no more antagonism. It's also been argued that the class problem has disappeared because societies now are basically societies of the middle class, so that is a reason why politics should take place at the center. Many different reasons go into explaining this transformation of politics, but I think that this is expressing simply the hegemony of the neoliberal discourse. It's an abandonment by the left-wing parties of what should be their task, which is to provide an alternative to neoliberal discourse. Because they don't have any alternative, they then occupy the same terrain and simply propose little differences.

I think we very much need to redraw a new frontier. I'm not saying that we should go back to the old frontiers because those old frontiers have collapsed, not only because of communism but also because social democracy has become inadequate in terms of many demands. So we need to rethink how we are going to define the difference between the left and the right, and that's what I call drawing a new political frontier. We need to draw a new political frontier and redefine who the adversary is, who is the "them" to which the "we" of the radical democratic forces need to be opposed in order to establish its unity. If we are unable to define that, there won't be any possibility of creating a chain of equivalence because the very condition for creating this chain of equivalence is to establish a "them." In fact, it is in the establish-ment of the "them" that the chain of equivalence can be estab-lished. By the way, what allows for this chain of equivalence to not erase differences is that its unity is not given by a common essence, because a common essence would reduce all the struggles to one single thing. The unity of this chain of equivalence is created by determining the "them" to which we are opposed. So there are still many different struggles, but they are linked together by the fact that we establish a frontier in which we are going to fight the one who we define as our adversary, and this is the condition for defining our unity. You can't have a democratic politics that is going to try to transform a given hegemony into a transformed relation of power if it's not on the basis of determin-ing who is the "them," the adversary, the one we are going to oppose. This is precisely what the politics of the center and the kind of consensus politics that is dominant today is making impossible. They are predicated on the fact that we no longer need those frontiers, that this was something good for old-style left-wing politics, but now the present condition of democracy goes against that. That is completely wrong.

I'd like to add something here that for me explains the urgency of this, even if we are not thinking in terms of the radicalization of democracy but only in terms of defending this miserable part of democracy that we've got at the moment against the danger of the extreme right. Those frontiers which the left is unable to redraw with respect to the right are now being redrawn by the extreme right, which is in fact re-presenting itself. I'm thinking of the situation in France and also in Austria, but to a certain extent there are similar movements in many European countries, movements of the extreme right which are presenting themselves as the only alternative to this wishy-washy consensus type of politics that the democratic parties of center-right and center-left are offering. They are redrawing the frontier between "them"—the alternative to the present order—and those who don't want to change anything. Those movements are getting more and more popular support precisely because they are able to redraw those frontiers while the other groups are not even trying. So, I think politics needs to have political frontiers. In a democratic setting it's going to be redrawn by the extreme right in a way that is going to undermine the very basis of the democratic system.

Q. In her extended critique of *Hegemony and Socialist Strategy*, Rosemary Hennessey argues that your focus on the deepening of the democratic revolution through the extension of equality and liberty to the historically marginalized masses is inadequate. She argues that "the systematic workings of power are invariably not dismantled by campaigns aimed solely at the redistribution of political liberties." The point she makes here is traditionally Marxist—that a truly radical politics, appropriate for the present context of global neocolonialism, requires the redistribution of material and economic resources by democratizing the economy. Given that we are in what has been called an advanced stage of capitalism, in which first world multinational corporations are rapidly and continually redrawing political frontiers and creating new colonies, how do you see an anti-colonial or postcolonial politics taking shape in your recent work on "liberal socialism"?

A. I don't know the work of Rosemary Hennessey, and I don't know what critique she makes of *Hegemony and Socialist Strategy*, but if what she argues is that the systematic workings of power cannot dismantle solely the redistribution of political liberties, and if she makes that as an argument against us, then I'm really puzzled because I agree with that. I don't think that we ever argued that it was only a question of political liberties. The deepening of the democratic revolution through the extension of equality and liberty is not at all simply a question of the redistribution of political liberties. *Hegemony and Socialist Strategy* makes quite clear that a very important component is the question of the extension of liberty and equality *in the sphere of the economy*. Unfortunately, this is not the only person who has not been able to understand that; we are often accused of having abandoned the economy or of having abandoned the question of class. But I really can't understand why people can read the book and say something like that because a very important part of hegemony is the question of the economy. Obviously, this is absolutely central. It's not only a question of political liberties. The question of democratizing the economy is very much part and parcel of the process of radical democracy.

For me it's absolutely evident—in fact, so evident that some liberals sometimes accuse us of being obsolete traditional Marxists because of the emphasis we are putting on the economy. We are also attacked for putting *too much* emphasis on the economy and for being unreconstituted Marxists, so it really depends on what you want to hear in our work. Also, the idea of liberal socialism is precisely where we are trying to make a plea that the question of the economy is central. This is probably more developed in my recent work where I engage with the work of Norberto Bobbio. Bobbio has been one of the very few who for a long time have been arguing that the socialist goals—in terms of the transformation of the economy—could be realized, and he also argues that they can only be legitimately realized within the framework of a liberal democratic regime. I agree very much with that position. In fact, this is what we are arguing in terms of the radicalization of the democratic project, that there is room within the framework of a liberal democratic regime—understanding that a certain symbolic ordering of social relations according to the principle of liberty and equality for all—for a radical transformation of the economic system. Or to put it another way, what we are arguing is that there is no necessary link between what is called political liberalism (what I prefer to call ethical-political liberalism) and economic liberalism or capitalism. Of course, many liberals argue that the two necessarily go together. But people like Bobbio and other liberals—in fact, even John Rawls, for that matter—argue that private ownership of the means of production is not a necessary condition for a liberal political system.

So I think it's very important to realize that there's been an historical articulation here, but it's contingent and it's perfectly imaginable that we could have a liberal democratic state (which would be liberal in the sense of pluralist and in the sense of defending the ideas of liberty and equality for all) that is not capitalist. That's also the kind of argument that Samuel Bowles and Herbert Gintis have been making in the United States, for instance—the way in which you can radicalize liberal democratic ideas, extending them to the economy. After all, I think that it's important to realize that we could not find a more radical principle to fight for than the one of liberty and equality for all. So the problem with liberal democratic societies—*really existing* liberal democracies—is not their ideals; their ideals are wonderful. The problem is that those ideals are not put into practice in those societies. So the question that I think radical democracy is very much about is how to force those societies to take those ideals seriously, to put them into practice. That, of course, will mean establishing some form of liberal socialism, and this means a democratization of the economy. So I don't see how we could be accused of not taking that dimension into account.

Q. In *The Return of the Political*, you are clearly working against any conception of politics that is rationalist, universalist, and individualist. At one point, you write, "The rationalist longing for an undistorted rational communication and for a social unity based on rational consensus is profoundly antipolitical because it ignores the crucial place of passions and affects in politics." A number of feminists, including feminists of color, as well as other left-progressive scholars have attempted to theorize what might be called "political emotions," or those emotions that are discursively produced to perpetuate relations of subordination or which may lead to a struggle to end such relations. Anger and outrage as well as empathy and sympathy are key emotions that feminists have explored in their efforts to build multicultural coalitions. In your own work on the articulation of political identities, do you see a role for political emotions?

A. I'm very sympathetic to this emphasis on political emotions because this is really part of my main struggle at the level of theory against a rationalist conception of politics, which takes two different forms. One is the traditional liberal one which believes that in the field of politics, people are basically moved by their interests; they are trying to maximize their interests. There are many different forms of that, the latest one being rational choice. But it's basically an argument proposing that what moves people to act is a calculus of interests. In reaction to this, we have been witnessing in recent decades the development of a new model of democracy called "deliberative democracy," which in different ways both John Rawls and Jürgen Habermas belong to. They are saying that it is not really interests but reason and rationality that should guide the democratic citizen. Democratic citizens are not going to act simply to try to maximize their interests, but they are going to act according to reason and rationality. What both models completely leave aside is the whole notion of what I call "passion" in politics because I think that is what moves people to act in politics. It's not that reason and interests have no place, but I think that these are not the main motives for people to act. It's what I call "passion." Outrage, anger, empathy, sympathy, and those kinds of emotions are part of the same family in criticizing the rationalist model. But once that's said, what I'm trying to say with this question of passion is different. I consciously use "passion" not "emotion."

Richard Rorty once said to me, "This is the Gallic form. We Americans speak about 'emotion'; you Gallics speak about 'passion,' but in fact we are speaking of the same thing." I say that we are *not* speaking about the same thing. Certainly, for Rorty emotion is a bit too soft; the whole dimension of antagonism is not present. As he says, for him democratic politics is about people being "nicer" to each other. I think that's a bit too simple a way to think about democratic politics. Emotions, of course, are important, but I want to insist on the notion of passion to reintroduce the adversarial "we/them" relation, the possibility of agonism.

I'm also particularly interested in thinking the whole of collective identity. In fact, this term *passion* is a kind of placeholder for many things. It's a placeholder in part for some emotions certainly, but also for desire and for the collective form of identification. That's where I think that my understanding of passion is very close to the Freudian notion of identification, but in the sense of "collective" identification. What makes people crystallize into a "we," a "we" that is going to act politically? I think that rationality is not going to allow this, and it's not the search for the maximization of your self-interests. That's why liberals are so bad at understanding the phenomenon of political masses. When suddenly there is an eruption of those collective forms, they see it as some form of archaism or irrationality because they feel that modern citizens should not act in that way. Well, I think that this is a dimension of the field of collective action that is basically what politics is about; it's central. We need to understand the dynamics of those passions in order to realize that it's very important not to try to erase those passions or, as some would say, to try to relegate them to the field of the private. The real issue for democratic politics is how we can mobilize those passions toward democratic designs.

To come back to the position of the extreme right, I think that they are very much aware of the importance of passion and are trying to mobilize those passions toward non-democratic designs. The way to fight them is not by appealing to reason, as if people should act rationally. No, it's trying to see how you can intervene in that field and mobilize those passions. The only way to impede those efforts by the right is to try to offer another outlet for those passions toward democratic designs. So it's not the same thing as political emotion, even though I think there is a certain common ground between what I'm trying to do and the insistence of those feminists about the whole notion of political emotion.

Q. In "Feminism, Citizenship and Radical Democratic Politics," you suggest that the objective of many feminist struggles is to make sexual difference irrelevant in the social relations in which it operates. Although you seem to agree with this objective, you also state that you are not in favor of the total disappearance of sexual difference as a valid distinction. As you know, a number of feminists on both sides of the Atlantic have argued that sexual difference cannot become irrelevant in any social relation until the institution that creates sexual difference and which makes it relevant—the institution of compulsory heterosexuality—is destroyed. What do you think about this view?

A. In order to answer this adequately, I think we would need to take much more time than we can here. I personally do not believe that the institution that creates sexual difference is compulsory heterosexuality. Of course, it's one of the forms in which it is created, but I think there are many many different ways in which sexual difference is made pertinent and relevant, and this is only one of them. I've been interested—particularly during the time that I was associated with the journal *m/f*—in insisting on feminism's need to recognize the multiplicity of forms in which sexual difference is discursively constructed and established. This can be through the discourse of the economy, of the law, of religion; there are many different forms through which sexual difference is created.

Also, and this will probably take us to the more general issue, I certainly don't believe that the aim of the feminist struggle is to abolish sexual difference; even if that were the aim, I don't think it's possible. If we take psychoanalysis seriously, I think this is what psychoanalytic theory tells us. It's not a question of abolishing difference. What I think we as feminists need to do is to fight against those forms of sexual difference which are constructed as forms of subordination, because obviously many of the forms of sexual difference are constructed that way. I don't think that sexual difference in itself necessarily implies a relation of subordination, but of course in our type of societies many forms of sexual difference are constructed as relations of subordination. That should be the aim of feminists. In some cases, the strategy is just to make sexual difference irrelevant. For instance, in the field of politics, certainly in the field of citizenship, I don't think that it should be relevant—in the same way that it should not be relevant if you are black or white or blue eyed or blonde or gray. It's not a question, as Carole Pateman would have it, of having a feminine concept of citizenship as opposed to a masculine one. It just should not make any difference.

In many cases, equality comes by making this distinction absolutely irrelevant. In other cases, it would be in constructing sexual difference in a way that is equalitarian but not by abolishing it, not by making it not pertinent. This, again, is a struggle which we can't have a blueprint for. I think that clearly feminists' aim should be to fight against forms of sexual difference that are constructed on the basis of relations of subordination. Of course, this links to the question of compulsory heterosexuality, but I don't think that there is any particular privilege to this. One can perfectly well imagine a society where there would not be compulsory heterosexuality and in which we would have many forms of sexual differences that are very negative for women and that are constructed on the basis of relations of subordination. So I definitely do not believe that there is some privilege there.

Q. Some of your work has been quite controversial and had led to various critiques and, perhaps, misunderstandings. Are there any specific misunderstandings of your work that you'd like to address at this time?

A. There have been so many; let me just mention three. One we have already dealt with, which is the question of the economy. That's clearly a widespread misunderstanding—that we are abandoning the question of class, abandoning the question of economy. All our development of hegemony has been to say that we need to articulate the struggle around issues of class with struggles against sexism and racism. So the economy is very much present in our work. That's basically why we define ourselves as post-Marxists. We think that there is something from the teaching of Marx that we want to keep because it's very important and we can't abandon. The second point—which again I find difficult to see how people cannot understand, particularly after the explanation we gave in "Post-Marxism Without Apologies"—is the question of our discourse being idealistic. We've tried often and repeatedly to insist that by "discourse" we don't just mean something related to speech and writing but something similar to what Wittgenstein meant by language games. It's something composed of practices, institutions, discourse; it is something that is very very material. But apparently people can't take the point, and they go on saying that this is an idealistic view. They want to say it's not materialist and that we don't take into account something like reality. Again, this is a basic misunderstanding that is the origin of many criticisms.

The third one, which I also find difficult to understand because I've so often been arguing precisely the contrary, concerns the question of pluralism. We've been accused of defending some kind of total pluralism. We are presented as defending some kind of extreme postmodernism for which there's no way of thinking about any kind of structure. In many papers and conferences I've said that I want to distinguish our form of pluralism both from the liberal view of interest group pluralism and also from what I call some extreme forms of postmodernism. I've been arguing that we need to be able to distinguish between differences that do exist but should not exist. We should fight against them because those differences are based on relations of subordination; and there are differences that do not exist but should exist because it's precisely by the nonrecognition of those differences that relations of subordination are created. But of course it means that not all differences are to be valued and it's not a total pluralism. I've made this argument in very many places. Nevertheless, I quite often see critiques that say I'm defending some kind of extreme pluralism. Those are probably the three more common misunderstandings. I can think of many others, but these probably are the more important ones to consider because they are saying exactly the contrary to what I think.

Stuart

Hall

Cultural Composition: Stuart Hall on Ethnicity and the Discursive Turn

JULIE DREW

Stuart Hall has been preoccupied with how to think questions of race for more than thirty years. From his own deliberate attempt to think of himself as a "black man" and as a black public intellectual, to his recent work on postcolonial theory, Hall continues to focus on the formation and material effects of concepts of ethnicity. The term *multiculturalism*, for example, is played out very deliberately in his writing in order to identify and work against what he sees as the negative meanings embedded in the term. Multiculturalism is often equated with an essentialized notion of ethnicity in which "everybody secure within his or her own ethnic group is competing with other ethnic groups on a hierarchy for resources" while each individual is "slotted into a pluralist space." Hall, however, supports the notion of an "adjectival multiculturalism" that expresses a "sliding and translation" between differences, a "mongrelization" of cultural identities without idealized, homogeneous, originary pasts. This attention to language is part of what Hall calls "the discursive turn." Like Raymond Williams, whom he speaks of with great admiration and affection, Hall sees language as an unavoidable game of meaning-making that cuts both ways. "Everybody," he argues in the interview below, "has an ethnicity because everybody comes from a cultural tradition, a cultural context." The essentialist notion of ethnicity is "extremely damaging" because it "doesn't allow for pluralization; it doesn't allow for hybridization." But since ethnicity as a concept is necessary, there must be, for Hall, a "contestation around the very term itself."

Hall believes that certain concepts are indispensable despite their traditional connotations, so we must use them under erasure until we develop a more adequate language. Those concepts can "no longer be said and thought in the paradigmatic position of their old theoretical constructs," according to Hall, and that is why we are in the "deconstructive moment." In order to think and act, we must position ourselves within contemporary language games on the "underside, the disturbed, subverted side of the positive concepts."

The cyclical nature of "the world of theory" is also characterized by both trace and emergent elements. New theories are not generated without "taking on board the baggage that the concepts are already carrying from older meanings." Hall sees scholarship that simply "operates on the new" without excavating and addressing the traces of older meanings as untenable—untenable and potentially damaging because theory is "a deadly serious matter." Hall cautions against "subscribing wholly" to one theory or theorist. Theory will always entail "dogmatic closures" that will try, as all closures do, to establish "identity positions," and those positions that are necessarily left outside will become "the excluded, constituted other that will return to haunt the field and disturb the paradigm." This, argues Hall, is "precisely why one cannot become the disciple of a theory.

The deliberate tension of Hall's relationship to language and to theory is echoed in his political work in Great Britain. As a black public intellectual and an activist of the New Left, Hall nevertheless has tried to avoid representing the life experiences of others. His own life was "deeply protected" in that he "did not share the experiences of people who were constantly refused housing and decent public services." He stresses that he was "deeply and profoundly . . . privileged in relation to the majority experience of blacks." To offer himself as a representative of "black experience" would have been "a categoric mistake," a "deep, profound misrecognition." Hall notes that we often misrecognize the way in which class intersects with race in precisely this way.

In the following interview, Hall declares that intellectuals are often party to such misrecognitions, that they sometimes "come on as if what they want to do is divest themselves of their intellectual responsibility and just be the guys in the hood—and they're not." The politics of academic work is found, not in intellectuals' "turning up in front of the factory gate and pretending they're Lenin," but, rather, in "turning ideas into everyday practice." "It has to do," he insists, "with their attention to the articulation between the philosophical and the popular."

Hall's comments regarding the pedagogical uses of the popular will be of particular interest to compositionists. In recent years the field of composition and rhetoric has paid a considerable amount of attention to pedagogical methods that incorporate popular culture into the classroom. While Hall certainly approves of the popular as an instrument of pedagogy and as an object worthy of critical inquiry, he cautions against what he sees as "academic repetition." He speaks of growing "disillusionment" with cultural studies now that it is no longer in its "ascendancy." He recognizes the unfortunate proliferation of pedagogical practices given a cultural studies tag that are "simply a waste of everyone's time." He offers, however, a firm admonition to remember why we went to the popular in the first place: "It's not just an indulgence and an affirmation; it's a political, intellectual, pedagogical commitment. Everybody now inhabits the popular ... so that does create a set of common languages. To ignore the pedagogical possibilities of common languages is extremely political."

Q. You have described identity as a "production," a "matter of 'becoming' as well as of 'being.'" You have been and continue to be a prolific writer; you write passionately, often personally, and you publish in various public and academic forums. How does your writing continue to construct your identity? And how does your cultural and historical identity continue to construct you as a writer?

A. The point that I have made about identity is, perhaps, a familiar one, but it is worth restating. It's the notion that identity is always in the making. There is one idea of identity as a fixed position, and another idea that identity is relative to the extreme. There is now a third position in that debate because I think those people have moved away from identity as process and have sometimes gone right over to the point where identity is nothing at all; it's a kind of open field where one just sort of occupies a particular identity out of habit. So it is that there's no fixed identity, but it's not that there's just an open-ended horizon where we can just intentionally choose. What that means is that there is no final, finished identity position or self simply then to be produced by the writing. Any cultural practice plays a role in the construction of identity. While it's true that you may have a very clear notion of what the argument is and that you may be constructing that argument very carefully, very deliberately, your identity is also in part *becoming through the writing*. It's inflected by the very language you use because in order to express something, to occupy language, you are necessarily playing a game—a language game that other people have played and used. Meaning is already sediment in that language, so you reactivate all those other marks of meaning as well as what *you're* trying to say. Of course, writing is also a production, a production of knowledge and a production of a version of the self.

Q. Historically and contextually, at the moment of writing.

A. Yes, exactly. And we therefore occupy our identities very retrospectively: having produced them, we then know who we are. We say, "Oh, that's where I am in relation to this argument and for these reasons." So, it's exactly the reverse of what I think is the common-sense way of understanding it, which is that we already know our "self" and then put it out there. Rather, having put it into play in language, we *then* discover what we are. I think that only then do we make an investment in it, saying, "Yes, I like that position, I am that sort of person, I'm willing to occupy that position." Then it becomes a kind of space of enunciation for further thoughts and a space for other kinds of practices. The reverse is also true: you can produce a self in writing that is not close to a position you want to hold for very long, and others that go off on tangents and don't engage the unconscious.

Q. Do you go back and read your own writing?

A. I do, yes—not to think how wonderful I was, but because I'm not a terribly good editor of my own writing. Three weeks later I will see things wrong with my writing that I didn't see at the time. So that's one kind of rereading. Another kind of rereading is sort of incidental. I've been winding up my work after being at the Open University for seventeen years, so I'm throwing away a lot of paper. I'm really surprised by all kinds of things, particularly a certain kind of recurrence, a certain consistency that I hadn't been aware of. And I say this because I'm not attached to consistency. I don't think it's a terrible thing that I'm saying something different now from what I said in the 1980s. Times have moved on, so why shouldn't one say that? So I'm a bit surprised to find that I still think about class what I thought in the 1960s. It's really quite sad to find out that one doesn't move on, or that one has only five thoughts in a lifetime. [Laughter.] Perhaps there are ten good things you might think in a lifetime and you sort of go on thinking around those same lines. But I am struck by the fact that I have been preoccupied by the same kinds of questions throughout many different kinds of writings, and I only see this retrospectively when I look back at things I've written.

Q. So there is a consistency, not so much in the answers but in the kinds of questions you ask.

A. Yes, exactly. The answers change, the answers *have* changed, certainly, but the questions have remained largely the same.

Q. You've written eloquently about Raymond Williams' influence on your own intellectual growth. You've also spoken very specifically about his commitment to using what he called a "shared" vocabulary and about his writing: his style, his ability to address a wider audience than just his immediate peers. How has Williams' writing, as such, influenced your own writing? I'm thinking particularly of your comments in "Only Connect" that address his sentence structure, his word choice, and so on.

A. His is a very distinctive style. He has more than one style, for one thing. He has a style that is directed toward a general public, a general readership rather than a narrowly academic or intellectual one; and he has a more serious, intellectual style that is unique in a number of ways. One is the ability to connect areas and experiences and structures, as he does with a phrase like "structure of feeling." This is an oxymoron because you know that structures don't have feelings and feelings don't have structures. But "structure of feeling of an age" is exactly the intangible ethos that is the complex, cultural outcome of a variety of different practices. If you can grasp what the structure of feeling is, grasp the sort of background, the emotional canvas on which other debates are taking place, you can perhaps also see that the people who are opposed in terms of their positions also share something vital, something immensely important, because they're both part of that structure of feeling. Although they may oppose one another in terms of their logical political argument, they also have a basis for a dialogue. So, Raymond is wonderfully suggestive, and I like *Key*

Words very much because it's neither a strictly lexicographical exercise nor an attempt to write a definitive history. Those things are extraordinarily rich for me in terms of his writing.

But there *is* a problem, and I would locate it around his generalizations. His generalizations are very abstract. Now, that may sound paradoxical, because aren't all generalizations necessarily abstract? If you look at some of the abstract notions—abstract, as it were, above the concreteness of the things that they're referring to—you can't help but ask yourself, "What is it about the nineteenth century that he's talking about here?" His writing, his generalizations, drive some people wild. I think his writing takes this maddening form for two reasons. First, British intellectual life is not very philosophical. It's not philosophical in the way in which French intellectual life is. It's full of moral, social, and ethical generalizations, but it's not full of philosophical concepts; it's not good at conceptual theory. Books like *Culture and Society* and *The Long Revolution* are Williams' attempts to inhabit an English idiom that is distinctive because it's morally and socially rooted, and they are attempts to think in a sort of general way. It's as if he wants to use moral, concrete concepts in a philosophically abstract way, and I think this is because he inhabits a particular discourse that relates to nineteenth-century moral philosophers and writers. That tradition, which comes out of thinkers such as Leavis, is very literary and doesn't have access to a continuous philosophical tradition.

But there's a second reason for the maddening form of Raymond's writing, which some people cite as a sort of evasiveness in his work. This is partly because the language Williams uses is negotiating his complicated relationship to Marxism. He wants to go on using certain basic Marxist ideas, but he refuses to be trapped in the whole series of Marxist concepts. So he will not use "mode of production" until very late because this term is already fixed in a certain way that he doesn't want, but he does want to talk about what he calls a "general mode of life," and this both is and isn't a proper Marxist concept. I think this tension in Williams is one that runs throughout most of British cultural studies, a tension that comes from being influenced by certain very important concepts in Marxism, being concerned about questions that Marxism put on the agenda, but steadfastly refusing the reductionist forms of Marxism that have dominated intellectual life. All of us have been inside and outside that vocabulary, wanting to use it without being trapped by it. Much of Williams' work is marked by this struggle. It's not so much in the later work, because the later work was written in the 1970s and 1980s when a particular kind of Marxism did become a permissible language through Althusser, Gramsci, and others. And although he's very much *not* an Althusserian, I think that in a work like *Marxism and Literature* he felt able to engage Marxist ideas much more directly than he had in his earlier work. The earlier work is a struggle to avoid being pigeonholed by a language that he nevertheless wants to echo.

Q. Almost like a rebellious son who is never quite able to leave the family.

A. Yes—never able to leave the family, never wanting to leave the family entirely, but wanting to refuse the patriarchal authority and the reductionism that a certain kind of canonical language has. This goes back to your original question. It's a production of a new kind of self in writing.

Q. You say in "Our Mongrel Selves" that the millions of currently displaced people are "obliged to inhabit at least two identities, to speak at least two cultural languages, to negotiate and 'translate' between them.... But they are also obliged to come to terms with and to make something new of the cultures they inhabit, without simply assimilating to them." You also cite Salman Rushdie's description of "mass migration" as a gift of great possibility for the world. Do such discussions, wherein the cultural "obligations" of the displaced and the cultural "possibilities" of hybridity are touted, cast the diasporic subject in the role of sacrificial lamb? Can such language really intervene in the diaspora experience?

A. I don't think it puts the migrating subject in the position of the sacrificial lamb, though genuinely living between and within two or more cultures is at best a difficult proposition. Nor do I think that I use the diasporic or migratory subject as a kind of celebratory figure, which is something that I've been accused of. Migration is a very troubling experience in terms of the sense of uprootedness, the sense of displacement, that the majority of people who migrate must contend with. Some people choose to do so, can afford to do so and have another life, but the majority of people who are migrating have no choice. Migration is a fantastic, mass phenomenon of the late twentieth century—both forced and free migration. There's nothing celebratory about it. So, this is to explain my use of this figure. It *is* a figure for me, and it is a metaphorical figure—not entirely but partly. What I mean by this is that what the migratory or diasporic subject has been obliged to go through is increasingly the condition of everybody, whether they're migrating or not. It's not that the migratory subject is some wonderful or special being, or has been selected by god—or punished by god—but simply that his or her experience now coincides with what is increasingly a global experience. Fewer and fewer cultures are originary; fewer and fewer cultures can identify any lines of stable continuity between their origins and the present. The more we know about all these cultures, including the ones that do their best to preserve their internal homogeneity, the more we understand how diverse their sources are, how much they've been influenced by others, how much they've borrowed across the borderlines. The borders have all been porous. So, our condition, the condition of all of us— even people who haven't moved an inch—is to discover our increasingly diverse cultural composition.

The migratory subject, then, who has been obliged to discover this condition and who is more self-conscious about it than somebody who has never moved physically, is at least in the position of pedagogical figure because that experience becomes a kind of representative experience from which we can draw lessons. Now, "What lessons?" you want to know. Not the lesson that these are wonderful people who have special gifts or anything like that, but just that they can do what everybody is now required to do, which is to produce culture, produce new cultures from old, produce new cultures out of the bringing together of diverse, other cultural traditions. That's what we're *all* doing, but the migration and diasporic experience highlights that process. There's no mistaking that every diaspora—no matter how much it is transfixed by the dream or myth (and sometimes the grim reality) of going back to where it came from (which usually involves displacing people who are now there)—has to come to terms with the new conditions in which it exists. Think of the cuisines of the Jewish diasporas. Jewish cooking is, of course, about Judaism and its extremely strict rules of transmission precisely about diet; and yet, Jewish cooking is an incredibly diverse field *because* it is a diasporic field. Ashkenazi Jews have taken on Middle

Eastern cooking, whereas Sephardic Jews have taken on North
African cooking. That's what Jewish cooking is: it is the sum of
these differences. The differences aren't nothing. They broadly
identify as a cultural configuration, something that is no longer
one thing. If you've ever been through a diasporic experience,
you would understand that this is how culture works. Of course,
what you often do is exactly the opposite: you manufacture a
myth of homogeneity, of purity, but the reality is that you live in
a mixed, mongrelized world. And, increasingly, everybody lives
in a mixed, mongrelized world. The non-diasporic English
subject who hasn't moved an inch from Hackney or East Bethnal
Green is living in a cultural world of which his or her grandmother
or grandfather could not have dreamed. They wouldn't recognize what this world is. The diasporic experience is a figure; it's
a figure for the increasing pluralization of cultural forms and for
the insistence that culture works not by perfectly reproducing
itself into infinity, but precisely by *translating between*. Nor is the
diasporic figure just an imitation, a mimicry of what it's supposed
to subscribe to; it's a third thing, shifting and in process, at once
making cultural meaning and being made by culture.

Q. Words like *imitation, mimicry, shifting*, and *in process* might just as
easily be used to describe "the postmodern."

A. It's very reflective of that. The postmodern has a certain twist to
it, conceptually, that I find myself not really being able to follow.
First of all, there's a kind of celebration of postmodernity that I
think is a deeply Eurocentric and Western phenomenon. The
"end of history" idea can only be embraced by those who've
benefitted thus far from history. If you've lost at history, you
need a little bit more history; you need history to go on for a bit
longer before you'll want to declare it to be at an end. If you've
done extremely well out of the historic process, you can declare,
"Here we stand and no further; there's nothing more to come."
It's a kind of Parisian, left-bank closure that says, "We have got
there, so this is the end of history for everyone."

Q. If we decide not to play, then there is no game.

A. Yes, then the game must be over. Then there's the celebration of
fragmentation, and I don't want to celebrate fragmentation. If
you've come, as I have, from a culture like the Caribbean where
everybody is diasporic, then you know that indigenous people no
longer exist. Everybody who's there came from somewhere else:

Africa, Europe, China, East India, and so on. If you've been through that, and you've been through the plantation and slave experience, you don't celebrate fragmentation. So I emphasize diversity rather than fragmentation: many elements, none of them wholly integrated, but not just shards, not just splinterings. The act of splintering doesn't suggest to me that anything emerges from it. Out of diversity, however, come new culture, new cultural forms. Out of cultural crossovers comes new music, not emptiness. So, I want to stay this side of validating a kind of postmodern excess that I don't find myself comfortable with. When I say that many of the ways that I'm trying to think questions of how culture operates and how identity operates are inflected by postmodern theory, I don't mean that sort of thing.

Q. But you do invoke theory, postmodern and otherwise. Do you find pleasure in the act of theorizing, as many intellectuals do? And why do you think we speak so seldom of that pleasure?

A. There's no question about that: it is a pleasurable intellectual activity, and we don't talk about it. On the other hand, in the end theory is a deadly serious matter, but not as theory. I'm not interested in theory as such. I'm only interested in theory insofar as it helps our common-sense understanding. There's a lot of playful postmodernism that is an innocent enough game; there are many more dangerous games than playful postmodernism. On the other hand, postmodernism applied to really thinking about the relations between the First and the Third World is an extremely dangerous operation, and so one has to be careful about subscribing wholly to one theory or theorist. When you're as old as I am and you've seen enough of them go by, you can never give yourself wholeheartedly to any one of them or you'll be out of date like an old Ford and at the next turn you'll be left behind. This is not just a question of keeping up; it's a question of recognizing that the development of theory goes through a certain cycle. It usually comes out of the break in the problematic of a previous dominant theoretical set of positions, and then there's a generative moment when it's putting genuinely new conceptions into the field. When you look at them, those new conceptualizations are never entirely novel; you'll find previous echoes. They are a reconfiguration of new and old elements rather than literally a discovered truth or method. There's never anything absolutely new. Then you get a kind of hardening into a doctrinaire, sectarian position, and you are either this kind of Foucauldian or that kind of Foucauldian, but it would be anathema to offer any sort of tentative criticism of anything that Foucault says. And that is a sure sign that it's about to be disrupted by another paradigm—we're just waiting for the next one to appear. But if you are really not interested in that game of succession but are interested in what theory can deliver, you have to plot a less extreme path, a path that does not allow you to give yourself entirely to any one theory. Rather, you must keep your antennae open to the truth in the previous theories that had to be destroyed but that then have to be taken over. For example, the predominance, the absolute exclusiveness, of the concept of class in Marxism prevented us from understanding questions about race, gender, and sexuality. The next move is not to abandon class altogether but to reintegrate it into another position that isn't all-encompassing and obscuring.

So, you haven't really lost anything. What Marx had to say about class has some relevance, though not within the paradigmatic framework in which he developed it. The next move is already open to hear some echoes and to read some people who have now gone out of fashion because they had something important to say. And, similarly, one has to have the antennae turned toward the future, where the dogmatic closure of the theoretical world will try, as all closures do, to establish an identity position among, say, all Foucauldians, or all Lacanians, or all Deluezians. And by that very act of closure, some positions will be left outside—because history is never finished—and those positions will become the excluded, constituted other that will return to haunt the field and disturb the paradigm, to ask some questions which can't be asked within that framework. So once you know that this is how theories work, you can't become the disciple of a theory—you can't. I'm profoundly influenced by Gramsci, but I'm not "a Gramscian" in the sense that I think everything Gramsci said was right or that I would defend everything that he said.

Theorizing requires a certain conceptual distance from an investment in the security of a paradigm that's all self-sufficient, in a sense an arbitrary closure, in order to act. That's how language works, and on a more general level that's how theory works. Of course, to write any particular piece or to think through any particular problem, you do have to locate yourself somewhere theoretically from which you can think. I remember in the very heady days of the early 1970s that I had graduate students who were rendered speechless by theory. They could not put down a sentence because they could already see the theoretical objections to it. They couldn't say, "This is really so," because "the real," you know, was being interrogated. They were completely paralyzed by theory. I'd reply, "It's not forever; just try to take a position and see what the strengths and weaknesses are. Think from it and see where it takes you in terms of different contexts, different conjunctures, different language games."

Q. You mention in "Cultural Studies and its Theoretical Legacies" that you carry around at least three "burdens of representation." You say, "I'm expected to speak for the entire black race on all questions theoretical, critical, etc., and sometimes for British politics, as well as for cultural studies. This is what is known as the black person's burden, and I would like to absolve myself of it at this moment." In a recent *JAC* interview, Michael Eric Dyson spoke at length about the complexities of privilege and obligation for a black public intellectual—particularly one who is well-known and highly paid—and the continual self-critique that must accompany such a position. What specific privileges and obligations are a part of being a world-renowned black public intellectual, and how do you balance those tensions?

A. If I think about it more personally and autobiographically, my biography precisely matches the postwar migration. In the early 1950s, there were already some black people living in London. People had come during the war, gone home and come back, but the big wave happened after I came. In 1953 and 1954 lots of people came for the first time to work. In a way, my politics and even my identity have been shaped very much in relation to that historical trajectory.

Q. The political identity of "black," to which you refer in your work?

A. Even the personal identity. My mother would have died at the thought that I might call myself "black." In the Caribbean, the distinction between black and brown, colored and not-so-colored, very light and dark is what the whole social structure was built on, and it still persists in spite of the fact that the Caribbean is now much more manifestly and self-consciously a black culture.

So, the taking on of a black identity was explicitly so. Thinking of myself as a black person, as a black intellectual, was only possible because this community, and with it my own identity, was forming around the dialogue between that community and what was called the "host society." And that host society had to negotiate, had to ask, "Who are these people? How long are they here for? What do we think about them? Why do they speak English?" "Because we colonized them five hundred years ago, that's why." "But why are they different?" "Because they come from Africa." What that society was negotiating, I was negotiating. It's different for someone like Michael Dyson, who is much younger then I am, who comes after civil rights, who comes out of a long, stable, African American community, an African American tradition of resistance and struggle. My identity was formed in relation to the formation of a community itself.

Now, there is a tradition in the Caribbean of what public intellectuals like me are supposed to do: we are supposed to lead; we are supposed to take office in organizations; we are supposed to shape the community. This occurred in a particular political era in the Caribbean, but I didn't think it was right to repeat that. To attempt to represent the life experiences of others was never something I felt called upon to do. There were those who knew what the experience of trying to make a life in Britain was like. I knew it, too, but my life was deeply protected: I went to Oxford, and I had a middle-class education. When I ventured out into the world, of course I was discriminated against, but nobody stopped me from getting a job. I did not share the experiences of people who were constantly refused housing and decent public services. So, how could I presume to lead them? I had a function, of course, which was to try to articulate what they wanted, or to try to find out how they were coping with this adaptation. I tried to learn what their aspirations were, what their problems were, what the problems of adaptation of the second generation were, what the problems of discrimination and racism were, and why this was so deeply embedded in the British response to them. *Those* were my skills, and I tried through writing, speaking, acting politically to use those skills in the service of that community. But I could not call myself, my experience, representative of theirs. That would have been a categoric mistake; it would have been a deep, profound misrecognition. This is precisely the way we misrecognize the way in which class intersects with race. Such a misrecognition would have pretended that because we were all black we were all having the same experience, but we were not all having the same experience. I was not having the same experience. I was deeply and profoundly, and remain profoundly, privileged in relation to the majority experience of blacks.

Of course you're connected with them, of course you politically identify with them, of course you share certain experiences with them; society is perfectly well aware that you are black and will treat you in that way in myriad and minute forms. But I can't say I was experiencing what others experienced. Those who were in the front line were in a much more exposed position. So, I tried to find a political role, a role for intellectual work that would genuinely enhance and identify myself, an organic formation that would operate in the areas that I had access to and they didn't. Public speaking, the television, the radio, committees of investigation, police investigations where I might be asked to give evidence—I had access to that. I had a responsibility, a duty, to try to voice as articulately as I could what I understood that experience to be. But I had to ensure to myself and to them that it was an interpretation; it was my interpretation of them. I couldn't sort of deliver myself on the plate as this sacrificial person that you're treating this way. So these are very complicated issues, very complicated issues. I think the problem in translation and adjustment of languages is how class intersects with it, how power and status cut into and make other forms of social division. Class cuts us in a different way from the ways in which race and gender cut us.

The identification across gender doesn't produce the same politics as the identification across race and class. We are disrupted by them rather than formed into a single kind of protesting subject. And, of course, the system then exploits that, and this is a longstanding issue for me. When I was at the Centre for Cultural Studies, young students wanting to get into politics were sometimes impatient, asking, "Why should we go through all of this and study books? Let's just get out there!" It took a lot of time to convince them. They were not street kids; they were extremely privileged, middle-class graduate students. To make a political link with other people requires a practice, not just an expression. They couldn't just dissolve themselves, pretend that

they were really ignorant, inarticulate kids hanging around the
street. They were Ph.D. students being funded by the state to do
nothing but read books in libraries. It was ridiculous! But they
could make contact with those kids in the street, with the workers
that they wanted to identify with, and build an organization in
which all of their different experiences could be put together to
educate one another about what could be shared—all in the same
organization, wanting something out of it. (That was Gramsci's
notion of the party, you know; it's not the big Communist Party,
with a capital *P*.) In other words, you have to go through the
translation rather than back to expression. You don't deny that
the divisions of labor, class, and education have already transected,
broken those organic links. You can't deny that and just pretend
we can reaffirm the links as if they will come back into being.
"We're not students, we're really workers," they wanted to claim.
Rubbish. They'd never worked a minute in their lives! But we
could, together, build an organization that would recognize, "I'm
a student and you're a worker," and that would then ask, "What
do we as students and workers want out of this society? Is there
something we could share, build together?" Intellectuals sometimes come on as if what they want to do is divest themselves of
their intellectual responsibility and just be the guys in the hood—
and they're not. If they *can* make a connection, superb; but that
in itself is a politics. It means learning from people you don't
know; it means trying to understand experience; it means constructing alliances across differences that are ineradicable.

Q. You suggest in "Gramsci's Relevance for the Study of Race and
   Ethnicity" that a group—be it raced, gendered, classed, or
   otherwise marked—may have a sense of its "basic conditions of
   life" but that it still requires the intellectual to "renovate and
   clarify" constructions of popular thought. You argue that "common sense" must be transformed by the intellectual into a "more
   coherent political theory or philosophical current." However, as
   more and more "popular thought" is staked out by academics in
   the humanities as legitimate intellectual territory, that territory is
   necessarily marked by specialized vocabularies, publications, and
   limited audiences. Can the appropriation and subsequent theorizing of the popular by academics struggling not only for raises,
   promotion, and tenure, but also for disciplinary identity threaten
   those intended political objectives?

A. I would like to have thought that they wouldn't. Gramsci's work is particularly interesting here and relates to the discussion in that he always emphasized the need for what he called "organic intellectuals" to operate at both ends of the spectrum and for them to operate in a more sophisticated manner. For them just to be the traditional intellectuals, as we called them, will simply no longer do. At the same time, we require them to understand that those ideas could never have any real political or social impact unless they could connect them, translate them.

It's not necessarily true that the same people are good at doing the translations; intellectuals may not be the right people. They may need to find other people who understand intellectual work and who also are themselves more in touch with popular currents. Gramsci is very interested in the village priest. Village priests in many remote Italian towns are not intellectuals, but because they've been through intellectual training, they have access to a dogma and to certain philosophical conceptions. But they also live the practical life of the people every day: they shop with them; they rear their children. *They're* the translators, not Aquinas. They're how Aquinas becomes a practical philosophy, because the philosophy shapes what people do in and with their everyday lives. This is why the popular became, under Gramsci's influence, such a very profound concept in cultural studies at a certain point in time. The efficacy, making ideas practical, is exactly the same link that one finds in Foucault between discourse and practice. Ideas become institutionalized in the practice of what happens every day in the local hospital, what happens in the clinic, what happens when a doctor encounters a patient in the operating theater—how those ideas become a practice. What he means by discourse is not just ideas; it's ideas translated into everyday practice. Everybody, I think, is aware that this is where one encounters the politics of academic work—not in academics' selling a paper, or turning up in front of the factory gate and pretending they're Lenin. It has to do with their attention to the articulation between the philosophical and the popular. And that, of course, has made the terrain of the popular a privileged object of analysis in a way in which it wasn't before. When we started out, people imagined we were interested in the popular because we watched soap operas and we thought we'd better write about them. In part that's true, but it's not just an indulgence; it is a sign that even intellectuals occupy the popular. Nobody occupies the philosophical pole only. Everybody reads novels, reads the newspaper, listens to the radio, has conversations; everybody is in both areas. This is why Gramsci says there are people called "intellectuals" who are paid to do intellectual work, and then there is the "intellectual function" which *everybody* does, including people who can hardly read and write. They conceptualize what they're doing, so they are intellectuals in the moment. That is the intellectual function.

In our society these things are separated into different roles, different statuses, different institutional settings, which have their own forms of promotion and demotion, inclusion and exclusion. Nevertheless, almost every individual is between the two, has a foot, a stake in both camps. To take the popular seriously is not just to indulge in a form of populism. The sort of position that says, "*East Enders* is wonderful, *ER* is wonderful, but Shakespeare is rotten," is just an inversion of the old elitism; it's just turned upside down. Nothing has been transformed. However, to notice that the modern novel is also always in part science fiction or thriller or romance as well as serious literature is to open the possibility of transformation.

That kind of work is valuable in a number of different ways, and the fact that that work is enjoyable is a value. I think intellectuals here are rather lucky since they get pleasure out of doing criticism: when they stop enjoying the film, they can enjoy talking about it. But for the people who really just enjoy watching the film and don't have access to a more privileged critical language, I suppose that our talking about film, or talking about television, or talking about rock music can be an appropriation of sorts. Kids used to act as if we had robbed them of their last refuge, their last resistance. The whole thing about rock and pop culture was that it wasn't school. Well, if school is now the domain of the popular, where can they escape to? So there are problems of tactics, too. You can practically hear the explosion of a kind of academic industry of popular culture. Caught up in promotion and tenure, there are those who will benefit from that industry, and I think people are beginning to smell a rat about this. Everybody knows that there are those engaged in various practices that they identify as cultural studies but that are simply a waste of everyone's time—the beetlebrowed, pious references to the analysis of three new rock lyrics, and so on. There's a bit of idiocy about that. One should not forget why one went to the popular in the first instance; that's why I talked about what Gramsci was interested in. It's not just an indulgence and an affirmation; it's a political, intellectual, pedagogical commitment. Everybody now inhabits the popular, whether they like it or not, so that does create a set of common languages. To ignore the pedagogical possibilities of common languages is extremely political.

Q. You insist in "Cultural Studies and its Theoretical Legacies" that "Cultural studies . . . refuses to be a master discourse or a metadiscourse of any kind. . . . It is a serious enterprise, or project, and that is inscribed in what is sometimes called the 'political' aspect of cultural studies." How do you answer critics who argue that cultural studies is, in many of its pedagogical applications, in danger of merely replicating the traditional English studies practice of "reading" texts? The first faint rumblings of what may prove to be a significant backlash against cultural studies is now being heard in rhetoric and composition.

A. That's interesting, because I think it's not only from the field of rhetoric that these critiques are emerging; we're hearing all over that people are becoming disillusioned. We're past the point where people are mesmerized by the ascendancy of cultural studies. Rather, they've got their teeth sunk into it, and they're beginning to shake it around a bit, take a bite. You should expect that and welcome it; it can lead to productive debates as well as sterile ones. This is a complicated question because cultural studies is, and should be, practiced in a multitude of ways. It continues to expand widely but also wildly. Textual analysis, however, is really about much more than a traditional notion of "close reading." What is behind the notion of textuality is what I would call "the discursive turn." Saussure has had a profound effect on almost everything, but the importation of the linguistic model, this discursive turn, is quite deeply misunderstood. The moment you affirm that everything is within discourse, it's very hard not to appear to be arguing that everything is discourse, and by "discourse" people are generally not thinking of the articulation between discourse and practice that I talked about before. Everything is not language; nothing operates outside of meaning. A lot of people are practicing cultural studies as if that were the case, however. And so there is something to the criticism that a lot of what is going on is not much more than old-style practical criticism, close textual reading of a good old Leavisian kind but with some fancy Saussurian or poststructualist terms and a bit of identity and subject position thrown in. The text is abstracted from its institutional context, from its historical context—that form of what I would call "literary cultural studies" is deeply troubling. You have to work on the text, but you also have to work on the context; you have to know something about the history of the society in which the institutions work as well as about what the technologies of the media are and how they're financed. So, I think there's been a kind of reduction to text in the narrow sense, not text in the broad sense, indicating what I call the discursive turn.

By "discursive turn" all I mean is that no practice is ultimately understandable outside of the context of its meaning. All human practices are embedded in meaning, which is not to say that there is nothing but meaning. There is food, there is nature, there is death, and there are all sorts of things apart from meaning; but no *practice* takes place outside of meaning or outside of the material world—but we don't say that. We're transfixed by the coming of meaning because the whole positivistic thrust of social thought for many centuries has been to downgrade meaning, to see meaning in language as subsidiary. So we are talking about the constitutive role that we want to give to language, discourse, textuality, the work of language itself, and we forefront that, but we are not saying there is nothing but text and endless text; rather, we are saying that no practice exists outside of the framework of its meaning. It comes from somebody who wants it to mean something, it occupies a language which only is a language because it communicates meaning, it is interpretable only because other people either share or bring to bear on it a framework of interpretation: it is discursive from beginning to end. But it's also something else: it's also materialist, economic, political, social, technological. It's not *only* textual because it *is* textual. This is a fine distinction that is absolutely critical. The reason why I'm insisting on it is that I think many people in cultural studies are themselves complicit with blurring the distinction because they don't want to think about that messy other bit. They just want to go on doing what they've always done but with a new trendy heading to it. We can all record five television programs and spend twenty hours looking at how the meanings work inside language. If we don't ask anything else about the efficacy of these structures out there either in circulating meanings across the globe or in making profits for CNN, if we aren't interested in any of those other questions, we are not doing anything other than a very sophisticated literary, textual, critical work, and we're therefore vulnerable to just those kinds of criticisms.

In our courses at the Open University, we start by talking about what we call the "cultural studies circuit," which is an intersection of many specific moments. We ask students to identify questions of representation that are about textuality and language—questions of production, questions of consumption. All of those are the moments of a cultural circuit, and for a phenomenon to become truly cultural, it has to pass through all of those and more. For an analysis to be adequate to the object of analysis, it has to refer to all of them. Now, we aren't all experts in all of them. But if your area is the area of production, you have to go to production with the notion that what is being produced is *meaning*, so it has some relation to the moment of representation. You must also see that what you're producing is going to be consumed and that it will be transformed in the consumption, so it also has a relation to the question of consumption. Each moment has an openness to the other moments of the circuit. You can say, "I'm only an expert in representation so that's what I'll do," but you then have to write your analysis in such a way as to reveal the fact that you are not dealing with a number of other things without which not a lot can be said about the cultural impact of the object that you're trying to study. So, you don't study the economics of production as if it's outside of meaning; you look at how economic processes also depend on representation, and so on.

Each of the moments, then, even the moment of technology that appears to be a hard engineering one, is lodged within technology *at a particular time*, and the multiple and competing discourses of technology at any given moment make of technological research and development, of technological consumption and production, a very different thing. The language of progress is one such discourse; the language of environmental damage is another. These are rival discourses out of which the technological emerges. You don't lose the reference to the discursive turn in each of the moments; it isn't just harnessing old style economics, old style technology, old style audience research to the moment of language and textuality, because each of those other moments has been transformed by the discursive turn which operates throughout. You've given culture and meaning and language a more constitutive place in understanding what the economic is and what the technological is and how the modes of regulation operate; so you've transformed them from a sort of hard, pulsivistic instance, but you *can't* leave them out—this is what we have to understand.

Theory is always closed, because theory can't be infinitely open. It can't match the infinite openness of the world—as I said before, you'd never think anything. So you have to understand the arbitrary closure that is required to make sense of a thing theoretically; but, nevertheless, you have to write as if it is possible to sketch in or indicate how this analysis might be transformed once we bring the other moments in, too. So the textual critic is not required to become an economist as well. On the other hand, the more interdisciplinary the work, the more varieties of these skills will be harnessed in analyzing the object. At any rate, the textual critic can say, "This is a reading of the text; those are the meanings which are potential in this text. Which ones did the audience take?" I don't know, because I'm an audience of one— that is, me. What I can give is a good guess about what a lot of people like me might have taken from the work, but we know very well that people take all sorts of meanings from messages because messages are not closed. The moment of representation is not closed from the moment of interpretation, consumption, and transformation. You have to leave open the possibility that people are watching the same thing that you are and reading something completely different from it. We have to be more tentative. A kind of certainty arises from textual criticism in which one says, "Those are the meanings and I have nothing else to say. There are a lot of symbolic meanings that you can't get, but this is the meaning of the text." What is that kind of critical analysis but a return to what Bauman calls "the critic as legislator"? This comes out of what I would call—and I use the phrase deliberately, with all its masculinist connotations—an attempt at "mastery" going on in cultural studies scholarship. In this the critic is sort of overcoming the text, squashing the text. It's a claim that one has got the full measure of a text, and it is a way of validating one's own practice as the master reflects back on his or her own genius. The claim and appearance of brilliance enhances one's institutional position in the field, but there's a lot more to practice than just identifying oneself as a professional of one sort or another. Critical practice has a lot of social implications as well.

Q. You explore the term *ethnicity* in "New Ethnicities," arguing that the word has been "deployed, in the discourse of racism, as a means of disavowing the realities of racism and repression." You argue that this "appropriation will have to be contested, the term disarticulated from its position in the discourse of 'multiculturalism.'" Do you see the discourse of multiculturalism as a negative force, then, in the work that a recuperated notion of ethnicity might do within a new politics of representation?

A. I'd like to answer that by saying something briefly about the negative aspects both of ethnicity and of multiculturalism, because I think they're linked. Multiculturalism very much invokes ethnicity because what does multiculturalism mean? Well, a society is multicultural and that is to say it is composed of different ethnic groups. Clearly, people have different cultures even if the concept of race is a bit dubious scientifically. Now, the form of multiculturalism that I have difficulties with is the one that has an essentialized notion of ethnicity.

Everybody secure within his or her own ethnic group is competing with other ethnic groups on a hierarchy for resources; so the Koreans are above the Hong Kong Chinese, who are above the Puerto Ricans, who are above the blacks, and so on. But each individual is slotted into a pluralist space here. I have no objections to the term *multicultural* used adjectivally—Britain has become a multicultural society—but not if it's organized in this hierarchical or stratified or essentializing way. What I mean by multicultural, then, is that society has been mongrelized. You look out and you don't know whether kids are black or white or North African; it's just the pluralization of kinds of people (not cultures) which now make up a city like London. You have no idea how London has been transformed in fifteen or twenty years; you have no conception. It did not look like this at one time. And it's different from an American city because the groups are not watertight. It's like New York in some ways, but it's unlike other American cities where one is very much aware of the fact that it's multicultural in the sense that there are lots of different "cultures," but each culture is very much protective of its own self. Of course, we have that here, too, but there's been a lot more sliding and translation between them. So, which of those two is strictly pluralist in the old sense—in segmented, clearly identifiable, originary, and essentialist ethnic segments?

If each individual is ascribed to one of those ethnic segments, the term *multicultural* simply describes the many segments, whereas adjectivally *multicultural* describes a society that has been messed up or mongrelized by the variety of peoples who probably do tend to locate themselves more in one group than in another but who are not so formally fixed into groups. That kind of fixing has not been located in institutional practices, so resources are not given out in that way. Resources here are allocated in radically different ways than in the U.S. It's very odd to have any government resources given out to Cypriots only, or to Bangladeshies only. We can't do that. You can give it to the East End, where mainly the people are Bangladeshi; but you have to do it because you're giving it to a poor community, not because you're giving it to an ethnic group.

It's about citizenship. And this is different from a pluralist society. It's a funny piece of history that the U.S. has a much longer tradition and history of ethnic pluralism—it's made out of it—whereas Britain has always conceived of itself as culturally homogeneous. But the impact of globalization and migration on the two societies has been a little different. In the U.S., recent migration has been absorbed into and has complexified the pluralist hierarchy, whereas in Britain what it has done is simply blur its homogeneous origin. This is not to say that informally there isn't group identification. For instance, at one time the term *black* covered both Asian and Afro-Caribbean people, but it doesn't any longer. So there's a bit of a strengthening of ethnic identity here because now people will say, "Black and Asian" (which, if you think about it, is an extremely odd mixture because one is racial and the other is ethnic), and by that they mean the two major minority groups are the Afro-Caribbean and the subcontinent of Asia (which of course doesn't hold up any longer because within that Hindu and Muslim are completely different). But the point is that they are beginning to make a distinction. So we are beginning to have more ethnic identification in Britain, but it is not anywhere so clearly stratified as in the U.S., and it's not legally and officially acknowledged. There's no law saying money can go to help Muslims. How ethnicity plays in Britain and the U.S. is rather different, and consequently what the term *multicultural* means is rather different. The critique of the use of the term *multicultural* in the U.S. wouldn't apply in quite the same way here. There are people here who say we don't like the term *multiculturalism*, but nobody in England would object if you said that this is a "multicultural society." Adjectivally, everybody understands that what has happened is cultural diversity, cultural pluralization.

The term *multiculturalism* can operate in very different contexts and have very different meanings. The same thing is true of the term *ethnicity*. In my terminology, everybody has an ethnicity because everybody comes from a cultural tradition, a cultural context, an historical context; it is the source of their self-production, so everybody has an ethnicity—including the British: Englishness. It's very important to say that because in the current discourse, Englishness is not an ethnicity; Englishness is like white, what the world is, and black is marked. Ethnic minority groups are marked, but Englishness is unmarked. One thing that has happened as a result of multiculturalism in Britain, as a result of its becoming a multicultural society, is that Englishness is increasingly contested. It has become aware of itself as a distinctive ethnic identity, and there's a big debate about what Englishness is, what Englishness is now. Does Englishness depend on having an empire, in which case can you be English in the same way in which you were in the nineteenth century? Can you be English and black? There is a huge contestation around the question of the nature of ethnicity. Now, there is also the essentialist notion of ethnicity, which is as I described it earlier: "You are what you are because you are a member of an ethnic group. That is your identity, so stay within it; its traditions are yours, and really you belong in your homeland, and if only you could get the money you would go back home. Unfortunately, you have to wander in the diaspora for a little bit, but that's who you really are." Now, that essentialist notion of ethnicity is extremely damaging because it doesn't allow for pluralization; it doesn't allow for hybridization. In the new generation, in the current youth cultures, there are amazingly generative things happening. They're combining black, jungle, Indian, and Hindu music—all kinds of extraordinary things. And the last element that could be identified in such work is, "Please go back to your cultural roots." That would be the end of any cultural creativity or productivity. So, I don't think we can do without ethnicity as a concept, but I think there are certain dangerous versions of ethnicity around. That is why I said there has to be a contestation around the very term itself. What do we mean by it? I mean the diverse version of ethnicity, the multicultural, adjectival version of ethnicity. I don't mean the back-to-one's-homeland version of ethnicity. The same term will actually occur in both sentences, but the distinction is very important.

This is where we are with respect to a whole variety of concepts. We can't do without them, but we don't mean them in the old way so we have to use them, as Derrida suggests, "under erasure." *Ethnicity* is one of the concepts that has come under erasure, and so have *modernity*, *Enlightenment*, and *identity*. If I simply say "identity," I don't make it clear whether I'm talking about identity in a Cartesian, Enlightenment sense or identity in a Rushdian sense. It's not clear because the same word can have both meanings. I don't have another word, so I have to use it in such a way as to close out certain connotations and open up others. That's what happened to the term *black*. People didn't find another word, and they had a contestation around that word precisely because it was already inserted in the discourse in a negative way. That was a word that had to be disarticulated from its older discursive configuration and rearticulated in a new one. The politics were exactly about disentangling it from its older, negative notions and reinvesting it with positive associations. The same is going on about concepts such as ethnicity, and one after another the panoply of concepts of post-Enlightenment social science are coming under erasure. They've not been replaced by an entirely new critical or theoretical conceptual vocabulary, but they are on the move; they no longer can be said and thought in the paradigmatic position of their old theoretical constructs. That is why we are in the deconstructive moment. That's what deconstruction means to me; that's what I understand Derrida to be saying: we have no other language but the language of the old metaphysics, the language in which philosophy has been conducted, and it no longer works; but we are not yet in some other language, and we may never be. We may simply have to occupy the underside, the disturbed, subverted side of the positive concepts—the negative side of a positive concept—in order to think with, rather than waiting for some new dispensation. That is exactly what the notion *post* means for me. So, *postcolonial* is not the end of colonialism. It *is* after a certain *kind* of colonialism, after a certain moment of high imperialism and colonial occupation—in the wake of it, in the shadow of it, inflected by it—it is what it is because something else has happened before, but it is also something new.

Q. So in a discursive sense, we can articulate new ways of thinking and being while using the same terms, the same vocabulary.

A. Exactly. Writing is kind of a game of defining one's terms against the uses one doesn't want as one goes. Every time I use *ethniciy* I have to make sure that I'm not being slotted back into the essentialist notion of ethnicity or what I'm saying could be completely misunderstood. And there *are* certain misunderstandings, whether deliberate or not, and I rather like that. Both Homi Bhabha and I use the term *hybridity*, and Robert Young has accused us both of occupying nineteenth-century racial theory because *it* uses the term *hybridity*. Of course, I'm not talking about hybridity in that sense; I'm using it metaphorically. But I have no other term. I can only take up *that* term, try to refuse its racialist connotations, and try to reinvest it with a new kind of cultural meaning. I don't know how else to talk. But you are always open to exactly that kind of misinterpretation. Someone will always say that if you're talking about ethnicity you're just in one of the old ethnics: "America is an ethnically pluralist society, what's wrong with that, we're a melting pot," and so forth. We are trapped by the deconstructive moment in some of the primary concepts with which cultural studies is trying to operate. These are its concepts. Each of them is no longer tenable in terms of an old vocabulary, but we have no entirely new dispensation with which to think. It requires a kind of double operation, rhetorically, discursively, in that one uses terms that are untenable; one occupies a conceptual world but one no longer believes in the translation.

Q. That kind of double operation would require not only a fairly in-depth and critical understanding of the older, negative discursive configurations—a history, really—it would require a broad and continually updated knowledge of contemporary critical theory.

A. Absolutely. This goes back to the point I made about new and old theories: you can't just generate a new theory without taking on board the baggage that the concepts are already carrying from older meanings. In that sense, theory is often abused in terms of scholarship. These are necessary functions, and just operating on the new is not tenable because the theoretical discourse itself is invested with cultural baggage inherited from the fact that language is thousands of years old.

Q. The work of Angela McRobbie, Hazel Carby, Patricia Williams, bell hooks, and Robin Kelly might all be classified as "cultural studies." Does the umbrella term and received notion of the political project of cultural studies as such water down a feminist agenda when that agenda is subsumed under the broader term?

A. I don't know whether it does. I don't think that this is necessarily so. Cultural studies does function as an umbrella term for a variety of different practices, not all of them the same by any means; a number of very different kinds of inquiries all get hobbled together under that umbrella. But it *is* part of the new critical theoretical family, so it has a certain relation to feminism, to psychoanalysis, to postcolonial theory, and to poststructuralism. It is part of a configuration of critical languages, rather than one. Now, I suppose the question is, why has it become the umbrella term, and what is the effect of that happening? I think, partly, it has become the umbrella term out of convenience. It's more neutral than feminism, and it's not so specific as psychoanalysis. Psychoanalysis mobilizes the anti-Freudians, whereas cultural studies—who can object to studying culture these days? And I suppose its references are broader. Women and the psyche and colonial relations are all part of culture. *Culture* is the broader term, so I suppose the fact that the term *cultural studies* has been adopted is a kind of convenience in that sense. It's a way of signaling something, of signaling that one occupies the terrain of new critical languages, new theoretical ideas, and where the people that you quote use it, it does inflect their work differently. I can think of many feminist theorists who are doing perfectly good feminist theoretical work, but they're not engaged with the way in which feminism has inflected our thinking about culture. They're not engaged in the kind of gendered aspects of cultural forms in the way in which those feminist theorists who use the term *cultural studies* would be. So I think it has made a difference, and I think you can see that. I think of important work in feminist epistemology—for instance, Sandra Harding's work—but it's not cultural studies. I don't mean to rule it out, but if your principal interest is in developing the argument that your project has a bearing on other cultural theories, I don't know if I'd call that cultural studies; I don't know what you'd be getting by calling it cultural studies. On the other hand, bell hook's work on the intersection of gender, race, and representation is about cultural identity and representation. These are classical cultural studies concerns, really.

I'm not giving a very satisfactory answer to this question, and I think the reason is that I've always been afraid of policing the term *cultural studies*. I've always been particularly afraid of my own role in such policing because I was close to the beginning when the term began to be used and because of the placement of Birmingham in the development of cultural studies generally. It's very hard not to have a kind of patriarchal relationship to it.

Q. Stuart Hall as owner and founder of cultural studies?

A. Exactly—owner, founder, and sort of stepfather. I think it would be quite wrong; I'm just not interested in doing that. I tend to be more flexible and fluid: I go not to the labels but to the work. Okay, you can call this cultural studies if you like, but is there something distinctive about the work which wouldn't have been done without the traditions of thinking and writing that have been inherited from cultural studies? If there is, then I think it's a perfectly valid usage.

Cultural studies is not a discipline in its own right; it never has been, and I don't think it should aspire to be. It identifies a field of work, a configuration of different theoretical traditions as defined by a set of preoccupations, but it's not a discipline in its own right and it doesn't aspire to disciplinary status. Cultural studies has always been interdisciplinary, and this was true in Britain right from the very beginning. The first cultural studies department came out of a rather contingent ensemble of different disciplines. It just happened that the people at Birmingham were in sociology, literature, and history. But the people in Portsmouth were in literature, history, and the visual arts or film. So you wind up with a different inflection. The people in Middlesex have always come out of a very strong visual arts history and tradition, but there are people at Birmingham who also belong to that. Dick

Hebdige is as much a member of that tradition as he is of anything else. So I don't think these labels should be too tightly articulated to a disciplinary label.

Q. *Policing the Crisis*, although twenty years old, continues to inform our notions of national identity and the nature of crime. Policing has come under massive public scrutiny in the U.S. in recent years, with recurring outcries against institutional racism and condoned violence fueling an already volatile situation. Discussions of policing and law and order in general are once again being talked about in the context of "community" in an effort to address localized charges of racism and brutality. What do you think is not being said in discussions of community policing? In other words, how would you envision an effective sequel to *Policing the Crisis*?

A. Well, I don't know about a sequel because in some ways *Policing the Crisis* represents a continuity in my work that already exists. I continue to work in and on concepts of race and ethnicity. It represents continuity also in terms of how I want to think questions of race because it doesn't autonomize race. I want to think race in relation to British politics and in relation to national identity. Did you know that *Policing the Crisis* was researched by myself and four graduate students and that all the graduate students were white? And that the project came out of the activity of one of those students who was researching the case of a particularly violent incident and the subsequent wave of moral panic? It was a mugging—one of the first cases where the American term *mugging* was used—and the kids were Irish. The key articulation was, "What's happening in the U.S. is now going to happen here, so we can import the terminology, the conception of urban violence, the racialized images of crime, and the forms of policing. Everything can be brought over. So, it deals with race but in a distinctive way. It's not a black text—I think I can put it that way. It engages with black questions and black politics and questions of race, but it's not a black text. Those are continuities because I've always wanted to write about race in that way. On the other hand, it represents a huge shift because what we saw as a result of *Policing the Crisis* was the coming of Thatcherism. We looked into the crisis of Englishness that was working itself out through these discourses on race, crime, and youth after 1968 and into the 1970s. You could see that law and order was the response, not just to the question of urban crime or to race but to the whole crisis of British national identity. People were panicking. They said, "This society is breaking apart, it's diversified by immigration, it's no longer an imperial society, it's declining economically. Communities are breaking down; how can we be sure of who and what we are?" A law and order response was made in an attempt to stop what was perceived as a hemorrhage. What *we* asked was, "Where is this law and order response coming from?" It was coming partly from the state in the form of policing and the judiciary and political spheres; it was coming partly from the demand of local communities themselves who felt threatened by change, white communities who thought of themselves as part of the imperial nation and therefore no longer the greatest nation on earth. They were living cheek by jowl with the people they had hoped to leave in Calcutta, and Delhi, and so on. They felt deeply threatened by change and their feeling was, "We can't walk on the streets." All of these inchoate feelings were indicators of a kind of social crisis. And what we said was, "If this move takes hold, the whole of what in Britain has been the postwar settlement from about the 1950s on, which has been a period of the construction of the welfare state—comprehensive schooling, social democratic kinds of approaches to social problems—will come to an end and a harder-edged, more competitive way of life will come about.

So, *Policing the Crisis* was a huge shift for me because it was a shift into my work on Thatcherism and all of what happened in the 1980s. *Policing the Crisis* is one of the few social science books that is predictively correct: it was right about the 1980s, that Britain was about to be transformed by the experience of Thatcherism. It justified our approach to race because if you'd just taken race as a black issue you'd have seen the impact of law and order policies on the local communities but you'd have never seen the degree to which the race and crime issue was a prism for a much larger social crisis. You wouldn't have looked at this larger picture. You'd have written a black text, but you wouldn't have written a cultural studies text because you wouldn't have seen this articulation up to the politicians, into the institutional judiciary, down to the popular mood of the people, into the politic, as well as into the community, into black poverty, and into discrimination.

So, I suppose an actual answer to your question would be that

if you were writing that book in America, you would have to try
to recognize the historical implications of slavery as well as the
changes that were made since the civil rights movement. You
would have to deal with the unsettled and unsettling business of
aspirations and disillusionment, but also with the fracture within
the black population into a more successful section of the black
middle class and into more bitter deprivation and poverty. A new
Policing the Crisis couldn't just say, "They're doing to us what
they've always done"—although that is, of course, part of it. But
saying only that is ineffective and incomplete.

Q. You have commented at various times, as have others, on the
importance of language for ongoing political action and systemic
change. New vocabularies and new metaphors enable us to
rephrase questions, repose problems, and organize experiences
and knowledges in ways that create new spaces for action. How
is cultural studies currently positioned to participate in the construction of innovative language?

A. It does touch on that, but the question is whether cultural studies
is still in a very creative, tension-filled relationship, and I find that
hard to generalize about, to tell the truth. As I said before, I think
it's not in its ascendancy any longer; it's lost some of its novelty.
That loss, as we're seeing now, is resulting in critiques of cultural
studies itself. There are a lot of questionable practices in writing,
publishing, and teaching that aren't doing very much. There's a lot
of what I would call "academic repetition." It's difficult for a
form of study that has become much more academically assimilated to retain its political cutting edge, and by "political" I mean,
very broadly, its image in the area where culture and politics
intersect. I don't mean taking up a particular political position in
respect to Tony Blair, for instance, but, rather, a concern with
questions of culture and power and difference.

My answer is not, I think, touching the heart of your question,
however. I don't have an overall sense of whether cultural studies
is really generating new ideas, new languages. At the moment, I
feel that it's not, but that may be because the political landscape
is rather complex, rather difficult to pin down. The new government is a strange beast, really, and people haven't gotten its
measure. In broader cultural terms, it's a modernizing force that
is socially conservative, and this is a very odd formation. Things
seem distributed in different ways; this is rather exciting in terms

of momentum for reform, but it has certain deep limitations lodged right at the center of the project. Old Left positions don't seem to have any purchase on it because those positions are not really engaged with the modern world, with the problems currently facing us. Cultural studies has got a lot of analytic work to do in teasing out underlying background assumptions; it has a lot of work to do in terms of trying to interpret how a society is changing in ways that are not amenable to the immediate political language. Blair will formulate those changes in a certain way, but there's a deeper level of shifts to be included in such analyses, shifts in the popular.

If you think about the response to Diana's death, it was utterly unpredicted and unpredictable—massive, absolutely massive, very different from the classical, public response to the death of a royal. The British response has been modern in some interesting ways, yet was nevertheless tied up with the mystique of sovereignty, of royalty, with the fact that she's a princess, and very beautiful; but it was simultaneously tied up with a confessional culture. She was the first princess who talked about adultery on television. She talked about her anorexia and her bulimia and her life, about going to see a feminist therapist, about going to the gym. This response to her death is a fascinating mixture of old English virtues, English idolatry of royalty, and modern romantic elements where people are turning out the notion of the upper classes. The commitment after fifteen years of Thatcherism to a public philosophy of compassion—of touching people with AIDS, of taking black children in Africa into your arms—is a fantastically complex shaft of light into the British cultural unconscious. For goodness sake, I certainly don't know whether cultural studies has any language for it, but it certainly has some work to do in telling us what is going on in this increasingly multicultural, increasingly diverse, rapidly shifting, regionalizing, British society. There is a lot to do, and not just in the British context. What Australia is doing about the rising, indigenous Australian society and about Australian identity is being looked at; the importation of cultural studies into southeast Asia, which is occurring at a tremendous rate, is another enormous project, and that's happening partly because globalization itself is so deeply tied in with cultural studies. It is deeply connected in cultural economic terms, in terms of hardware, in terms of satellite technology, in terms of the world investment in the global dissemination of meanings, images and messages. "Culture" has never been such an intensely interesting, complicated object to contend with. I just don't know whether cultural studies is quite up to it, whether it has seen the dimensions of the genie that it let out of the bottle. It was responsible for taking the stopper out of culture's bottle, but now culture doesn't belong to it anymore. There's more talk about culture in management theory: everybody there is talking about cultural change. The politicians and management gurus only talk about cultural change. They don't talk about anything else. They're reading Foucault like crazy, and particular forms of neoliberalism. New-liberal forms of governance—which Foucault is very interestingly and complexly related to—are being taken on by accountants. There's a huge school of Foucauldian accountants. So, I think we're about to be engulfed by culture; it's as if there's almost nothing else but culture left to us now. Cultural studies requires a huge bootstrap operation to lift itself out of its earlier agenda with national cultures and communities so that it can come face to face with these much larger, much wider, much broader, more extensive social relations. I am struck by how much potential work there is, and I feel that cultural studies is not aware of its new vocation. It could be called on to be at the leading edge of measuring new ways of both understanding and implementing social and historical change.

Q. While your work is heralded internationally as vastly important to the humanities, you have been criticized as well. Are there any criticisms or misunderstandings of your work that you'd like to address?

A. You know, I have to say that I don't read criticisms of my work. I have limited time for reading. When I left the Centre for Cultural Studies, I decided that I would contribute in other ways. I participated in compiling a history of cultural studies and of what happened at Birmingham. I don't want to privilege my view over other people's, but I do have a view about what occurred. But when I decided that I wouldn't really participate in the attempt to police the boundaries of cultural studies, what I did was to move to new substantive areas: back into questions of race. I thought it was more important for me to contribute to a particular area of work in cultural studies than to try to be responsible for deciding where the field was going. In the time that I've had available to read, I have preferred to read in the areas in which I'm thinking and writing, to read what others are doing in such areas rather than what others think about me and my work. I've been more interested in reading the debates about ethnicity and postcolonial theory and its developments than in tracking and responding to the criticisms of my own work. This is not a justification for it, and I think it's not a very good practice because people will think I'm disdainful of my critics, but I just don't know the rude things that they're saying because I haven't read them. Occasionally, I do come across criticisms, and I have the usual prickly responses when people misunderstand me. As you could tell by something I said previously, I was very wounded by Robert Young, that someone as sophisticated as he would willfully misunderstand me, would think that because I use the word *hybridity* I am complicit with nineteenth-century racial theory. But there are many other valid criticisms that I would take on board, but I can't. I am sometimes thought to be not very consistent—eclectic, really—for which I've already offered you a sort of an apologia. I think a certain kind of theoretical eclecticism in our period of heady intellectual and theoretical innovation can be a useful strategy. A friend of mine who says he is forever trying to keep up with these intellectual maneuvers asked me once if I thought that if he ducked he could miss the Lacanian moment! [Laughing.] Sometimes I've felt like ducking and that perhaps it would just go away and be over before I'd had to come to grips with it. So, eclecticism may be an excuse for a sort of lazy intellectual practice, a form of skillful intellectual ducking.

I don't think of myself as a theoretician. I don't have a philosophical mind that would allow me to stay at a certain level of abstraction for a long period of time. I can't sustain that. But that works for me because I'm interested in the dialogical relationship between theoretical concepts and the concrete. I put it that way because I'm not an empiricist either. It's not theory or empiricism; it is theory and concrete conjunctures—that's the interface that I find meaningful and productive. I suppose that's why I've remained more of a Gramscian than many other people who started out that way and have since abandoned Gramsci. Gramsci is interesting in exactly that interface between theory and the concrete, material world. So, it's necessary to know what you're good at and not pretend you're good at something else. In terms of my work, then, I've come to recognize that texts are only momentary stabilizations and then you give them back to the flow of meaning. They are appropriated by other people who will take from them what they will regardless of your intent. Every reading of a text is basically a translation, not a transmission of originary truth from one moment to another. One must give them away freely. People quite often get something different—but, you know, I got something different from Gramsci than what he'd intended me to get. I use Derrida in a way that would drive formal deconstructionists wild. My own work—and everyone else's, too—must be surrendered to that flow of meaning that will continue to create and recreate something new of the old.

Selected Bibliography

Gloria E. Anzaldúa

Books

Borderlands/La Frontera: The New Mestiza. San Francisco: Spinsters/Aunt Lute, 1987.

Making Face, Making Soul/Haciendo Caras: Creative and Critical Perspectives by Feminists of Color. San Francisco: Aunt Lute, 1990.

This Bridge Called My Back: Writings By Radical Women of Color. Watertown, MA: Persephone P, 1981. (ed. with Cherrie Moraga; 2nd. ed. Kitchen Table/Women of Color P, 1983)

Articles and Book Chapters

"Foreword." *Cassell's Encyclopedia of Queer Myth, Symbol, and Spirit: Gay, Lesbian, Bisexual, and Transgender Lore.* Ed. Randy P. Conner, David Hatfield Sparks, and Mariya Sparks. London: Cassell, 1997.

"Ghost Trap." *Currents From the Dancing River: Contemporary Latino Fiction, Nonfiction, and Poetry.* Ed. Ray Gonzalez. New York: Harcourt, 1994. 116-18

"The Homeland, Aztlan/El Otro Mexico." *Aztlan: Essays on the Chicano Homeland.* Albuquerque: Academia/El Norte, 1989. 191-204.

"Metaphors in the Tradition of the Shaman." *Conversant Essays: Contemporary Poets on Poetry.* Ed. James McCorkle. Detroit: Wayne State UP, 1990. 99-100.

"Life Line." *Growing Up Gay/Growing Up Lesbian: A Literary Anthology.* Ed. Bennett L. Singer. New York: New Press, 1994. 90-92.

"Ms. Right, My True Love, My Soul Mate." *Lesbian Love Stories,* vol. 2. Ed. Irene Zahava. Freedom, CA: Crossing P, 1991. 184-88.

"People Should Not Die in June in South Texas." *Growing Up Latino: Memoirs and Stories.* Ed. Harold Augenbraum and Ilan Stavans. Burlington, MA: Houghton, 1993. 280-87.

"Puddles." *Currents From the Dancing River: Contemporary Latino Fiction, Nonfiction, and Poetry.* Ed. Ray Gonzalez. New York: Harcourt, 1994. 118-20.

"En Rapport, In Opposition: Cobrando cuentas a las nuestras." *Making Face, Making Soul/Haciendo Caras: Creative and Critical Perspectives by Feminists of Color.* San Francisco: Aunt Lute, 1990. 142-48.

"La Conciencia de la Mestiza: Towards a New Consciousness." *Making Face, Making Soul/ Haciendo Caras: Creative and Critical Perspectives by Feminists of Color.* San Francisco: Aunt Lute, 1990. 377-89.

"Tlilli, Tlapalli: The Path of the Red and Black Ink." *Multi-Cultural Literacy.* Ed. Rick Simonson and Scott Walker. Saint Paul, MN: Graywolf P, 1988. 29-40.

"La Prieta." *This Bridge Called My Back: Writings By Radical Women of Color.* 2nd. ed. Ed. Gloria Anzaldua and Cherrie Moraga. New York: Kitchen Table/ Women of Color P, 1983. 198-209.

"Chicana Artists: Exploring Nepantla, el Lugar de la Frontera.*" Report on the Americas* 27.1 (1993): 1-37.

"To(o) Queer the Writer—Loca, escrotora y chicana." *Inversions: Writing by Dykes, Queers, and Lesbians.* Ed. Betsy Warland. Vancouver: Press Gang, 1991. 249-64.

Homi K. Bhabha

Books
The Location of Culture. London: Routledge, 1994.

Nation and Narration. London: Routledge, 1990.

Articles and Book Chapters
"Anxious Nations, Nervous States." *Supposing the Subject.* Ed. Joan Copjec. London: Verso, 1994. 201-17.

"Are You a Man or a Mouse?" *Constructing Masculinities.* Ed. Maurice Berger, Brian Wallis, and Simon Watson. New York: Routledge, 1995. 57-65.

"Articulating the Archaic: Notes on Colonial Nonsense." *Literary Theory Today.* Ed. Peter Collier and Helga Geyer-Ryan. Ithaca: Cornell UP, 1990. 203-18.

"The Commitment to Theory." *New Formations* 5 (1988): 5-23.

"Editor's Introduction: Minority Maneuvers and Unsettled Negotiations." *Critical Inquiry* 23.3 (1997): 431-59.

"Freedom's Basis in the Indeterminate." *October* 61 (1992): 46-57, 78-82.

"Frontlines/Borderposts." *Displacements: Cultural Identities in Question.* Ed. Angelika Bammer. Bloomington: Indiana UP, 1994. 269-72.

"The Home and the World." *Social Text* 10 (1992): 141-53.

"Interrogating Identity: The Postcolonial Prerogative." *Anatomy of Racism.* Ed. David Theo Goldberg. Minneapolis: U of Minnesota P, 1990. 183-209.

"Life at the Border: Hybrid Identities of the Present." *New Perspectives Quarterly* 14.1 (1997): 30-31.

"Of Mimicry and Man: The Ambivalence of Colonial Discourse." *October* 28 (1984): 125-33.

"The Other Question: Difference, Discrimination, and the Discourse of Colonialism." *Out There: Marginalization and Contemporary Cultures.* Ed. Russell Ferguson, et al. New York: The New Museum of Contemporary Art and MIT P, 1990. 71-87.

"Postcolonial Authority and Postmodern Guilt." *Cultural Studies.* Ed. Lawrence Grossberg, Cary Nelson, and Paula A. Treichler. New York: Routledge, 1992. 56-68.

"Postcolonial Criticism." *Redrawing the Boundaries: The Transformation of English and American Literary Studies.* Ed. Stephen Greenblatt and Giles Gunn. New York: MLA, 1992. 437-65.

"Postmodernism/Postcolonialism." *Critical Terms for Art History.* Ed. Robert Nelson and Richard Shiff. Chicago: U of Chicago P, 1996. 307-22.

"A Question of Survival: Nations and Psychic States." *Psychoanalysis and Cultural Theory: Thresholds.* Ed. James Donald. New York: St. Martin's, 1991. 89-103.

"Remembering Fanon: Self, Psyche, and the Colonial Condition." *Remaking History.* Ed. Barbara Kruger and Phil Mariani. Seattle: Bay P, 1989. 131-48.

"Representation and the Colonial Text: A Critical Exploration of Some Forms of Mimeticism." *The Theory of Reading.* Ed. Frank Gloversmith. Brighton: Harvester, 1984. 93-122.

"Signs Taken for Wonders: Questions of Ambivalence and Authority Under a Tree Outside Delhi, May 1817." *Critical Inquiry* 12.1 (1985): 144-65.

"Unpacking My Library ... Again." *The Post-Colonial Question: Common Skies, Divided Horizons.* Ed. Iain Chambers and Lidia Curti. London: Routledge, 1996. 199-211.

Michael Eric Dyson

Books
Between God and Gangsta Rap: Bearing Witness to Black Culture. New York: Oxford UP, 1996.

Making Malcolm: The Myth and Meaning of Malcolm X. New York: Oxford UP, 1995.

Race Rules: Navigating the Color Line. Reading, MA: Addison-Wesley, 1996.

Reflecting Black: African-American Cultural Criticism. Minneapolis: U of Minnesota P, 1993.

Articles and Book Chapters
"Be Like Mike? Michael Jordan and the Pedagogy of Desire," *Cultural Studies* 7.1 (1993): 64-72.

"Contesting Racial Amnesia: From Identity Politics Toward Post-Multiculturalism." *Higher Education Under Fire.* Ed. Michael Berube and Cary Nelson. New York: Routledge, 1994. 336-52.

"Essentialism and the Complexities of Racial Identity." *Multiculturalism: A Critical Reader*. Ed. David Theo Goldberg. Cambridge, MA: Blackwell, 1994. 218-29.

"'God Almighty Has Spoken From Washington, D.C.': American Society and Christian Faith." *DePaul Law Review* 42.1 (1992): 129-59.

"Inventing and Interpreting Malcolm X." *The Seductions of Biography*. Ed. Mary Rhiel. New York: Routledge. 43-53.

"Malcolm X." *The American Radical*. Ed. Mari Jo Buhle, Paul Buhle and Harvey Kaye. New York: Routledge, 1994. 321-27.

"Performance, Protest and Prophecy in the Culture of Hip-Hop." *Black Sacred Music: A Journal of Theomusicology* 5.1 (1991): 12-24.

"The Plight of Black Men." *Race, Class, and Gender*: An Anthology. 2nd ed. Ed. Margaret L. Andersen and Patricia Hill Collins. Belmont, CA: Wadsworth, 1995. 110-20.

"The Politics of Black Masculinity and the Ghetto in Black Film." *The Subversive Imagination: Artists, Society and Social Responsibility*. Ed. Carol Becker. New York: Routledge, 1994. 154-67.

"A Postmodern Afro-American Secular Spirituality: Michael Jackson." *Black Sacred Music: A Journal of Theomusicology* 3.2 (1989): 98-124.

"Probing a Divided Metaphor: Malcolm X and His Readers." *Teaching Malcolm X*. Ed. Theresa Perry, New York: Routledge, 1996. 231-41.

"Rap Culture, the Church and American Society." *Black Sacred Music: A Journal of Theomusicology* 6.1 (1992): 268-73.

"Reflecting Black." *Brotherman: The Odyssey of Black Men in America*. Ed. Herb Boyd and Robert L. Allen. New York: Ballantine, 1995. 158-68.

"Reflections on the Presidential Election, '88." *Social Text* 8.22 (1989): 16-20.

Stuart Hall

Books

The Hard Road to Renewal: Thatcherism and the Crisis of the Left. London: Verso, 1988.

New Times: The Changing Face of Politics in the 1990s. London: Lawrence and Wishart in association with *Marxism Today*, 1989. (ed. with Martin Jaques)

Policing the Crisis: 'Mugging,' the State, and Law and Order. London: Macmillan, 1978. (with C. Critcher et al.)

Politics and Ideology: A Reader. Philadelphia: Open UP, 1986. (ed. with James Donald)

The Politics of Thatcherism. London: Lawrence and Wishart in association with *Marxism Today*, 1983. (ed. with Martin Jaques)

The Popular Arts. New York: Pantheon, 1964. (with Paddy Whannel)

Representation: Cultural Representations and Signifying Practices. London: Sage, 1997.

Questions of Cultural Identity. London: Sage, 1996. (ed. with Paul du Gay)

Resistance through Rituals: Youth Subcultures in Post-war Britain. London: Hutchinson, 1976. (ed. with Tony Jefferson)

State and Society in Contemporary Britain: A Critical Introduction. New York: Polity, 1984. (ed. with Gregor McLennan and D. Held)

Articles and Book Chapters

"Brave New World." *Socialist Review* 21.1 (1991): 57-64.

"Cultural Identity and Cinematographic Representation." *Frame Works* 36 (1989): 68-81.

"Cultural Identity and Diaspora." *Identity: Community, Culture, Difference.* Ed. Jonathan Rutherford. London: Lawrence and Wishart, 1990. 222-37.

"Cultural Studies and Its Theoretical Legacies." *Cultural Studies*. Ed. Lawrence Grossberg, Cary Nelson, and Paula A. Treichler. New York: Routledge, 1992. 277-94.

"Cultural Studies: Two Paradigms." *Media, Culture and Society* 2 (1980): 57-72.

"The Emergence of Cultural Studies and the Crisis of the Humanities." *October* 53 (1990): 11-23.

"Gramsci's Relevance for the Study of Race and Ethnicity." *Journal of Communication Inquiry* 10.2 (1986): 5-27.

"Marxism and Culture." *Radical History Review* 18 (1978): 5-14.

"New Ethnicities." *Black Film, British Cinema* 7 (1988): 27-31.

"Notes on Deconstructing the Popular." *People's History and Socialist Theory*. Ed. R. Samuel. London: Routledge and Kegan Paul, 1981. 227-40.

"Popular Culture and the State." *Popular Culture and Social Relations*. Ed. Tony Bennett, Colin Mercer, and Janet Woollacott. Milton Keynes: Open UP, 1986. 22-49.

"The Rediscovery of 'Ideology': Return of the Repressed in Media Studies." *Culture, Society, and the Media*. Ed. M. Gurevitch et al. London: Methuen, 1982. 56-90.

"What is This 'Black' in Black Popular Culture?" *Black Popular Culture*. Ed. Gina Dent. Seattle: Bay P, 1992. 21-33.

Ernesto Laclau

Books
Emancipation(s). London: Verso, 1996.

Hegemony and Socialist Strategy: Towards a Radical Democratic Politics. London: Verso, 1985. (with Chantal Mouffe).

The Making of Political Identities. London: Verso, 1994.

New Reflections on the Revolution of Our Time. London: Verso, 1990.

Politics and Ideology in Marxist Theory: Capitalism, Fascism, and Populism. London: Humanities P, 1977.

Articles and Book Chapters

"Community and Its Paradoxes: Richard Rorty's 'Liberal Utopia.'" *Community at Loose Ends.* Ed. Miami Theory Collective. Minneapolis: U of Minnesota P, 1991. 83-98.

"Converging on an Open Quest." *Diacritics* 27.1 (1997): 3-12.

"The Death and Resurrection of the Theory of Ideology." *Modern Language Notes* 112.3 (1997): 297-321.

"Democratic Antagonisms and the Capitalist State." *The Frontiers of Political Theory: Essays in a Revitalized Discipline.* Ed. Michael Freeman and David Robertson. New York: St. Martin's, 1980. 101-39.

"The Impossibility of Society." *Ideology and Power in the Age of Lenin in Ruins.* Ed. Arthur and Marilouise Kroker. New York: St. Martin's, 1991. 24-27.

"Minding the Gap: The Subject of Politics." *The Making of Political Identities.* Ed. Ernesto Laclau. London: Verso, 1994. 11-39. (with Lilian Zac).

"Politics and the Limits of Modernity." *Universal Abandon?: The Politics of Postmodernism.* Ed. A. Ross. Minneapolis: U of Minnesota P, 1988. 63-82.

"Power and Representation." *Politics, Theory, and Contemporary Culture.* Ed. Mark Poster. New York: Columbia UP, 1993. 277-96.

"Preface." *The Sublime Object of Ideology.* Slavoj Zizek. London: Verso, 1989. ix-xv.

"Psychoanalysis and Marxism." *The Trial(s) of Psychoanalysis.* Ed. Francoise Meltzer. Chicago: U of Chicago P, 1988. 141-44.

"The Signifiers of Democracy." *Democracy and Possessive Individualism: The Intellectual legacy of C.B. Macpherson.* Ed. Joseph L. Carens. Albany: State U of New York P, 1993. 221-33.

"Totalitarianism and Moral Indignation." *Diacritics* 20.3 (1990): 88-95.

"The Uses of Equality." *Diacritics* 27.1 (1997): 3-12. (with Judith Butler and Reinaldo Laddaga)

Mouffe, Chantal

Books
Deconstruction and Pragmatism. New York: Routledge, 1996.

Dimensions of Radical Democracy: Pluralism, Citizenship, Community. London: Verso, 1992.

Hegemony and Socialist Strategy: Towards a Radical Democratic Politics. London: Verso, 1985. (with Ernesto Laclau)

The Return of the Political. London: Verso, 1993.

Articles and Book Chapters
"Citizenship and Political Identity." *October* 61 (1992): 28-41.

"Politics, Democratic Action, and Solidarity." *Inquiry* 38.1-2 (1995): 99-108.

"The End of Politics and the Rise of the Radical Right." *Dissent* 42 (1995): 498-502.

Contributors

Andrea A. Lunsford is distinguished professor of English at Ohio State University, where she serves as acting director of the Center for the Study of Teaching and Writing. She has written extensively on issues related to composition theory, collaborative practices, and intellectual property.

Sidney I. Dobrin is assistant professor of English at the University of Florida, where he teaches graduate and undergraduate courses in composition. His most recent books are *Constructing Knowledges: The Politics of Theory-Building and Pedagogy in Composition* and *Composition Theory for the Postmodern Classroom* (with Gary A. Olson), both published by SUNY Press. Currently he serves as co-editor of *JAC: A Journal of Composition Theory*.

Julie Drew is assistant professor of English at the University of Akron, where she teaches in the graduate program in composition and in the undergraduate program in writing. She has just completed a book-length study entitled *Reenvisioning Composition's Radical Scholarship: Ideology, Disciplinarity, and Feminist Standpoint Theory*.

Gary A. Olson is professor of English and coordinates the graduate program in rhetoric and composition at the University of South Florida. His most recent book, *Publishing in Rhetoric and Composition* (with Todd W. Taylor), was published by SUNY Press in 1997.

Lynn Worsham is professor of English at the University of South Florida, where she teaches graduate courses in rhetoric and critical theory and undergraduate courses in writing and cultural studies. Her *Feminism and Composition Studies: In Other Words* (with Susan Jarratt) was published by MLA Press in 1998. Currently she serves as book review editor of *JAC: A Journal of Composition Theory*.

Index